DYING TO KILL

The ALLURE of SUICIDE TERROR
With a NEW PREFACE

MIA BLOOM

COLUMBIA UNIVERSITY PRESS   NEW YORK

COLUMBIA UNIVERSITY PRESS
Publishers Since 1893
NEW YORK   CHICHESTER, WEST SUSSEX

Copyright © 2005 Columbia University Press
Preface and acknowledgments to the paperback edition,
Copyright © 2007 Columbia University Press
All rights reserved

Library of Congress Cataloging-in-Publication Data
Dying to kill : the allure of suicide terror / Mia Bloom
p. cm.
Includes bibliographical references and index
ISBN 978–0–231–13320–3 (cloth : alk. paper)
ISBN 978–0–231–13321–0 (pbk. : alk. paper)
ISBN 978–0–231–50986–2 (electronic)
1. Terrorism. 2. Suicide bombers. 3. Nongovernmental organizations
HV 6431.B576   2005
303.6—dc / 25 22   2004063474

Columbia University Press books are printed on permanent and
durable acid-free paper
Printed in the United States of America

c 10 9 8 7 6 5 4 3
p 10 9 8 7 6 5 4 3 2

DYING TO KILL

For **BETTY** *and* **JOE**

In **LOVING MEMORY** *of* **JOE,** *my father,*
and **EHUD SPRINZAK,** *my mentor, and*
ALL *the* **VICTIMS** *of* **SUICIDE TERROR**

CONTENTS

PREFACE TO THE PAPERBACK EDITION

Dying to Kill: The Allure of Suicide Terror was originally completed in December 2004 and published in May 2005. Its publication coincided with rapidly developing real-world events in Europe and South Asia. Many of the "doom and gloom" predictions I made about the likelihood of increasing Islamic sectarian violence exceeded my own expectations. This paperback edition offers an opportunity to revisit the book's original analysis and predictions in light of subsequent events and to highlight both developments foreseen in the book and those that call for revision or extension of the original arguments.

Even as the December 2004 elections in Iraq provided a glimmer of hope for a peaceful transition to democracy, I predicted that sectarian violence would soon overtake any claims to positive developments there. For months, I was criticized for my pessimistic viewpoints and cautioned to be more careful about my predictions and policy recommendations. However, from research I had previously conducted on the Iraqi Anfal campaign against the Kurds (as part of my doctoral study at Columbia University), I was familiar with the deeply entrenched historical roots of Iraqi sectarian conflict. I also knew that there had been too many incidents of violence perpetrated against the Kurds, the Marsh Arabs, and the Southern Shi'a, which created incentives for *revanchismo* at a later date. Saddam Hussein's removal, like the death of Yugoslavia's Josef Tito, created an opportunity for instrumentalist mobilization of ethnic grievances, giving rise to civil conflict that threatens the state's political and territorial integrity and has unleashed a maelstrom of ethnic hatred and tit-for-tat violence.

From May 2003 until January 2006, there were 578 multiple-casualty bombings—suicidal or otherwise—in Iraq. Of these, at least 273 were suicide attacks, although the real number is likely higher as the source of this information, the Brookings Institution's Iraq Index, omits attacks with fewer than three casualties. Diego Gambetta suggests that the figure might be as high as 487, meaning that nearly half of all the suicide attacks worldwide between 1981 and 2005 have taken place in Iraq in two and a half years.[1]

Six weeks after the publication of *Dying to Kill*, on July 7, 2005, London's equivalent of 9/11 dramatized the proximate dangers of homegrown suicide terrorism and the potential for backlash in Europe against a growing Muslim population that existed on society's economic and social fringes. The controversy over the September 2005 *Jyllands Posten* (a Danish newspaper) publication of cartoon images of the prophet Mohammed, the March 2006 violent street demonstrations in France, and suicide bombings in Iraq conducted by European converts to Islam generated fears of a growing radicalization of European Muslims.

For terrorism researchers, it has been a busy two years as many of us developed into an epistemic community of scholars, sharing our work, our primary research, and our results and often meeting at academic conferences. As we debated preconditions and motivations of and patterns in suicide terrorism, we have also formed supportive professional relationships and close friendships. Our understanding of terrorism has been deepened and enhanced by these interactions. With a barrage of books published on the subject over the last two years, often with strikingly (and not so surprisingly) similar titles, several competing theories have been bandied about—some based on fact, some on fiction. Some were good, others were awful, but all of this research and analysis has served to increase interest and awareness to such an extent that the field of terrorism and suicide terrorism studies has become increasingly sophisticated and well developed.

Certain trends in suicide terrorism have become evident to most of us: (1) that foreign occupation is a necessary although insufficient prerequisite for the evolution and spread of suicide terrorism; (2) that suicide terror was increasingly morphing into a sectarian strategy to be used against Shi'a by Sunni extremists (often associated with the Deobandi order); and (3) that as long as certain religious authorities justified and provided credibility for this form of violence, it will likely persist throughout the Islamic world.

The majority of targets in Iraq to date have been civilians, and the majority of these civilians have overwhelmingly been Shi'ite. As Gambetta asserts, "In Iraq ... it is unlikely that Shi'ites would have been so relentlessly targeted had the motives for the attacks been aimed only at fighting the occupation"; additionally, "radical Salafis in Saudi Arabia are said to nurture a hatred for Shi'ites that rivals that for the US."[2] However, perhaps the most surprising transformation of suicide terrorism over the past few years has occurred in Afghanistan and Pakistan. Afghanistan, occupied for ten years by Soviet troops, did not see the tactic used against the Russians between 1979 and 1989. Since then, religious justifications and ideological contagion from other countries suggest that suicide bombing has taken hold in Afghanistan. To date there have been 132 suicide attacks using a variety of delivery mechanisms: improvised explosive devices (IEDs), vehicle-borne IEDs (VBIEDs), bicycle bombs, taxi bombs, and even *donkey* bombs against a spectrum of targets including Coalition troops, Afghan civilians, rival tribal associations, mosques, and villages.

In Pakistan, where there is no foreign occupation, we have witnessed an additional three dozen attacks in recent years,[3] as suicide terrorism has become the tactic of choice for sectarian conflict in which Shi'as are more likely to be targeted than foreigners or military targets. The bombers' motto is allegedly "Kill a Shi'a, Go to Paradise!";[4] in 2005 and 2006, areas previously immune to the scourge of suicide terrorism witnessed attacks as part of internecine strife in Bangladesh (2005) and Somalia (2006). According to a jihadi leader in Pakistan, "the decision to launch suicide operations in Afghanistan and Pakistan was taken at a single meeting in Karachi in November 2001, six weeks after the start of the post September 11th bombing [campaign]."[5] Before 1998, the only confirmed instances of suicide terrorism in Pakistan were related to the Sunni-Shi'a sectarian conflict and were perpetrated by the Sunni extremist Sipah-e-Sahaba Pakistan (SSP) group and its militant wing, the Lashkar-e-Jhangvi (LEJ), or by the Shi'a extremist group Sipah Mohammad.

Pakistan's first suicide bombing was carried out by the Al-jihad group on a crowded street in Peshawar in December 1995, killing thirty. It was followed in 1996 by two more car bomb attacks: an attack on a bus in Lahore by Kashmiri separatists, followed by a radical-Islamist attack on the Egyptian Embassy in Islamabad.

The Pakistani suicide attacks since 2001 demonstrate certain patterns and common characteristics. A Karachi-based leader of the outlawed Jaish-e-Mohammed movement told police interrogators that it was only after the Taliban's fall that militants who fought alongside the Taliban were forced to sneak back into Pakistan, where they decided to carry out *fedayeen* missions within the country. He claimed that there are "hundreds" of *mujahideen* prepared to carry out suicide missions and that while they derive inspiration from the Palestinians and the Chechens, they have easier access to manpower and explosives.[6]

Since 2002 Pakistan has been "wracked by suicide bombings" according to some analysts.[7] According to Pakistani reports, the bombers are mostly unknown, lacking the cult-hero status afforded to perpetrators in places like Palestine or Sri Lanka. Indeed, a major challenge in studying Pakistani bombers is the lack of reliable evidence about them. Unlike bombers in

Palestine and now Iraq, Pakistani bombers rarely leave any of the "last will and testament" videos. Three Afghan suicide bombers videotaped their farewell statements, and so their names and addresses are known, and we can even begin to piece together some of their motivations.[8] However, many of the Pakistani bombers remain faceless and nameless: "We don't know how many of the [Pakistani suicide bombers] were Pakistani, Afghan or Arabs. But it is more likely for Afghans to undertake suicide missions in Afghanistan and for Pakistanis to do so in Pakistan."[9] This stands in stark contrast to Iraq, where the majority of suicide bombers, according to studies by Scott Atran, Reuven Paz, and Mohammed Hafez, are overwhelmingly foreigners who have come to Iraq for the purpose of the Global Jihad.

According to law-enforcement personnel, Pakistan is sitting on a powder keg, with hundreds of trained and highly motivated youths belonging to outlawed religious groups, often in hiding. According to one government official, "These men are like misguided missiles. It's easy for any international terrorist organization such as Al Qaeda to recruit them and create manifold problems for the country's security." Judging from recent events, intensive recruitment has begun, and many pundits have begun heralding the "era of the suicide bomber" in Pakistan. With the stated aim of purging the land of "infidel forces," this new terrorism has been used overwhelmingly against the Shi'a minority in the country, against other Sunni sects, and "against" government and military representatives of the state.

The history of sectarianism in Pakistan dates back to political cleavages in the 1970s, but it intensified in the 1990s as a spillover effect of the war in Afghanistan. According to Mary Anne Weaver, "Sunni and Shi'ites have been slaughtering each other for 30 years but suicide bombings are relatively new. It's the legacy of the anti-Soviet jihad in neighboring Afghanistan and spillover from Iraq."[10] Before September 11, 2001, Lashkar-e-Jhangvi (LeJ) capitalized on cross-membership among the various groups associated with Al Qaeda and the Taliban to find a foothold in Afghanistan. LeJ subsequently reinvented itself in Pakistan as a purveyor of suicide terrorism. Pakistan's sponsorship of the Taliban in Afghanistan in the 1990s ideologically "Talibanized" Pakistani society. Islam—previously a unifying force in Pakistan—became an element of division and destabilization, with decreasing tolerance of competing Islamic interpretations. As a result, each sect and each school of thought considers its own brand or interpretation of Islam to be the only legitimate form. This has led to greater sectarian and ideological schisms. The genesis of the problem can be traced to the 1970s when, under pressure from the fundamentalists, the Ahmadiyas were declared non-Muslims. Today, Wahhabis and Deobandis clamor for a similar edict against the Shi'a.

Nasra Hassan asserts that the targets of Pakistani suicide bombers vary along a spectrum from foreign to local: "The targets are first and foremost enemy structures and authorities: their own, if considered un-Islamic or tyrannical; or external ones such as foreign troops, external or internal allies of the enemy (the latter represented by the army, police, or civilian officials), and sectarian or ideological enemies."[11] Pakistani officials claim that the militants have the resources to carry out suicide missions on a daily basis. The only reason this has not happened, they claim, is that they are selective, preferring to wait and strike the right target at the right time. Moreover, the militants' most desirable targets—Western nationals—are a rarity in the country. Those Westerners who remain have severely restricted their movements. A car bomb attack on March 2, 2006, that killed David Foy, an American embassy consular officer, occurred the day before a visit by President Bush. This attack was an indicator of the growing anti-American sentiment in Pakistan and disapproval of U.S. policies in Iraq—all of which intensified after the failed U.S. attempt to kill Al Qaeda leader Ayman al Zawahiri by a missile strike in a border village that did, however, kill eighteen civilians.[12] As a result of the general difficulty in finding Western targets, the militants have apparently set their sights on the Shi'a minority, who orthodox Sunnis denounce as *kafirs* (infidels)—that is, a legitimate target for "Jihad."[13]

The shift in terrorist tactics has been perceptible across Pakistan. A May 31, 2005, attack in Karachi during evening prayers inside Ali Raza Imambargah, a Shi'a mosque downtown, killed as many as nineteen and wounded thirty-eight. The force of the blast was so severe that it cracked the building's dome. This attack came just weeks after one on May 7 at another Shi'a mosque, which killed twenty-three and injured almost one hundred people during Friday prayers. Most Pakistani officials believe that the Ali Raza Imambargah attack was perpetrated in retaliation for the assassination of a Sunni Muslim cleric, Nizamuddin Shamzai, the previous day, which triggered rioting across Karachi and prompted police to step up security patrols at Shi'a mosques amid fears of sectarian violence.

Overall, it seems that measures taken under international pressure and for international consumption, such as the banning of sectarian groups and curriculum reform in religious schools, have been half-hearted and have had little impact on the growing sectarian violence in Pakistan. Banned groups simply rename themselves and continue to operate with impunity.[14] In May 2005, jurists in Pakistan forbade suicide attacks at home but said their decree did not apply to Indian-controlled Kashmir—a declaration repeated in April 2006 when the leader of Egypt's Muslim Brotherhood condemned suicide bombings in the Sinai against other Egyptians but justified them against

Israel. Fifty-eight Pakistani clerics from different schools of Islamic thought issued a fatwa (religious ruling) that banned suicide bombings in Pakistan and Kashmir—places where the victims were likely to be other Muslims. A counter fatwa by forty religious parties permitted attacks in Kashmir (though not in Pakistan).[15]

Another major challenge in analyzing suicide terrorism in Pakistan is the sheer diversity of the phenomenon in terms of varying tactics, the diversity of terrorist groups, and the range of targets. The various groups appear to have loose structures, with suicide squads displaying a wide range of ideologies and motivations. They mutate rapidly, hide inside other groups, disappear, dissolve, and reappear. Sometimes members of one group perpetrate an act on behalf of another, calling organizational loyalties into question.

Finally, it is worth noting that suicide bombing in Pakistan is now spreading to conflicts in neighboring countries with no previous history of the tactic. Two suicide attacks occurred in November 2005 in Bangladesh—a wave of bombings that targeted judges, journalists, and politicians in Gazipur on November 15 and 24, 2005. The authorities believe that the courts and judges are targeted because they symbolize secular laws in the country. Most laws in Bangladesh are secular, based on the British legal code inherited from colonialism. The police suspected Jamaat-ul-Mujahideen, one of three outlawed Islamic groups, which wants to establish Islamic law in the country.

The Gazipur bomber used an IED strapped to his body. Although Chief of Police Abdul Qaiyum asserted that this was the country's first suicide bombing attack, there had been a series of smaller attacks the previous August in which more than 400 mini-bomblets went off across the country within the space of half an hour, killing two and injuring more than one hundred. The attacker entered the law library in Gazipur wearing a lawyer's black gown to evade security. A second attack in the port city of Chittagong occurred at the same time, and thirteen policemen were among the sixteen people wounded or killed. Tactical innovation is evident in the Chittagong case, primarily the use of a secondary IED on the same bomber. When suspicious police tried to search the bomber, he threw one of the bombs at the police and then exploded the other.

As indicated above, beginning in 2006 suicide terrorism spread to Somalia, where Islamist groups employed foreign fighters and at least one female perpetrator. In September, Somalia's first suicide bombing targeted President Abdullahi Yusuf outside the parliament in Baidoa. Although President Yusuf was not hurt in the attack, his brother and four other bodyguards were killed. Two people were arrested in connection with the attack. The Union of Islamic Courts (UIC), an Islamist group that briefly controlled most of southern Somalia, denied any responsibility. Nevertheless, the government accused the UIC of links to Al Qaeda—charges the group rejected. However, the UIC's advance into Baidoa and the attack on President Yusuf highlighted the powerlessness of the government.[16] Baidoa was the last outpost held by Somalia's weak transitional government, which was challenged by the Islamists who at that time controlled Mogadishu and most of the southern regions.

Two months later a second car bomb exploded in Baidoa, leaving eight people dead. The perpetrator was reportedly a veiled female suicide bomber who detonated herself at a checkpoint; however, initial reports contradicted one another on specifically how many bombs and bombers were involved. The deputy defense minister, Salad Ali Jelle, alleged that three car bombs had exploded at police checkpoints as they tried to inspect the vehicles, killing the drivers and three others, and that the surviving perpetrators—foreign members of Al Qaeda—were in custody. However, the police commander, General Ali Hussein, claimed that at least twelve people had died and that there "were two suicide cars full of explosives."[17] The three men captured appeared to be African but not Somali. Somali information minister Ali Jama stated, "We do not want to jump to conclusions, but all indications are that the attack was carried out by the Islamists in Mogadishu because they are the ones who have invited foreigners with this kind of expertise."[18]

While some predictions made in this book have materialized, others have not. What seemed to be a hopeful and promising peace process in Sri Lanka in 2002 and 2003 has all but unraveled by early 2007, with neither the leadership of the LTTE nor the current government under President Mahinda Rajapakse demonstrating commitment to the peace process or treating the Oslo agreements as a constraint on their respective actions. Although news of events in Sri Lanka since the December 2004 tsunami rarely make headlines in the American press, the current government's political intransigence, a bombardment campaign against Tamil civilians on the East coast in July 2006, and the LTTE's return to suicide terrorism have complicated prospects for peace.

On July 7, 2004, a female attacker struck a Colpetty police station after a failed attempt to target Minister for Hindu Affairs Douglas Devananda. There were three attacks against military and naval targets in the first three months of 2006 and two further attacks during May and June. On April 25, 2006, a woman feigning pregnancy, Kanapathipillai Manjula Devi, seriously wounded the chief of the army, Lt. General Sarath Fonseka, when she detonated her bomb inside a military hospital in Colombo. Most recently, a particularly deadly attack against several buses filled with naval personnel at Habarana killed one hundred people in October 2006. The increase in the number, scale, and lethality of the attacks make political compromise less likely in the short and medium terms.

The Rajapakse government, itself a political coalition including several hard-line extremist parties, has little incentive to make concessions that could endanger the coalition's internal political balance. Rajapaske might also be considering Ranil Wickremasinghe's April 2004 electoral defeat, in part because he was seen as too accommodating to Tamil political aspirations. Indiscriminate attacks by both the government and the LTTE, with the latter using suicide attacks in the capital city of Colombo, have contributed to the escalation. Attacks against Colombo allow the LTTE to bring the insurgency to the mainland. According to Christine Fair, "because Colombo is the capital, targeting this city inflicted costs upon the entire Sri Lankan polity ... attacking Colombo has rich dividends. It makes leaders question the value of countering the LTTE. A single blast in Colombo has more value psychologically than full scale conflict in the North and northeast."[19] The deteriorating political situation in Sri Lanka does not bode well for what appeared to be the one case of success described in this book, as the peace process is grinding to a halt. The problem for the government is that it has failed to convince Tamils that there is a viable alternative to the LTTE. According to Jehan Perera, executive director of the National Peace Council: "So far the Sri Lankan state has not been able to convince the Tamil people that their grievances for equality, for power sharing, for a form of federal autonomy, would indeed be delivered to them."[20]

Notes

1. Diego Gambetta, ed., *Making Sense of Suicide Missions* (New York: Oxford University Press, 2006), 305-6.
2. Gambetta, *Making Sense of Suicide Missions*, 310-11.
3. Diego Gambetta lists fourteen attacks from January 2004 until February 2006, which killed 228 people, *Making Sense of Suicide Missions*, 304.
4. Nasra Hassan, "Suicide Terrorism," in *The Roots of Terrorism*, ed. Louise Richardson, Club de Madrid Series on Democracy and Terrorism (London: Routledge, 2006), 36-37.
5. Hassan, "Suicide Terrorism," 30.
6. Zahid Hussein, "Suicide City," *Newsline*, June 2004 (cover story).
7. Erik Schechter, "Reaping a Bloody Harvest." *Jerusalem Post* (Israel), May 12, 2006, 21.
8. More than thirty suicide assaults have been reported from different parts of Afghanistan during the past six months. The figures appear unbelievable considering the fact that suicide bombings were unheard of in Afghanistan during the years of Soviet military occupation from 1979 through 1989, the Afghan jihad, and the civil war.
9. Rahimullah Yusufzai, "Suicide Bombers From Palestine to Afghanistan," *The News*

(Pakistan), May 12, 2006.

10. Mary Anne Weaver, *Pakistan: In the Shadow of Jihad and Afghanistan* (New York: Farrar, Straus and Giroux, 2003).

11. Hassan, "Suicide Terrorism," 31.

12. James Rupert, "Pakistan Bomb Kills US Official," *Newsday*, March 3, 2006.

13. Schecter, "Reaping a Bloody Harvest," 21.

14. Ali Dayan Hasan, "Playing with the Fire of Sectarianism; Pakistan," *International Herald Tribune*, February 13, 2006, 8.

15. Hassan, "Suicide Terrorism," 31.

16. BBC News, "Somalia Suicide Bombing Arrests, " September 26, 2006, http://news.bbc.co.uk/go/pr/fr/-/2/hi/africa/5389636.stm.

17. BBC News, "Car Bomb Blast Rocks Somali Town," November 30, 2006, http://news.bbc.co.uk/go/pr/fr/-/2/hi/africa/6160603.stm.

18. Middle East Online, "Somalia on Edge After Baidoa Suicide Attack" December 1, 2006, http://www.middle-east-online.com/English/?id=18585.

19. Christine Fair, *Urban Battle Fields of South Asia: Lessons Learned from Sri Lanka, India and Pakistan* (Washington, D.C.: Rand, 2005), 48.

20. Dumeetha Luthra, "Discipline, Death, and Martyrdom," BBC News, June 9, 2006, http://news.bbc.co.uk/2/hi/south_asia/5051652.stm.

ACKNOWLEDGMENTS FOR THE PAPERBACK EDITION

I dedicate this new edition of *Dying to Kill* to Dr. John Horgan, who has improved my life and my work, correcting many of my previous errors both professionally and personally. A stór mo chroí.

I want to express my deep gratitude to my new academic home, the School of Public and International Affairs at the University of Georgia, and all of my colleagues there. UGA has provided the best working atmosphere any academic could hope for and the most collegial group of professors ever to work together. Since *Dying to Kill* first appeared in May 2005, I have had the opportunity to present my findings to policymakers, the military, and various academic audiences throughout the United States and the United Kingdom. I thanked almost everyone I knew in the first edition, and I want to thank them all again for their continued support, especially Michael Lipson, and add to the list David Burbach, Zak Taylor, Victor Asal, Mo Hafez, and Thuy for their comments and encouragement.

January 15, 2007
Atlanta, Georgia

ACKNOWLEDGMENTS

There are many people who deserve special thanks. First and foremost, I dedicate this book to my parents Betty Bloom and Joe Grynwald, for all their love and support over the years.

I am grateful to Columbia University Press and to Anne Routon and Peter Dimock for their advice, comments, and suggestions. I thank Leslie Bialler for all of his assistance making the manuscript much more readable. Anne, you made what should ordinarily have been an ordeal, a pleasure! Peter, your enthusiastic support of this project was the difference between a few random ideas and a coherent work.

To my mentors, without whom I would have given up a long time ago, Dick Bulliet, Roy Licklider, Chaim Kaufmann, Ed Rhodes, and Dick Ullman. You were such excellent advisors. I cannot thank you enough for your immeasurable patience and good will. I am likewise grateful to Martha Crenshaw and Ehud Sprinzak who inspired this research and Bruce Hoffman whose comments and encouragement have been invaluable over the years. Ehud saw in me, at very young age, the potential to be a serious scholar and was extremely proud when I finally fulfilled his vision. He is sorely missed by friends and colleagues alike.

I am indebted to the granting agencies and institutes who provided assistance or research money to fund portions of this book, including the SSRC MacArthur Foundation, Global Security and Cooperation Award, the United States Institute of Peace, the International Center for Ethnic Studies in Sri Lanka, the Council on Foreign Relations, and the Center of International Studies at Princeton University, especially the support of Richard Ullman and Robert Gilpin. I thank the staff of the Office of Counter Terrorism in Trenton, NJ, for their support of my work. I am grateful for the research assistance of Shanthi Divakaran and Minari Fernando in Sri Lanka and Nicole Cordeau and Patrick Hynes in Montreal.

Over the years, teaching has inspired much of my research. I had some terrific students at Cornell University for the two years I taught there and at McGill University where I taught in 2004. My students' questions from Government 397 and 385 and Poli Sci 522 forced me to delve deeper into this material and student requests for clarification demonstrated that I needed to understand it better in order to explain it to them. A few in particular deserve special mention: Tovah Meredith Nagin, James Pincow, Kate Stinson, Nathan Naidoo, and Jeff Dalziel. Not only did you help keep my faith in teaching but became my friends through life's trials and tribulations. At times, teaching me as I taught you, I am so proud of you all.

I thank the many universities who generously invited me to give talks throughout 2002–2004 and provided terrific insight and comments on early versions of the chapters. Special mention goes to the University of Chicago, Program on International Security Policy, and several members of the UC faculty who were particularly helpful and encouraging: Stathis Kalyvas (now the Arnold J. Wolfers Professor of Political Science at Yale), Robert A. Pape, John Mearsheimer, Rashid Khalidi (now the Edward Said Professor at Columbia University), and Daniel Drezner as well as the UC grad students who participated in the PISP seminar and read through the preliminary version of chapter 2.

I thank David and Barbara Rapoport and the Burkle seminar at the University of California in Los Angeles and the members of the Institute for Social and Economic Research Policy (ISERP) seminar at Columbia University and Charles Tilly who were all exceedingly helpful. I am grateful to Stephen M. Saideman, my colleague at McGill University, for ensuring theoretical rigor and acknowledge my academic home, the University of Cincinnati and my wonderful colleagues there who helped me even before I arrived: Laura Dudley Jenkins, Dinshaw Mistry and Richard J. Harknett deserve great appreciation for their comments on earlier drafts. Last but not least, my long time academic home at the Center for Global Security and Democracy at Rutgers University, and Ed Rhodes in particular, have been crucial during the completion of the manuscript.

To all of my colleagues and friends who have had to suffer through years of extended conversations about violence, genocide, rape, and suicide terrorism—replete with all the gory details over brunches and dinners. You have been remarkable sounding boards, read through my onerous prose (sometimes on very short notice) to help me condense and clarify the chapters. Nichole Argo, Sammy Barkin, Magnes Bernhardsson, Robin Bhatty, Dan Byman, Tim and Sarah Büthe, Beth De Sombre, David Del Conte, Aleka Filindra, Kelly Greenhill, Amaney Jamal, Colin Klein, Melinda Kovacs, Alan J. Kuperman, Adrienne LeBas, Assaf Moghadam, Ruby Rios, (Kenneth) Steve

Rose, Chris and Lori Rudolph, Itai Sneh, Amy Shuster, Jeff Taliaferro, Chris Twomey and especially Joe Foudy, and Michael Lipson, thank you all for your insights, ideas, friendship, and eleventh-hour editing.

There have been several women who have inspired me in a number of ways in their amazing ability to balance professional and family lives while always maintaining their femininity, dignity, humanity and grace. Their imprimatur has stayed with me all these years and I send them my gratitude and deep affection: Hazel Cohen, Lesly Lempert, Teri Schure, Nina Raben, Hillary Klein, and Fagie Goldberg.

Inspiration can stem from both positive and negative sources. Adversity can be a great source of strength. To quote M. Branch, "Are you happy now?" David Sohmer, Jennifer Zoschak, and Jay Kuris have all shown me that a particular insignificant and irritating speck of dust can metamorphose into a pearl with sufficient tenacity and spirit. Jay, thank you for always helping me make lemonade out of lemons, of which there were many.

Finally, I thank my parents again because I can never thank them enough.

M.B.
January 28, 2005

A SELECTED GLOSSARY OF TERMS AND ABBREVIATIONS

A.H. (Arabic): After the Hijra. It is the reference used in the Islamic calendar, instead of A.D. which is used in the Christian calendar, or C.E. used in the Jewish calendar.

Al Sa'iqa: "The Storm." Palestinian armed group created by Syrian Ba'athist party in 1966.

Al Qaeda (or Al Qaida): Radical Islamist terror network loosely organized by Osama Bin Laden.

Al Quds (Arabic): "The holy;" Arabic name for Jerusalem.

Alawi (Arabic): A sect of Shi'ite Muslims in Syria, considered heretical by the mainstream.

'Aliyah: "Going Up." Refers to immigration to Israel.

Allah (Arabic): God.

Ansar (Arabic): "Helpers;" the people of Medina who responded to the Prophet's call to Islam and offered Islam a city-state power.

ASALA: Armenian Army for the Secret Liberation of Armenia

Ba'ath (or Ba'th): Pan Arab party with extreme Arab nationalist leanings founded in 1940's in Syria by a Michel Aflaq and Salah Edin Bitar. Both Syria and Iraq were ruled by Ba'athist regimes, but the regimes were rivals. Lebanese Ba'ath party split from the Syrian party in 1966 and moved to Iraq in 1968. The U.S.-led coalition ended Ba'ath rule in Iraq in 2003.

BKI: Barbar Khalsa International, Sikh terrorist group in India.

Burqa: Long garment covering the entire body worn by extremely religious Muslim women. Also known as *hijab*.

Dar-al Harb (Arabic): "The house of war;" the part of the world not subject to Islamic rule.

Dar-al-Islam (Arabic): "The house of Islam." The part of the world subject to Islamic rule.

Dhimmi (Arabic): Christian, Jew or Zoroastrian living in a Muslim state. *Dhimmi* are supposed to wear special dress and pay the *jizyah* (poll) tax. They are exempt (or forbidden) from fighting and from paying the Muslim *Zakat* (charity) tax.

DFLP: Democratic Front for the Liberation of Palestine (Damascus—led by Nayif Hawatmah), Palestinian Marxist radical movement. DFLP was founded in 1969 when it split from the Popular Front for the Liberation of Palestine (PFLP). Believes Palestinian national goals can be achieved only through revolution of the masses. In early 1980s, occupied political stance midway between PLO and the rejectionists.

DMK: Dravida Munnetra Kazhagam (Southern Indian) Radical Indian Political Party which supported Tamil insurgents' bid for autonomy.

Druze: A religion that broke away from Islam about 1000 CE following the teachings of Darazi, Hamza ibn Ali ibn Ahmad, and Baha El-Din. Druze call themselves Mowahhid, which means "monotheistic." They believe in reincarnation and in abstract concepts of heaven and hell. Druze are loyal citizens of whatever state they live in. Large Druze minorities live in Israel, Syria and Lebanon.

EPRLF: Eelam People's Revolutionary Liberation Front formed in 1980 under K. Padmanabha.

EROS: Eelam Revolutionary Organisation of Students formed in 1975 under V. Balakumar.

ETA (Basque): Euzkadi Ta Askatasuna, Basque Fatherland and Liberty. Founded in 1959 with the aim of establishing an independent homeland based on Marxist principles encompassing the Spanish Basque provinces of Vizcaya, Guipuzcoa, and Alava, as well as the autonomous region of Navarra, and the southwestern French Departments of Labourd, Basse-Navarre, and Soule.

FARC (*Fuerzas Armadas Revolucionarias de Colombia*): a Marxist guerrilla organization in Colombia.

Fatah (or Al-Fatah): Palestinian radical movement founded approximately 1957, but officially founded about 1965. It has the declared aim of destroying Israel and replacing it with a secular democratic state. Fatah means victory in Arabic. The name is also a reverse acronym for Harakat Tahrir el Wataniyeha Filistiniyeh—Palestine Liberation Movement. Fatah is the party founded by Chairman Yasser Arafat, and represents the moderate end of the Palestinian political spectrum. Their slogan is "Revolution until Victory." Fatah is now led by Abu Mazen (Abu Abbas).

Fatah Revolutionary Council: Organization led by Sabri al-Banna ("Abu Nidal") and hosted by Iraq. Split from PLO in 1974 to become the Black September Organization (BSO), named after the 1970 massacre of Palestinians in Jordan.

FIS: Islamic Salvation Front, Fundamentalist Islamic Political Party in Algeria.

GIA: Groupe Algerien Islamique, Radical Islamic Organization in Algeria.

Gush Emunim (Hebrew): "Bloc of belief or Bloc of faithful." Radical right-wing religious movement of settlers formed in 1964 that gained popularity after the 1967 war.

HADEP: pro-Kurdish People's Democracy Party in Turkey.

Hamas (Arabic): Hamas is the Arabic acronym for the "Harakat al Muqawamah al Islamiyya" (Islamic Resistance Movement), formed in 1987 by Sheikh Ahmed Yassin.

Haram: (Arabic) Not lawful according to Islam. Engaging in an act that is Haram (i.e. eating food like pork, drinking alcohol, having sex outside of marriage) would lead to punishment.

Hijab (Arabic): Headdress of Muslim women prescribed by Qur'an.

Hijra, Hejirah (Arabic): The migration of Muhammad from Mecca to Yathrib, re-named Medina ("the city') in 622, A.H. (after Hijra) establishes the date on the Islamic calendar.

Hizb'allah (Arabic): (also *Hisbulla*, Hezbollah, *Hisbolla*, etc.) "The party of God." Shi'ite extremist group formed in Lebanon with the original aim of ending the Israeli oc-cupation of Lebanon.

Hudna (Arabic): Self-policed cease fires.

IDF: Israel Defence Forces (Tzahal—"Tzva Hagana Leyisrael"). The abbreviation is the official name of the Israeli Army.

IED: Improvised Explosive Device, another name for a suicide bomb device.

IRA: Irish Republican Army.

IPKF: Indian Peace Keeping Force sent to the northern provinces of Sri Lanka in 1987 to halt violence between Sinhalese and Tamils.

Ismaili: A Shi'ite Muslim sect centered in Pakistan with minority populations in East Africa.

Jihad (Arabic): "Struggle;" usually applied to an Islamic war. According to Muslim sources, "*Jihad is not a war to force the faith on others, as many people think of it. It should never be interpreted as a way of compulsion of the belief on others, since there is an explicit verse in the Qur'an that says: 'There is no compulsion in religion' Al-Qur'an: Al-Baqarah (2: 256). Jihad is not a defensive war only, but a war against any unjust regime. If such a regime exists, a war is to be waged against the leaders, but not against the people of that country. People should be freed from the unjust regimes and influences so that they can freely choose to believe in Allah.*" Also applied to the struggle of the human soul against sin.

JVP: Janata Vimukti Peramuna (Sinhalese), Right wing Sinhalese party opposed to Tamil separatism in Sri Lanka.

KADEK: Kurdistan Freedom and Democracy Congress.

LTTE: Liberation Tigers of Tamil Eelam, one of several Tamil insurgent organizations established in 1976 to work towards Tamil Independence.

Maronite: Ancient Christian sect, centered primarily in Lebanon.

MB: Muslim Brotherhood, *Mujamma al Islami* established in Egypt by Hasan al Banna in 1974 to provide much needed social services to Palestinians under oc-cupation.

Nakba (Arabic): Disaster; the Palestinian name for the exodus of refugees from Pales-tine in the 1948 war against Israel and the establishment of the state of Israel.

PFLP: Popular Front for the Liberation of Palestine, founded in 1967 by George Habash as a member of the PLO. Marxist radical movement that has the goal of eliminating the state of Israel through terror and other means. Joined the Alliance of Palestin-ian Forces (APF) to oppose the Declaration of Principles signed in 1993 and sus-pended participation in the PLO. Broke away from the APF, along with the DFLP, in 1996 over ideological differences.

PFLP-GC: Popular Front for the Liberation of Palestine-General Command—A group that split from the PFLP in 1968 to focus more on fighting and less on politics. Led by Ahmad Jibril, a former captain in the Syrian Army. Closely tied to both Syria and Iran.

PIJ: Palestinian Islamic Jihad (Harakat al Jihad al Islami al Filastini) was founded in 1979–1980 by Fathi Shiqaqi, 'Abd al Aziz 'Odah and Bashir Musa. Committed to the creation of an Islamic Palestinian state and the destruction of Israel through holy war, PIJ specializes in suicide bombings. It is a series of loosely affiliated factions rather than a cohesive group, highly influenced by the Iranian Revolutionary movement and focused exclusively on terrorism. There is an Egyptian *Islamic Jihad* associated with the Al-Qaeda group and Osama Bin Laden.

PKK: *Partia Karkaren Kurdistan,* Kurdish Worker's Party in Turkey.

PLC: Palestine Legislative Council. Officially it is the chief lawmaking body of the Palestine National Authority.

PLO: Palestine Liberation Organization. The umbrella organization of Palestinian political groups founded in 1964 as an initiative of Arab states, it evolved into an organization advocating a sovereign separate Palestinian nation after the 1967 Six-Day War. Initially headed by Ahmed Shukairy. Yasser Arafat became the head of the PLO in 1968. The PLO charter called for the destruction of Israel and its replacement by a secular democratic state, in which non-Zionist Jews would have equal rights. The parts of the charter calling for destruction of Israel were declared to be annulled after the 1994 Oslo agreements. Led by Abu Mazen after Arafat's death.

PLOTE: People's Liberation Organization for Tamil Eelam formed in 1979 under Uma Mahaswaran.

PNA: Palestine National Authority or Palestinian Authority. The name of the governing authority of the Palestinian autonomy created under the Oslo Agreements.

PNC: Palestine National Council. The governing body of the PLO.

PTA: Prevention of Terrorism Act, promulgated in 1979 the Sri Lankan Government permitted the army and the police to hold prisoners incommunicado for up to 18 months without trial.

Qur'an (Arabic): The holy book of Islam.

Sha'ria (Arabic): Muslim religious jurisprudence and law.

Shahid (Arabic): A holy martyr. Used to refer to suicide bombers as well as saints.

Shi'ite: (or Shi'a): A sect or branch of the Muslim religion centered in Iran, with large followings in southern Iraq and sub-sects (Alawi, Ismaili) in Syria and Lebanon. Shi'ites.

Sunni (Arabic): The mainstream Muslim religious sect.

TELO: Tamil Eelam Liberation Organization

TFP: Tamil Federal Party

TNT: Tamil National Tigers emerged in 1973 under Vellupillai Prabhakaran, was renamed the Liberation Tigers of Tamil Eelam (LTTE) in May 1976 when they split from the TULF in 1978 with greater calls for secession and independence

TULF: Tamil United Liberation Front political party, established in 1972 began calling for a separate Tamil state in 1976 to be achieved constitutionally.

TUF: Tamil United Front, All Ceylon Tamil Congress (ACTC), the Tamil Progressive Front, and the Ceylon Worker's congress joined forces in 1972 to campaign for parity status for the Tamil language. In May 1973 the TUF decided to work for an independent state, "Tamil Eelam," Tamil Homeland.

Umma: A people. Used to designate the community of Muslim believers and also the community of Arabs or Arabic nation.

UN: United Nations

Wahabbi (also Wahhabi, Wahabi) (Arabic): Muslim Sunni reform movement founded mid-eighteenth century by Abdul-Wahhab. Wahabi is the English name and the name used for them by other sects. They call themselves Muwahidun (Unitarians) and believe in strict asceticism, dominant religion of Saudi Arabia.

DYING TO KILL

CHAPTER ONE

Introduction:

The Historical Antecedents of

Suicide Terrorism

Imagine a situation in which choosing to blow yourself up along with dozens of other people seems like a great idea. How bad must your life be if you think that it is better to be a sacrifice than to live, have a family, and be a productive member of society? Imagine what goes through the minds of people right before they become suicide bombers. Are they scared, are they angry, do they fully understand what they are about to do?

This book investigates what motivates young men and a growing number of young women to do this. Terrorist groups appear to use suicide bombing under two conditions: when other terrorist or military tactics fail, and when they are in competition with other terrorist groups for popular or financial support. Suicide bombing is generally found in the second stage of conflicts— and only spreads in countries where the population is receptive to terrorists targeting civilians (which has been the case in Iraq, Israel, and Chechnya, less so in Sri Lanka, and not the case in Spain or Northern Ireland.)

Other scholars have attempted to explain this phenomenon as the result of brainwashing, extreme poverty, emotional dysfunction, or feelings of despair. These are partial explanations at best. Mark Juergensmeyer and Yoram Schweitzer argue that these "martyrdom operations" are acts of religious extremism.[1] Indeed, the organizations who recruit young people to detonate themselves in crowds of civilians have manipulated religious fervor by wedding the ideas of heavenly reward to martyrdom, encouraging their followers to believe they will ascend straight to heaven and enter paradise. This is presented as the absolute sacrifice leading immediately to the ultimate reward.

Suicide terror has historical precedents. Nonetheless, the 1983 attacks in Lebanon against the American Marine Barracks signaled the beginning of the modern use of suicide terror. Historically, Muslim (Shi'ite and Sunni), Christian, Hindu, Sikh, Jewish and secular organizations all employed suicide attacks, especially in the Middle East, but also in many other regions of the world. A partial list of terrorist groups that actively use suicide terror includes Hamas, the Palestinian Islamic Jihad, the al-'Aqsa Martyrs Brigades, Al-Ansar Mujahidin in Chechnya, Hizb'allah in Lebanon, Lashkar-e-taiba in Pakistan/Kashmir, Barbar Khalsa International (BKI) in India, the Liberation Tigers of Tamil Eelam (LTTE or Tamil Tigers) in Sri Lanka, the Kurdistan Worker's Party (PKK) in Turkey, and al Qaeda.[2]

There is an increasing and disturbing trend towards Islamic suicide terrorism. Abd Al-Rahman Al-Rashed, former editor of the London daily *Al-Sharq Al-Awsat* and general manager of the Arab Satellite network, Al 'Arabiya made a controversial comment after the Beslan attack in Ossetia in September 2004, under the title *The Painful Truth is that All of the Terrorists are Muslims,* he wrote:

> Obviously not all Muslims are terrorists but, regrettably, the majority of the terrorists in the world are Muslims. The kidnappers of the students in Ossetia are Muslims. The kidnappers and killers of the Nepalese workers and cooks are also Muslims. Those who rape and murder in Darfur are Muslims, and their victims are Muslims as well. Those who blew up the residential complexes in Riyadh and Al-Khobar are Muslims. Those who kidnapped the two French journalists [in Iraq] are Muslims. The two [women] who blew up the two planes [over Russia] are Muslims. Bin Laden is a Muslim and Al-Houthi [the head of a terrorist group in Yemen] is a Muslim. The majority of those who carried out suicide operations against buses, schools, houses, and buildings around the world in the last ten years are also Muslims.
>
> What a terrible record. Does this not say something about us, about our society and our culture? If we put all of these pictures together in one day, we will see that these pictures are difficult, embarrassing, and humiliating for us. However, instead of avoiding them and justifying them it is incumbent upon us first of all to recognize their authenticity rather than to compose eloquent articles and speeches proclaiming our innocence . . . Islam has suffered an injustice at the hands of the new Muslims . . . We have to realize that we cannot correct the condition of our youth who carry out these disgraceful operations until we have treated the minds of our sheikhs who have turned themselves into pulpit revolutionaries who send the children of others to fight while they send their own children to European schools.[3]

In this book, I will demonstrate that there is nothing inherently dysfunctional about the Islamic faith per se that predisposes its adherents towards violence, but increasingly groups are emulating each other's tactics and so suicide terrorism has mistakenly been associated with this one religion in particular. This chapter will show that all religious groups have been susceptible to terrorism at one point or another. Further, many groups engaged in suicide terror described in this book are decidedly secular and, for them, religion is incidental.

One can define terrorism as both an "act-based" event (targeting of civilians) as well as an "actor-based" phenomenon in which non-state actors engage in political violence in order to affect desired political outcomes. The U.S. State Department acknowledges that there is no single definition of terrorism. It uses the term "terrorism" to mean premeditated, politically motivated violence perpetrated against noncombatant targets by sub-national groups or clandestine agents, usually intended to influence an audience. "International terrorism" means terrorism involving citizens or the territory of more than one country. On the other hand, the definitions used by scholars tend to place more emphasis on the intention of terrorists to cause fear and terror among a target audience with the aim of persuasion that transcends the harm caused to the immediate victims.[4]

Although the individual bombers might be inspired by several—sometimes complementary—motives, the organizations that send the bombers do so because such attacks are an effective means to intimidate and demoralize the enemy. I will show how the organizations are rationally motivated and use violence to achieve their goals. The operations are carefully calculated and aimed at ending a foreign occupation, increasing the prestige of the organization that uses them, and leading to regional autonomy and/or independence. The book will present the individual's motivations for terrorism as well as why insurgent organizations adopt suicide terror as a strategy, whether this is successful, and why some groups have abandoned suicide terrorism.

Mark Juergensmeyer writes that there are few instances where terrorism has been effective in leading to prospective statehood. He lists only Ireland and the Palestinian Authority [and I would add Tamil Eelam] as cases where terrorism has advanced the cause of statehood. Even there, the terrorists have had to first abandon their violent tactics and transform their agenda to political means (negotiations) in order to achieve their goals.[5] In two of those cases, negotiations have been stymied by the continuation of violence and the goals of independence, statehood, or autonomy, which has yet to be realized. The "martyrdom operations" in many of the cases are deemed the only answer to opposing the vastly superior military capabilities of the other side. In the words of the founder and spiritual leader of the Islamic Resistance Movement Hamas (assassinated by Israel in March 2004), Sheikh Ahmad Yasin, "Once we have warplanes and missiles, then we can think of changing our means of legitimate self-defense. But right now, we can only tackle the fire with our bare hands and sacrifice ourselves."[6] Sheikh Lutful-lah of Lebanon's Hizb'allah (Party of God) echoed Yasin's sentiment after the 1983 bombing of the U.S. Marines' Barracks in Lebanon when he commented: "oppressed people cannot always be expected to behave in a reasonable manner."[7]

Many of the key elements linking the modern and historical antecedents of terrorism have not changed considerably. Consider the description of nineteenth-century anarchist Sergei Gennadievich Nechayev by the Russian revolutionary Bakunin in 1869:

> I have here one of those young fanatics who know no doubts, who fear nothing and who have decided quite definitely that many, many of them will have to perish at the hands of government but who will not let this stop them until the Russian people arise. They are magnificent, these young fanatics, believers without God, heroes without rhetoric.[8]

Suicide terror predates the modern manifestation of car bombs that began in Lebanon. It is neither unique to the modern period nor confined to any single region or religion. The early historical antecedents of terrorism include the Jewish Zealots and Sicarii in the first century AD, during the time of the Second Temple until its destruction in 70 AD, the Hindu Thugs in India from the time of Herodotus until 1836, the Ismaili Assassins of the twelfth century, anti-colonial movements in Malabar, and the Japanese Kamikaze during World War Two. By examining these early examples of terrorism we can deduce certain general patterns that emerged and draw similarities between these early illustrations and the more recent phenomena. The common themes that emerge from the early case studies provide a template of what is happening today: the role of early education in creating adherents, the appearance of charismatic and ambitious leaders, disputes over occupied territory, and the ways in which religion was manipulated to induce followers to kill in the name of God.

Although, in modern times, both secular and religious groups perpetrate suicide terrorism, before the nineteenth century, religion provided the primary rationale.[9] The early groups, although inspired by religious fervor, were diversified by their fundamental goals. Each of the early cases demonstrates a different religion that justified violence. The (Hindu) Thugs, (Muslim) Assassins and (Jewish) Zealots were all principally motivated by religion, yet the Thugs were a status quo organization with no political purposes while the Assassins opposed the status quo and wanted to bring about revolutionary change. In their world view, the leaders of the day had strayed from the divine path and their purpose was to set the leadership straight. The Zealots were the quintessential anti-Colonial struggle—centuries before the advent of "colonialism." Zealot violence, although having religious, puritanical, and messianic underpinnings, was intended to shake off the Roman (and Gentile) occupation.

One of the earliest examples of terrorism comes from India, where the Thugs strangled their victims and buried them—a deliberate assault on orthodox Hinduism—in order to please the Goddess Kali (known as Bhowanee). Thugs, also called the Phansigars or stranglers, are linked to the ancient Sagartians who served in the Persian army according to Herodotus.[10] The organization would thrive for 2500 years, until the advent of the British Raj, making them the longest lasting terror group in history. The Thugs believed they needed to supply Kali, the goddess of time and universal energy, sustainer and destroyer of all life, with blood to keep the world balanced between good and evil. Thugs were expected to kill to accomplish this task and new members were drawn from the families of Thugs—making it an inherited profession. The more terror the victims experienced, the more Kali enjoyed their deaths.[11]

The Thugs were regulated by their methods of attack, division of labor, disposal of the corpses, distribution of booty, and training of new recruits. They normally targeted travelers, but were constrained from attacking certain civilians: women, the homeless, lepers, the blind, the infirm, and artisans (considered to be descendents of Kali and favored by her). Europeans were largely immune from attack, thus limiting the Thugs' political purposes vis-à-vis national liberation. The Thugs' victims were sacrifices; nevertheless they avoided brutalizing them. As sacrifices, they had to be without blemish and could not be abused in any way.[12] According to their ideology, the victims entered paradise in exchange for their lives.

In the Muslim Middle East, Bernard Lewis writes about the Ismaili Islamic sect known as the Nizari (and more commonly known as the Assassins). For 800 years, the sect was shrouded in mystery, glimpsed through a mist of rumor and speculation. Philip K. Hitti writes that the whole mysterious legend of the Assassins was most fancifully presented by Marco Polo, who passed through Persia in 1273. Speaking of the Assassin chief, Polo wrote:

> He had caused a certain valley between two mountains to be enclosed, and had turned it into a garden, the largest and most beautiful that ever was seen ... flowing freely with wine and milk and honey and water; and numbers of ladies and of the most beautiful damsels in the world, who could play on all manner of instruments and sung most sweetly, and danced in a manner that it was charming to behold. For the Old Man desired to make his people believe that this was actually

Paradise. . . . 'So when the Old Man would have any Prince slain,' Polo continues, 'he would say to such a youth: Go thou and slay So and So; and when thou returnest, my Angels shall bear thee into Paradise. And should'st thou die nevertheless even so, I will send my Angels to carry thee back into Paradise. . . .' And in this manner the Old One got his people to murder any one whom he desired to get rid of.[13]

The derivation of the word Assassin, still used today to describe a political murderer, originated with the Arabic word *hashishiyyin* (because they reputedly smoked hashish before engaging in acts of terror). Lewis corrects this misconception and argues that there is no evidence of the use of drugs. Their primary goal was to purify Islam. They inflicted relatively few casualties, although they posed a serious threat to the governments of Seljuk Empire in Persia and in the Levant in their heyday.

In order to spread their notoriety, they attacked prominent victims at venerated holy sites and at the royal court; they would strike on Muslim Holy Days when many witnesses were present. Lewis writes that their weapon was "always a dagger, never poison, never a missile . . . and the Assassin usually made no attempt to escape; there was even a suggestion that to survive the mission was shameful."[14]

The Assassin understood that he would not survive the attack. Since Assassins were drawn from a heretical Shi'a sect that venerated Ali, the nephew and son-in-law of the prophet Muhammed and Hussein, martyred at the Battle of Karbala (in modern day Iraq) in 680 AD, the "cult of sacrifice" was reinforced by a deeply embedded Shi'a admiration for martyrs—especially those who died trying to kill an enemy of Islam. Assassins' education prepared them for this martyrdom and reinforced the belief that their sacrifice would lead them to paradise.

The use of terror appears in many ways to be a "weapon of the weak"[15] for the Assassins. With one carefully planned attack, a small force prepared to die in the course of killing others could cripple their more powerful enemy. They realized, too, that the fear or memory of such an attack could be as paralyzing as the attack itself.

From 1090 to 1256 AD, the Assassins terrorized those who opposed them—killing grand viziers and kings, attacking the Muslim hero Salah ad-Din[16] and eventually doing battle with the forces of Genghis Khan during the Mongol invasion of the Middle East. It was even alleged that they served as hired mercenaries for the English Crusader King, Richard the Lion Hearted. They originated in Persia although many Assassins emerged from the Egyptian missionary schools during the Fatimid (an Ismaili) dynasty. Trained in remote Persian mountain fortresses, they later moved to Syria, prepared to follow to the grave—and beyond—charismatic leaders such as Hasan-i Sabbah and Sinan ibn Salman ibn Muhammad (commonly known as the "Old Man of the Mountain"). When the Fatimid Dynasty ceased to promote their millenarian ideology (to cleanse the empire of impure, corrupt, and hypocritical elements of Islam) the founder of the Assassins broke off and seized several mountain fortresses where he developed a particular Gnostic theology promising a messianic fulfillment of history.[17]

The Assassins were hardly a mainstream Islamic group and they existed for the most part on the fringes of Islamic society. The Muslim Philosopher al-Ghazali wrote extensively about them and devoted many works to the confutation of those he termed Batinites, in seven anti-Ismaili tracts.[18] The core of al-Ghazali's anti-Batinite criticism consisted of underlining the absurdities and heretical innovations which followed from their blind submission (*taqlid*) to the authoritarian teachings of their religious leaders or Imams. For al-Ghazali, the only living guide for the Muslims was the Prophet Muhammad, whose acts and utterances make up the *Hadith* and *Sunnah* which were sufficient to guide the lives of the Islamic Community of Believers.

The Assassins' goal was to return the Islamic Community of Believers (Umma) into a single community (as had been the case under the first four rightfully guided Caliphs, the successors to the Prophet, in the seventh century) and they rebelled against the existing Sunni order and sought to establish their own state—consisting of a series of fortresses and city states. The city state's raison d'être was terror. To facilitate operations they established a network of supporting cells in sympathetic neighboring urban centers. Rapoport describes the efficacy of their methods. They placed a young Assassin in the service of a high official at a very young age. Through devotion and skill over the years he would acquire his master's trust, and then, at the appropriate time, the faithful servant would plunge a dagger into his master's back.[19] Nevertheless, the Assassins were constrained in their methods. When attacked by the ruling Sunni elites, they engaged in retaliatory violence but rarely escalated the conflict. The tradition of the Assassins was dictated by the abhorrence of fitna among Muslims. "Fitna has the opposite and negative connotation from Jihad," explains Giles Kepel. "It signifies sedition, war in the heart of Islam, a centrifugal force that threatens the faithful with community fragmentation, disintegration and ruin." [20]

When the Assassins' supporters were indiscriminately targeted by the Sunni elites because of their heresy, they responded with restraint. They believed that additional assassinations were the only legitimate response. The political consequences of their restraint meant that after forty years, support for the Assassins among urban elements waned and the massacres ceased. However, because of their physical isolation and autarkic methods, they survived until the Mongol invasions of the thirteenth century led by Hulagu.[21]

We can draw many similarities between the Assassins and the contemporary manifestation of suicide terror. Similar to the Assassins, many of the current movements indoctrinate their followers at an early age and rely upon adherents' dedication to charismatic leaders which make them notorious and seemingly irrational. The Assassins used religious schools to propagate their message and their operational tactics could be compared to sleeper cells that would be activated years after being assigned to a particular target. In many ways, this early group demonstrates a degree of sophistication years ahead of its time.

There are likewise similarities among the early antecedent groups: Like the Assassins, the Jewish sect known as the Sicarii (or Zealots) were identified by their use of a particular weapon (a dagger or *sica*); both were inspired by hopes of messianic redemption and designed their attacks to be well publicized.[22] Beginning in 48 AD, the Zealots carried out terrorist campaigns to force insurrection against the Romans in Judea. These campaigns included the use of *sicarii* (dagger-men), who would infiltrate Roman-controlled cities and stab Jewish collaborators or Roman legionnaires with a *sica*, kidnap the staff of the Temple Guard for ransom, or poison their enemies. The Zealots' justification for their killing of other Jews was that their acts demonstrated the consequences of the immorality of collaborating with the Roman invaders, and exposed the fact that the Romans could not protect their Jewish collaborators.[23]

Rapoport differentiates the Sicarii from the Zealots since the focus of Sicarii anger was Hellenized Jews whereas the Zealots generally targeted the enemy occupiers — Romans and the Greeks.[24] The Zealots or Sicarii operated for approximately a quarter of a century during the time of the Second Temple. They ostensibly had three primary goals: to cleanse Judea of foreign influences and bring about messianic redemption, to incite rebellion among the Jews and Greeks of the Holy Land by making the Roman occupation so intolerable that rebellion was inevitable and, finally, to prevent any possible reconciliation between the Romans and Jews (i.e., spoil any potential for peace).

The origin of their ideology derived from the days of Moses when Phineas, a vigilante High Priest, averted a plague intended to punish Israel's apostasy and "the whoring acts of Moabite women." Phineas took matters into his own hands, and killed a tribal chief and his concubine.[25] The name *Sicarii* comes from the Latin word for Phineas' spear which he used as a dagger (*sica*), and also meant "bandit." Phineas' actions prepared the way for Holy war (*herem*) which God commanded Israel to wage against the Canaanites for control of the Promised Land[26] *Herem* (Holy War) was a war without constraints vis-à-vis civilians and did not exempt women, children or the elderly. The Zealots and Sicarii utilized a wide range of tactics. They typically assassinated prominent Jews, and, especially Temple priests, who had succumbed to Hellenistic culture.[27] They took hostages and terrorized wealthy landowners to compel them to redistribute their lands according to the Biblical traditions. Finally, they attacked Jewish moderates willing to negotiate with the Romans and those who argued in favor or moderation and restraint.

Flavius Josephus wrote about the group that:

> The Sicarii committed murders in broad daylight in the heart of Jerusalem. The holy days were their special seasons when they would mingle with the crowd carrying short daggers concealed under their clothing with which they stabbed their enemies. Thus, when they fell, the murders joined in cries of indignation . . . and were never discovered. The first assassinated was Jonathon, the high priest. After his death there were numerous daily murders. The panic created was more alarming than the calamity itself.[28]

Rome's desire to avoid conflict encouraged the militants' violent behavior and weakened Jewish moderates. Demonstrators became more aggressive and bands of rock throwing children broke off from the crowds to stone the Roman occupiers. When the Romans responded, their restraint and discipline dissolved. The panic which engulfed the crowds in Jerusalem led to a number of occasions when innocent bystanders were trampled to death.

> This pattern kept repeating itself, and the atrocities seemed especially horrifying because they normally occurred on holy days when Jerusalem was crowded with pilgrims, many of whom were killed while attending religious services. The massive outrage generated by Roman atrocities and the [Zealots'] assassination campaign against the moderates intimidated reluctant priests into refusing to allow Roman Sacrifices at the Temple.[29]

In addition to a policy of "targeted assassination," the Zealots engaged military forces on the battlefield, and slaughtered their prisoners without hesitation. Josephus writes that the final insult to Rome came when the Zealots massacred the Jerusalem garrison after the Romans had laid down their arms and were guaranteed safe passage. Rapoport explains:

> The Zealots saw themselves as revolutionary catalysts who moved men by force of their audacious action, exploiting mass expectations that a

cataclysmic messianic deliverance was imminent. To generate a mass uprising, they escalated the struggle by shock tactics to manipulate fear, outrage, sympathy and guilt. Sometimes these emotional affects were provoked by terrorist atrocities which went beyond the consensual norms governing violence; at other times, they were produced by provoking the enemy into committing atrocities against his will.[30]

Because of the massacre, the Romans and their Greek recruits retaliated against the Jewish civilian population. A cycle of violence resulted in which reprisals and counter reprisals spread throughout the Eastern portions of the Empire. Given that most of the Jewish residents of the Empire preferred peace, Rome believed that the Sicarii's violence against other Jews would destroy their popular support. Yet the Zealots and the Sicarii had designed their actions to deliberately provoke a massive uprising. "Consecutive atrocities narrowed the prospects for a political, or mutually agreeable, solution serving to destroy the credibility of moderates on both sides while steadily expanding the conflict, which enlisted new participants."[31]

Several different Zealot and Sicarii groups existed resulting in a multiplicity of organizations engaged in outbidding—similar to the modern manifestation evident on the Palestinian-Israeli conflict in which religious and secular groups vie with one another to win Palestinian popularity through the use of violence. As is the case among Palestinians, "the effect of multiplicity was to encourage each element toward even more heinous atrocities, in order to prove the superiority of its commitment and in time the groups decimated each other."[32]

Zealot leaders then burned the food supply of their own forces during Jerusalem's long siege as a show of religious dedication and in an attempt to force God's hand to act against the Romans. God would have no choice but to intervene to preserve his adherents. Divine intervention was not forthcoming and many of Jerusalem's residents starved to death. Josephus' position was that the Zealots' tactics were to blame for all the calamities that befell the Jewish people including their exile, expulsion, the massacres of Jewish communities in Egypt and Cyprus, and the destruction of the Second Temple.

Finally, Josephus blamed the mass suicide at Masada on zealot intransigence. When Roman general Flavius Silva decided to attack Masada at the end of 72 AD, there were 960 insurgents and refugees in the fortress including men, women, and children. Silva surrounded the mountain with the tenth Roman legion plus auxiliaries. Once the fortress' fall was inevitable the following year, Eleazar, the leader of the zealots, persuaded Masada's defenders to engage in an act of mass suicide. (Two women and their five children survived to describe the events by hiding in a cave.) The Zealots on Masada preferred to die by their own hand rather than be captured by their Roman enemies. The symbolic act demonstrated the commitment of the Jews and their steadfast opposition to Roman oppression. Mass suicide was common after military defeats; Josephus joined the Romans' side because he refused to participate in one after his army was beaten.[33]

The Thugs and Assassins alternated between periods of inactivity and periods of intense activity. The Thugs were expected to kill a minimum number of people per year although they tended to focus their attacks during specific seasons. The Assassins, as an offshoot of Shi'a Islam, were able to practice quietude and dissimulation (*Taqiya*) and appear to work within the system, until such time that they were activated to carry out their mission.[34] Both the Thugs and Assassins were indoctrinated as children and were shockingly effective in their operations. Neither the Thugs nor Assassins carried out operations against foreigners, only individuals from within their own community. Practically speaking this meant that the Thugs were never a viable opposition to British rule in India and the Assassins rarely attacked Christians—not even the invading Crusaders.

In contrast to this, the Zealots focused their anger on the Roman occupation and Jews who collaborated with them. Among these ancient groups, the Zealots had much in common with the modern manifestation of suicide terror because their goal was to oppose a foreign occupation of the Holy land and to shake off Roman rule. The use of stone throwing children resulting in unrestrained soldiers massively retaliating against them should resonate with the modern conflicts and with many images in today's news. The Zealot focus on Roman occupiers and on collaborators and moderates willing to negotiate is strikingly evocative of the present Palestinian-Israeli conflict.

The Jewish Zealots, Hindu Thugs, and the Muslim Assassins are early examples of terrorism and religiously inspired sacrifice. A lesser known example of the early antecedents of suicide terror date to the eighteenth and nineteenth centuries when it was effectively used by the Muslim communities of Malabar, Aceh, and the Philippines against foreign colonial occupation. Dale writes that there were:

> Protests against Western hegemony or colonial rule by Muslims who felt that they had no other means of fighting against superior European or American power. The suicidal attacks by Muslims in Asia represent a pre-modern form of terrorism—as a more politicized variant of a type of anti-colonial resistance that long antedates the twentieth century. . . . These suicidal *jihadis* in the eighteenth century Malabar . . . were one of the few means by which they could injure

and intimidate those who had usurped trade and otherwise assaulted their community.[35]

The suicide terrorism in Malabar took the form of directed attacks against specific individuals for social, economic, or religious purposes, blending the two variants of suicide terror, in the sense that they had both religious and nationalistic justifications. The Jihadis, called *juramentados*, would rush the enemy, trying to kill as many Spaniards as possible, until they themselves were killed. Dale writes that there is no record of a *juramentado* who ever returned home alive.[36] Like the Hamas *Shahids* (Martyrs) of today, the Malabari Martyrs underwent extensive recruitment, training, and preparation for their suicidal attacks. They signaled their commitment by divorcing their wives, dressing in a white, uncut cloth (the garment used for the Muslim pilgrimage for the Hajj and for burial) and participating in a religious ceremony to make their commitment irreversible. A martyr was not permitted to change his mind and there were significant social pressures by family and friends to fulfill his duty. Their individual acts were memorialized in heroic literature (e.g., the *Hikayat Prang Sabi*)[37] which detailed the rewards of paradise. This literature functioned as a means of mobilizing young men to become martyrs.

Like Palestinian *Shahids* or the Hindu Tamil Tigers in Sri Lanka:

> The prevalence of the very young, only occasionally the extremely aged, and nearly always the impoverished, whatever the age, confirms the importance of youthful enthusiasm, naïveté and recklessness, aged depression, and despair and poverty [were] critical influences that led individuals to sacrifice themselves.[38]

By the mid twentieth century, the Muslims in Malabar, Aceh, and the Philippines had abandoned suicidal terror. In all three areas, terrorism's end was due to the shift in the political environment in which the Muslims found themselves—one which now offered Muslims an alternative means to realizing their goals and not because of increasing coercion on the part of the colonial power.[39] The shift from suicidal violence to political activism demonstrates how the tactic could transform over time and under which conditions it did so. The example of how Muslims in Asia abandoned suicide terror provides an opportunity to learn from the lessons of the past. It is particularly noteworthy that the British, French, and Spanish authorities were incapable of stopping suicide terror by using more sophisticated policing tactics or punitive military actions. The British and Dutch authorities managed to "solve their terrorist problems by allowing nationalist movements to develop. . . . these movements offered the promise of altered political systems and then realized their goals only with the withdrawal of the colonial governments."[40]

In the contemporary period, religious groups and nationalist movements have used suicide terror to accomplish their goals and have come from several major religions, besides Islam. There are further historical examples of sacrifice, based on the complete dedication and commitment to a particular leader and/or to a nationalist cause. Previously successful tactics have been reintroduced. Even the particular method that the terrorists of September 11 used did not come out of the blue, figuratively speaking. Hijacking of commercial aircraft has, of course, been a time-honored method of international terrorism, and was especially prominent during the first couple of decades of the modern era of international terrorism.

The September 11th operation was not the first time that terrorists succeeded in crashing airliners into well-chosen targets to cause significant casualties on the ground. Throughout the Pacific War, aircraft crashed into enemy ships. The Japanese *kamikaze*[41] who flew their planes into the American fleets demonstrated a similar blind devotion to their leadership and the nationalist cause.

From October 1944 to August 1945, more than 3,000 Japanese Army and Navy pilots died intentionally crashing their planes into Allied ships. Smaller numbers died manning weapons specifically designed for suicide missions— which offered no hope of survival. Although not strictly accurate, the term *kamikaze* has come to refer to all premeditated suicide missions conducted by the Japanese military during this period (and not just the "Divine Wind" attack corps.) In many cases the planes were damaged as a result of enemy fire and would not have been likely to make the journey back home safely. Some crashes were deliberate attacks by undamaged planes. The vast majority of these acts were committed by Japanese pilots but not all. There are at least two incidents of American attacks on Japanese ships, one during the battle of Coral Sea in May 1942, the second at Midway that June. Although far less numerous, suicide missions were also conducted by other countries.[42]

In 1941, Russian commanders instructed fighter pilots to crash their planes into enemy planes when Hitler's invasion caught them completely off guard. Germany established squadrons of *Rammjäger* (battering-ram) aircraft to crash into enemy bombers once they were losing the war. The planes were not originally designed for suicide missions. The craft had been specially reinforced to better withstand aerial collisions, and pilots were instructed to bail out of their planes if they were downed. According to Goebbels' diary for March 31, 1945, however, "the *Rammjägers[sic]* are now to make suicide attacks. . . . 90 percent casualties are expected." Initially these were composed of volunteers but later those found guilty of military infractions were sent on suicide missions.[43]

In April 1945 Germany used planes to crash into bridges to impede the Soviet armies closing in on Berlin. The pilots were reported to have signed the statement "I am above all else clear that the mission will end in my death."[44]

Individual kamikazes wrote about their motives, providing us with insight into how they felt. Second Lieutenant Shigeyuki Suzuki wrote to his parents before taking off on his final mission:

> People say that our feeling is one of resignation, but they do not understand at all how we feel, and think of us as a fish about to be cooked. Young blood does flow in us. There are persons we love, we think of, and many unforgettable memories. However, with those, we cannot win the war. . . . To let this beautiful Japan keep growing, to be released from the wicked hands of the Americans and British, and to build a "free Asia" was our goal from the Gakuto Shutsujin year before last; yet nothing has changed. . . . The great day that we can directly be in contact with the battle is our day of happiness and at the same time, the memorial of our death.[45]

As Japan's military situation deteriorated there was increasing discussion about the efficacy of this tactic versus more conventional attacks. Both middle and higher ranking officers sent proposals to Tokyo that suicide attacks be formally employed and suggested the use of 'special attack'[46] methods. General Ushiroku, senior deputy chief at Army General Staff, proposed the use of backpack-bombs by infantrymen in New Guinea and Bouganville.[47] Had this suggestion been implemented, the backpack-bomb would have been the original Improvised Explosive Device (IED) which is now common in the Middle East and Sri Lanka.

The mastermind behind the kamikaze attack is not known with any certainty, but it is often thought to be Admiral Takijiro Onishi, who commanded the first squadron, known as *Shinpu Tokubetsu Kogekitai*. The reasoning was that Japan was nearly defeated, short on resources, and had nothing to lose by sending its young pilots on cost-effective suicide missions in the hope of deterring the enemy.

Mako Sasaki provides the following statement, made by Onishi after the plan to use kamikazes was approved by the Imperial War Ministry: "If they [young pilots] are on land, they would be bombed down, and if they are in the air, they would be shot down. That's sad. . . . Too sad. . . . To let the young men die beautifully, that's what Tokko is. To give beautiful death, that's called sympathy."[48]

Suicide attacks were rejected by most senior officers but not because of their distaste for sending men to a certain death. Rather, as Vice Admiral Yokoi later pointed out, there were three significant flaws with kamikaze missions. The first problem was that it was a highly expensive tactic to use a trained pilot and his aircraft in a single attack. This strategy conflicted with the basic military principle of achieving maximum goals with the minimum loss to one's own resources (though the suicidal infantry counterattacks by the defenders on islands in the Aleutians, Philippines, and elsewhere suggests that a time comes when such calculations break down).

Secondly, plane-crash attacks lacked sufficient penetrative power to strike a mortal blow to the aircraft carriers. To be effective they had to strike when the decks were fully laden with aircraft. Thirdly, Yokoi argues that it was enormously difficult to evaluate the success of missions as the pilots were dead and their commanders had incentive to overestimate the gains achieved by their men's deaths.[49] Naitō suggests that professional military pride was another factor: the officers of the high command believed they could win by conventional means.[50]

In many instances, the Japanese Kamikaze were pressured or coerced into their missions. In most of the cases the pilots cited a complete dedication to the Emperor Hirohito as the divine representation on earth as they completed their task. Most significantly, the fact that Japan could not win against the American juggernaut resulted in pursuing a tactic against which the American Navy could not defend itself. In addition to the kamikaze pilots, Japan used manifold forms of suicide terror including suicide motorboats, Ōka, rocket powered piloted bombs made mostly of wood, airborne saboteur assaults, and suicide submarines. According to Peter Hill, these tactics, aside from aircraft crashing attacks, were not particularly effective.[51]

Thus, the Japanese resorted to this tactic only as a last resort and its efficacy is highly debatable although it had a significant negative psychological impact on the Navy's morale. So significant was the psychological warfare that U.S. commanders stopped warning their crews when attacks were imminent. Hill cites Hanson Baldwin that the "strain of waiting, the anticipated terror, made vivid from past experience sends some men into hysteria, insanity, breakdown."[52] Those planes that were able to penetrate the protective American cordon did considerable physical damage; Vice Admiral Brown of the U.S. Navy claimed that the kamikaze "inflicted more casualties in the US fleet off Okinawa than the Japanese Army did to the invading troops in the long battle ashore."[53]

Ben Ami Shillony asserts that 83 percent of all pilots who died in kamikaze attacks were university students.[54] At the early stage of the use of suicide missions, Japan had used fully-trained combat pilots. Once the use of the kamikaze became a large-scale operation, instructions were issued by the High Command that less valuable personnel be used and shifted to university students drafted in 1943 who had undergone minimal training.[55] The best pilots were used to escort the kamikaze to their targets. In doing so the escorts played a number of support roles: they guided the navigationally untrained kamikaze; they protected them from enemy fighters; they observed their attacks; and they provided an environment encouraging completion of the mission (the realization that someone was watching bolstered the resolution of pilots). Many of the escort pilots resented their secondary role and protested that they should be allowed to fully participate in suicide missions.[56]

Although the kamikaze bombers were dedicated to a nationalistic rather than religious cause, those soldiers who died in battle were enshrined at Yasukuni Jinja and became *national gods*. A cult of personality, akin to that of Palestinian and Tamil martyrs, developed around them. Comparable to the posters that are immediately put up after every Palestinian martyrdom attack and the pamphlets of Black Tigers distributed at the annual Heroes' Day celebrations, the kamikaze were lionized in the press and in communiqués in which they were referred to as "god-heroes" and their photos were publicized in the newspapers. One young kamikaze pilot wrote to his parents that a film crew had visited his unit (He wrote: "I hope I looked photogenic today"). Kamikaze pilots received fan-mail and handmade dolls from schoolgirls to take on their missions. Civilians would approach them in the street and express their appreciation.[57]

This book's arguments regarding the process of outbidding might even be applicable in this case. There was interplay between the war party and peace faction in late-war Japan. In part, the encouragement and use of kamikazes made it more difficult for the peace faction to negotiate a settlement. After all, how could you dishonor the sacrifice of the kamikazes by negotiating with the enemy?

Analogous to the historical religious examples, the kamikaze made use of psychological operations although the military effectiveness of the tactic remains hotly debated. In the Japanese case, suicide terror was intended to complement military operations. It is in this respect that the differences between the historical examples and cases to be presented in this book become obvious.

Suicide terror can be nuanced, as Rohan Gunaratna suggests, into on-the-battlefield and off-the-battlefield operations.[58] In certain instances, suicide terror is part of the overall military campaign. These on-the-battlefield operations tend to target military personnel, military infrastructure or symbols, and are marked by being a tactic of last resort when power imbalances are so great that only shocking methods by groups with little to lose will have any effect. In off-the-battlefield operations, the attacks are ends in themselves, designed to terrorize the civilian population and provoke some political change. The targets are overwhelmingly of a nonmilitary nature (noncombatant civilians) and locations are chosen to have the maximum devastating effect in order to cause panic and wide-scale fear. In such cases, the use of suicide terror as a tactic will often be observed during periods of stalemate when something is required to tip the balance. Such highly publicized actions are effective in shaking actors out of their lull and shifting the existing status quo.

The early examples of suicide terror provide a glimpse of the range of tactics used in the past and, in many of the cases, rediscovered in the present. The terrorists' desire for publicity, the indoctrination of young children, the targeting of foreign occupiers and attacks against collaborators are all surprisingly similar to the tactics we observe in the Middle East, Sri Lanka, and Chechnya. The cases presented in this book will expound upon different examples of suicide terror in which I contrast on-the-battlefield and off-the-battlefield operations, differentiate between religious and nationalist groups using suicide terror, and develop a theory of how different groups use violence in order to achieve their goals.

I argue that under specific conditions endogenous to each of the cases, suicide terror will either be sanctioned or prohibited by the civilian population. The use of violence will either resonate effectively with the rank and file or will be rejected and, eventually, abandoned by the groups. I discuss to what extent organizations influence one another, and learn from each other's tactics, providing reciprocal training, and operational and financial support. Finally, the lessons of the past should not be ignored. In several of the early antecedents of terror, harsh counter terror tactics had the inverse effect. It was not until after the political backdrop against which the terrorists operated shifted that accommodation and a solution to the problem was possible.

In the following chapters I endeavor to *explain the unexplainable* and contrast the different motivations for suicide terror in several countries. The book critically examines cases across the Middle East, South Asia, and Europe in which suicide terror has been used or abandoned, and assesses whether it was a success or failure. The cases under review include the Palestinian-Israeli conflict (chapter 2), the Tamil-Sinhalese conflict in Sri Lanka (chapter 3) and the use of suicide terror by the Kurdish Worker's Party (PKK) in Turkey (chapter 5). In chapter 4, I set out to devise a theory of suicide terror in which I nuance how different sources of support, both financial and from the larger public, have a demonstrable impact on whether civilians are targeted and whether suicide terror will become the instrument of choice for insurgent and militant groups. In chapter 6, I discuss the development of a suicide terror "contagion" in which organizations far a field learn from each other and reproduce one another's tactics. Events in Iraq, Chechnya, the Philippines, Morocco, Turkey, and Saudi Arabia establish that suicide terror appears to have a clear "demonstration and diffusion effect" and seems to be catching on. In chapter 7, I examine the role of women suicide bombers in Chechnya, Sri Lanka and among the Palestinians. Finally, in chapter 8, I discuss the threat of further suicide terror against the United States. I assess what strategies have been developed in the aftermath of 9/11 to prevent the phenomenon from happening again or the nightmare scenario wherein suicide terror would become a systematic campaign against soft targets as it has become in other parts of the globe. Lastly, I explore to what extent the US-led war in Iraq might have unintended consequences for the war on terror at home.

CHAPTER TWO

PALESTINIAN SUICIDE BOMBING:
PUBLIC SUPPORT, MARKET SHARE,
AND OUTBIDDING[1]

Since November 2000, Palestinian public opinion has increasingly supported suicide bombing, even though support for such operations fluctuated in the past, it has alarmingly shifted toward radical Islamic organizations. This shift has occurred for a number of reasons that are endogenous to Palestinian society.[2] With such mounting public support, the bombings became a method of recruitment for militant Islamic organizations within the Palestinian community. They serve at one and the same time to attack the hated enemy (Israel) and give legitimacy to outlier militant groups who compete with the Palestinian Authority (PA) for leadership of the community.

Multiple organizations are engaged in a competition and use violence to increase their prestige. With every major attack since November 2000, support for suicide bombings increased and support for the Palestinian Authority decreased. In addition to support for martyrdom, groups that used the tactic became more popular. The support for militant Islamic movements appears to capture previously "nonaligned constituents" demonstrating that martyrdom operations boost the organizational profile of the groups using them.

Palestinian suicide bombing is a violent, politically motivated attack, carried out by people who deliberately blow themselves up together with a chosen target. Support for suicide operations works against the stated goals of a better future for Palestinian civilians. According to public opinion polls, Palestinians are, by every indicator, worse off now than they were before the Al 'Aqsa Intifada. Yet, the majority of Palestinians support the continuation of the Intifada and martyrdom operations regardless of Israeli retaliatory policies.[3] In this conflict, success has shifted from military victories, and toward the capacity to inflict harm on the other side. Suicide bombings and Israel's policy of targeted assassination both fall under this category. The targets of suicide bombings vary, ranging from government officials to military or economic targets, from scores of attacks to solitary or sporadic ones.[4] However, there is no single theory about what makes suicide bombers do what they do, and no firm opinion about their usefulness among Palestinians.

Conventional explanations of Palestinian suicide bombing regard it as a way for radical Islamic organizations to slow or stem the improvement of relations between Israel and the Palestinian Authority. In this capacity, the bombings play a strategic "spoiler role" to the peace process. Hamas urged more violence as relations between Israel and the Palestinian Authority improved. According to a Palestinian Authority document released in January 2004, "the suicide bombings are a key element in the arena of the struggle between the Israelis and Palestinians and an analysis of the circumstances of the timing and execution of the vast majority of the bombings, particularly the major ones conducted by the Hamas and Islamic Jihad, makes clear the timing was much more a purely political matter than a practical military one."[5] According to the report, Hamas and Islamic Jihad had agents who provided information on political developments, including inside information about negotiations with Israel, and the United States, thus enabling Hamas and the Islamic Jihad to respond accordingly.

An alternative explanation follows from the logic that violence is often retaliatory.[6] This school of thought traces Palestinian suicide bombings to Israeli provocations beginning with the Hebron Massacre by Baruch Goldstein in 1994. As Mazin Hammad commented: "The al Ibrahimi Mosque Massacre opened the doors of revenge in Palestine like never before."[7] Other "provocations" include the 1996 opening of the Hasmonean tunnel under the Al 'Aqsa Mosque, and the targeted assassinations of Palestinian militant leaders such as Hamas' bomb maker, Yahiyeh Ayyash (see photo insert 7) and Izz Eddin al Qassam Brigade leader Salah Shehada and his family in the spring of 2002. Ayyash himself prepared the improvised explosive devices, planned the attacks, trained the attackers and others to prepare suicide attacks. He was eliminated in Gaza when he was handed a booby-trapped cell phone, apparently by an Israeli General Security Services (GSS) agent. Ayyash's assassination took place at the end of a six-month period in which no suicide attacks had occurred (though several were allegedly thwarted during this period). About fifty days after "The Engineer" was eliminated, four painful attacks took place in Israel within a week (three of them were suicide attacks in Jerusalem and Tel Aviv), leaving dozens of people dead and hundreds injured. The Council on Foreign Relations described the five bus bombings in 1996 following his death as a boomerang effect.[8]

The news media implies causality and linkage between the two explanations: "signs of progress recorded by Middle East peace-brokers were obliterated in an orgy of terror as six Israelis were killed in a Palestinian suicide attack in January after Israelis killed Raed Karmi, the local militia leader in Tulkarm of Arafat's Fatah organization."[9]

Andrew Kydd and Barbara F. Walter have argued that violence plays a spoiler role to the peace process and is to be expected when negotiated settlements become imminent. "The purpose is to exacerbate doubts on the target side that the moderate opposition groups can be trusted to implement the peace deal and will not renege on it later on."[10] For Kydd and Walter, suicide bombing is a complex game depending on uncertainty between moderates and the target state and whether moderates are weak or strong vis-à-vis their opposition. They posit that when weak moderates are less capable of stopping terrorism from within their own ranks the other side becomes uncertain, may cancel peace negotiations, and shift Israeli voting in favor of anti-peace candidates. Although their model appears to explicate the bombings that surrounded the 1996 Israeli elections, it fails to explain the whole story.

The attacks carried out in February and March 1996 were among several factors that influenced the outcome of the Israeli Prime Ministerial election of May 1996—bringing right-wing Benjamin Netanyahu into power as well as his delayed implementation of the Oslo and Wye Agreements. Netanyahu's victory was in fact unexpected and his margin of victory was less than 0.5 percent. His victory was due to several factors, including a boycott of the election by a left voting bloc. Israeli Arabs, who comprise 20 percent of the electorate, boycotted after 102 men, women, and children were accidentally killed in an Israeli artillery attack of a UN compound in Kana, Southern Lebanon on April 18, 1996—six weeks before the election.

In addition, the Kydd and Walter model fails to explain why bombings in 1995 did not have the same effect when Yitzhak Rabin was still alive[11] nor can it rationalize how a left-wing government under Ehud Barak was elected in 1999 despite what Kydd and Walter cite as two episodes prior to the election. According to my data, there were no suicide attacks during this period and it is documented that "there was relatively little Palestinian terror on Netanyahu's three-year watch. Due to Arafat's combination of threats, policing and political cajolery, Arafat got Hamas to cut down its violence."[12]

Kydd and Walter are able to partially explain what motivates the organizations but do not and cannot account for why public opinion supports or rejects the tactic. Finally, they conflate the results of suicide bombing campaigns with their underlying motivation. There have been times when Hamas has willingly honored ceasefires (*Hudna*) to allow Arafat to pursue peace negotiations with the Israelis. For example, Arafat convinced Hamas to suspend military actions after September 11, 2001 on the condition that Israeli targeted assassinations stop. The Israelis continued their policy and

Hamas proceeded with their attacks.[13] In December 2001, Arafat delivered a speech in which he called for the terror to stop. He had done this several times before, but always with what seemed a wink. "In the aftermath of September 11, Arafat, according to many reports, was desperate not to repeat his mistake of the Gulf War, when he sided with Saddam Hussein. When Colin Powell called for the future establishment of a Palestinian state, his speech was seen as an achievement for Arafat, at least among his followers."[14]

Three weeks of calm followed. Ariel Sharon then ordered the "targeted killing" of Arafat's lieutenant, Raed Karmi, and Palestinian protests erupted throughout Israel and Gaza. "Arafat's activists became convinced that there was no way that they could reach even a limited understanding with Sharon; the only way to fight was to adopt Hamas' tactic of using suicide bombers."[15] At that point, Arafat joined in the dispatch of suicide bombers into Israel so as not to lose his control over the Palestinian Authority.

This pattern was repeated after the assassination of Raed Karmi, in the spring of 2002 with the assassination of Salah Shehada in Gaza, in 2003 when Hamas called a *Hudna* from May to July only to resume operations after attacks on Dr. Abdel Aziz Rantisi.[16]

Hamas may use suicide terror to deter policymakers from reaching agreements but only as long as Israeli policymakers transparently equate violence with non-negotiation, providing Hamas with its own "road map" of how to spoil a peace process that would, by definition, exclude them. Kydd and Walter correctly identify extremist violence as being strategic, and that the target of the violence is not only the moderates negotiating peace treaties. There are actually two audiences for the violence, one domestic (within the Palestinian community) and one external (the "Zionist Entity").[17]

These existing interpretations (spoiler or retaliatory) ignore the internal state building process and discount the competition for leadership underway within the Palestinian community that accounts for both the occurrence of bombings as well as the absence of attacks in the period from November 1998 to November 2000. Furthermore, the significant increase in attacks in March 2002 took place against a political backdrop with few substantive peace negotiations between Israel and the Palestinian Authority—limiting the explanatory power of the *spoiler* rationale to explain this phenomenon as a whole. James Bennet commented "having seen peace initiatives melt before previous waves of violence, Israelis, like Palestinians, were already deeply skeptical of the new plan [Bush's Road Map]. Many on both sides do not seem to be paying much attention to the renewed diplomacy" so it is unclear how effective the attacks are at spoiling a peace no one believes in.[18] Finally, these existing interpretations cannot account for the variance in public support for these operations over time.

Two Phases of Support for Suicide Terror

In the first period, 1994–96, support for suicide operations never exceeded a third of Palestinians polled whereas after November 2000, support for operations jumped to two-thirds or more. For example, see figures 2.1a and b in the appendix.

The bombings are not just the result of impending implementation of peace treaties or as part of tit for tat violence. Suicide bombings are more than just a reaction to external stimuli; we have to acknowledge the motivations for violence within Palestinian society. One should nuance support for the bombings and explain each phase separately. To do this we need to better comprehend the internal dynamics of the Palestinian polity and the ways in which radical organizations have effectively penetrated civil society.[19]

Palestinians' disillusionment with Arafat, the Palestinian Authority, and the deadlocked peace process provided radical groups with an opportunity to increase their share of the political market by engaging in violence. Finally, Israel's heavy handed responses to the violence (incursions into Area A, targeted assassinations, use of helicopter gun-ships, and civilian casualties) make Hamas' rhetoric appear valid and prescient.[20]

The frustrations associated with the Oslo Process, with Camp David II and the provocative visit in September 2000 of Ariel Sharon to the Haram al-Sharif, and the al 'Aqsa Mosque, exacerbated relations between Palestinians and Israelis. Israeli sharpshooters inflicted heavy casualties on Palestinian demonstrators, at first merely otherwise unarmed youths engaged in symbolic stone-throwing. On the first day thirty Palestinians were killed and hundreds injured, as opposed to only two Israeli casualties.[21] Israel relied on excessive force, generating a cycle of violence that has been escalated at each stage, inflicting disproportionate casualties on the Palestinian side.[22]

Extrapolating from Richard Ned Lebow's "justification of hostility,"[23] Zeev Ma'oz explains that in some cases, political leaders want to initiate a war but cannot afford—for domestic or international reasons—to launch an attack or be portrayed as the aggressor. Instead they try to provoke their opponent. If the opponent responds by escalating the crisis, this provides the initiator with an *ex post facto* justification to ramp up the violence. Ma'oz contends that there have been three instances when Israel used limited force as a means to provoke escalation and asserts that the Israeli response to the Al 'Aqsa Intifada demonstrates how "Israel used targeted killing during times of relative tranquility in order to provoke escalation. The cases involved conscious and deliberate provocations through the use of limited operations." He adds that Israel's key tactic to ignite escalation is its policy of targeted assassinations. "In each of the cases [of targeted assassination], the Palestinian response was a series of suicide bombings which brought about increased Israeli pressure on Palestinians in the form of encirclement of the major population centers, entry into the Palestinian cities and refugee camps, mass arrests, and long curfews of the Palestinian population in the West Bank."[24]

In the first period (1994–1996) suicide bombings were intermittent and, according to Hamas' leaders Sheikh Ahmed Yassin and Dr. Abdel Aziz Rantisi, they *were* intended to both undermine the legitimacy of the Palestinian Authority and negatively affect the peace process.[25] The timing of the attacks was correlated to respond to Israeli actions which provided *defensive* justifications for Hamas violence—in accordance with Islamic law. However, responsibility for the attacks in the first period was often not claimed by any group. Later on, groups vied with one another to make claims of responsibility.

Popular support for the bombings during this first period remained low and Hamas was unable to mobilize Palestinians by using violence. In 1996 the attacks were intended to disrupt the Israeli elections but the missile attack on Kana and the subsequent Israeli-Arab boycott of the elections also had a significant impact on the election results.

In the second period (after November 2000 and increasingly since) support for suicide operations increased exponentially and the waves of bombings demonstrate a competition between groups vying for power against a backdrop where violence resonates with the rank and file. Furthermore, we can observe increasing popular support for groups after they perpetrate martyrdom attacks. See for example figures 2.3 and 2.6 in the appendix.

The bombings have effectively undermined Arafat's monopoly of the legitimate use of force in an emerging Palestinian state entity.[26] According to one Palestinian Cabinet Member:

> When there is an ongoing peace process, the Palestinian Authority is empowered enough to exercise its control over all of the citizens . . . but after ten years of negotiations, Jewish Settlements have doubled since the signing of the Oslo agreement. . . . Hamas and the Islamic Jihad are political organizations that now have substantial standing in the [Arab] street.[27]

In the period immediately after Oslo, Arafat suppressed Hamas and the Islamic Jihad; arrested more than two thousand operatives and killed twenty of its leaders. The period between the signing of the September 28, 1995 Interim Agreement ("Oslo II") until the suicide bombings of February and March of 1996 represented the high point of the PA. The January 1996 elections for an 88-member Palestinian Council and the election of Yasir Arafat as President of the Palestinian Executive Authority endowed the PA with sorely needed political legitimacy. The smooth transition to Shimon Peres after Yitzhak Rabin's assassination, and the Israeli public reaction, increased Palestinian hopes for genuine peace. The Palestinian opposition's decision to boycott the PA institutions and elections led to its further marginalization and increased dissent within its already fragmented ranks.

During the Oslo process, opinion polls consistently showed the majority of Palestinians opposed "martyrdom operations." In November 1998, 75 percent ceased to support suicide operations altogether. In 1999 when over 70 percent of Palestinians had faith in the peace process, support for suicide bombings fell to 20 percent and support for Hamas was at its lowest point ever (below 12 percent). When it appeared that the peace process would yield positive results, the bombings did not resonate for the majority of Palestinians who preferred statehood and peace to violence and continued occupation. [28]

In the aftermath of Wye, Arafat had the mandate to crack down on militants and reign supreme on the Palestinian scene. President Bill Clinton's visit to Gaza in December 1998 helped give Arafat the legitimacy to implement the Wye Accord and the Palestine National Council (PNC) voted to amend the PLO Charter to rescind the call for the destruction of the state of Israel. In January, the Israeli Knesset members from across the political spectrum rebuked Netanyahu, and called for new elections. On May 17, 1999, Ehud Barak won a landslide victory. The majority of Palestinians were cautiously optimistic that they would get statehood.[29] See for example figures 2.5 and 2.7 in the appendix.

By the summer of 1999 Arafat neutralized the Izz Eddin Al Qassam Brigades (the military wing of Hamas) in coordination with Israeli intelligence forces and cut off millions of dollars that Hamas received from outside aid organizations. Hamas' popularity fell to 10 percent and the organization began to fracture and disintegrate from within. Because of their funding shortage, Hamas' extensive network of social services, which bolstered its popularity among impoverished Palestinians, declined overall.[30] In 1999 major schisms in Hamas emerged when its spiritual leader, Sheikh Ahmad Yassin, recognized Arafat's leadership and openly participated in meetings of the Palestinian National Council (PNC) proffering legitimacy to the PA. Yassin even publicly endorsed Arafat's decision not to unilaterally declare independence in May–June of 1999 for which he was severely criticized by hardliners within his own organization.[31]

As Ehud Barak increasingly ignored the Palestinian issue in favor of a "Damascus first strategy," Arafat's rule was increasingly questioned because of the peace deadlock and the Palestinian Authority's corruption. While Arafat was the unchallenged Palestinian leader in 1994–96, this was not the case during the second phase (1996–2000) when he appeared weak and incapable of "delivering" Palestinian agreement/support for his policies—partially explaining the much-touted refusal of Ehud Barak's peace deal in 2000.[32]

> In the second phase, Arafat's popularity occasionally plummeted to below 27 percent. The period of peace deadlock was closely correlated with an increase in Palestinian unemployment, decreasing per capita GNP, and economic stagnation which contributed to a poisoned atmosphere in which suicide bombings became more popular.[33]

Finally, the poor performance of the Palestinian Authority, the rife corruption of its leadership, and its inability to improve the daily lives of most Palestinians meant that, by November 2000, the Islamic Jihad and Hamas had reemerged to initiate a new cycle of violence. In the absence of funding to finance their benevolent activities, Hamas shifted the major focus of its efforts to martyrdom operations to raise its profile and win external donor support.

After the outbreak of the Intifada, support for the bombings and radical Islamic groups increased after every suicide bomb, and Arafat's support declined. According to Khalil Shiqaqi, the director of the Palestinian Center for Policy and Survey Research (PCRS) in Ramallah, young zealots hijacked the *Intifada* and exploited Palestinian instability "to weaken the Palestinian old guard and eventually displace it."[34] Israeli intelligence officials predicted that PA rule in the Gaza Strip would "disintegrate and that Arafat will [eventually] be replaced by Hamas and the Islamic Jihad."[35]

Public opinion polls show a steady increase in support for martyrdom operations as Palestinian hopes for a peaceful future plummeted. After a series of suicide bombs in 2000, popular support for Hamas rose to over 70 percent and continued to rise over the last two and a half years. See figure 2.6 in the appendix.

"Drawing sustenance from the demise of peace and Fatah's disarray and general despair the group's popularity soared, reaching parity with [that of] Fatah's."[36] *The Economist's* prediction of Hamas reaching parity with Fatah was realized by April 2003 when polls placed their popularity at precisely 22 percent each.[37]

Violence resonates with the larger population because of some of the Sharon government's counter-terror tactics. Fewer than 17 percent of Palestinians were optimistic that the violence will end and peaceful negotiations begin again. Since the outbreak of the Al 'Aqsa Intifada in September 2000, Israel has stepped up attacks on civilians, militants, the government and civil infrastructure.

Under Sharon's government, Israeli soldiers have bombed Palestinian cities, sent tanks into Palestinian villages, assassinated Palestinian leaders, killed Palestinian youths, demolished Palestinian homes, blockaded Palestinian towns, mined Palestinian fields, and made Arafat a virtual hostage in the West Bank. But the suicide bombers kept coming.[38]

Most Palestinians view violence as their only option to achieve the goals of independence. Munir al Makdah, who trains suicide bombers is quoted as saying, "Jihad and the resistance begin with the word, then with the sword, then with the stone, then with the gun, then with planting bombs, and then transforming bodies into human bombs."[39] Thus suicide bombing develops as a strategy over time after other tactics fail to yield results.

By claiming responsibility for the attacks, Hamas made the PLO look moderate by comparison. The *New York Times* argued that Arafat benefited personally from extremist violence and the suicide bombings gave him leverage in final status negotiations with Sharon.[40] Far from benefiting, Arafat was weakened by suicide bombing. Ziad Abu Amr, the chairman of the political committee of the Palestinian Legislative Council and Cabinet Minister, confirmed this:

Arafat should be empowered politically, not undermined. Only then can he move against the militants. Arafat was the only one who signed an agreement with Israel, and he is the only one who can. But Arafat is losing his popularity to suicide attacks. If there is nothing for him to brag about ... nothing that he has accomplished ... he has no standing. It all boils down to politics, power, and interests.[41]

Although directed at Israeli civilian and military targets, suicide bombings undermined Arafat's legitimacy within the Palestinian community. The attacks increased when Arafat was weakened by his inability to fulfill promises made to the Palestinian people and incapable of maintaining the monopoly of legitimate force.[42] With the absence of monopoly over force, groups compete and outbid each other with more spectacular bombing operations and competition over claiming responsibility for them. At the same time, the operations whip up nationalist fervor and swell the ranks of the Islamic Jihad and Hamas who use the bombings, in conjunction with the provision of social services, to win the hearts and minds of Palestinians.[43]

Hamas spokespersons acknowledge that the group sees its sizeable social programs as a means of building and maintaining popular support for its political goals and programs, including its militant and armed activities. "The political level is the face of Hamas, but without the other divisions

Hamas would not be as strong as it is now," according to Ismail Abu Shanab. ". . . it needs the three parts to survive. If nobody supports these needy families, maybe nobody would think of martyrdom and the resistance of occupation."[44] Another Hamas leader, Ibrahim al-Yazuri, characterized Hamas' objective as "the liberation of all Palestine from the tyrannical Israeli occupation . . . which is the main part of its concern," he said. "Social work is carried out in support of this aim."[45]

The Israeli policy of West Bank and Gaza closures causes severe economic stagnation. Terje Roed-Larsen, United Nations representative, estimated that there is a 75 percent poverty rate in Gaza and a 53 percent unemployment rate in the Palestinian territories—exacerbated by restrictions on movement imposed by the Israeli security regime.[46] Even Prime Minister Benjamin Netanyahu had reservations concerning the government's use of closure, "I am not a big believer in using closure. Closure produces frustration in the population, and the damage caused is larger than the benefit received."[47]

Thus the bombings resonate against a dual backdrop of economic hardship and the disappearance of any potential peace dividend. Palestinians are convinced that military operations are the only way to wear down the Israeli resolve and weaken their desire to hold onto the Territories. In sharp contrast to this, during periods of "peace progress," few Palestinians responded positively to the bombings in public opinion polls. It is precisely during periods of deadlock that suicide bombings proliferate to augment the organizational profiles of Hamas or the Palestinian Islamic Jihad at the expense of the Palestinian Authority.[48]

Furthermore, the martyrdom operations allow Arafat's rivals to gain international prestige, foreign financial support, and increased domestic "market share" at his expense. The emerging groups of the Palestinian electorate—the young and the urban college educated groups—typify this most clearly. Among the Palestinian youth, Arafat's popularity slips as suicide bombings proliferate. Arafat's approval rating was at 70 percent (in September 2001), but within three months slipped to 57 percent (in December 2001) and continued its decline until Israeli PM Sharon's incursions into the major West Bank towns in late March 2002 resuscitated Arafat's sagging popularity.[49]

In most of the polls, more than 30 percent of the Palestinian public say that they "do not trust any of the current leaders"—leaving the field wide open for incumbents. This group has potential for mobilization. Evidence suggests that with every suicide attack, the parties responsible for the bombings and other Islamic groups opposed to the Palestinian Authority are able to capture the support of people from this market share. Levels of support for Fatah might remain the same, but support for Hamas and for Sheikh Yassin increases while those polled who say they "don't trust any candidate" decreases at the same rate. Although there is some defection from Arafat's support base[50] it is safe to assume that Hamas is winning the hearts and minds of the undecided "voter." This is explained by the fact that groups engaged in suicide bombing appear to be proactive and capable of hurting the Israelis where they live. This positive image is something over which Palestinian organizations compete.

INTRA-GROUP COMPETITION AND OUTBIDDING

The suicide bombings have become bases of mobilization from which Hamas and the Islamic Jihad compete for leadership by capturing the Palestinian imagination. Over time more groups jumped on the suicide bombing bandwagon. There has been a proliferation of organizations using this tactic—some of which previously eschewed it. New groups emerged and previously secular groups started using the language of religious holy war (*Jihad*) to bandwagon onto Hamas' popularity including: the Marxist DFLP (Democratic Front for the Liberation of Palestine), the PFLP (Popular Front for the liberation of Palestine),[51] the Al ‘Aqsa Martyrs' Brigade and a new group calling itself *An-Nathir*, (The Warning). See figures 2.2 and 2.3 in the appendix.

All of the groups vie for the right to claim each attack as their own. "Several Palestinian groups rushed forward to claim responsibility for the bus bombing—an indication of the competition among Palestinians for militant credibility."[52] Hamas and the Islamic Jihad issued competing claims for responsibility for the August 9, 2001 attack on the Sbarro pizzeria (and rival claims that Izzedine Al Masri was *their* operative) and Hamas and the PFLP issued competing claims for the May 19, 2002 attack on the Netanya market. No fewer than four groups claimed credit for the bus bombing on July 17, 2002.

> Al Jazeera television said [the attack] was carried out by ... the Al Aqsa Martyrs' Brigade, in cooperation with Hamas. The Democratic Front for the Liberation of Palestine (DFLP) also claimed responsibility for the attack in a statement faxed to Reuters whose authenticity was confirmed by a DFLP spokesman in Beirut. "The military wing of the Democratic Front for the Liberation of Palestine announces its responsibility for the courageous attack that targeted a bus full of settlers," it said. Hamas and the Islamic Jihad also claimed [separately] they were responsible.[53]

The PFLP and Hamas both claimed credit for the bombing of Mike's Place on April 30, 2003. Violence has become *the* source of all honor among Palestinians. According to Nichole Argo, martyrdom is now a public good and a major source of honor in Palestinian society. Individual esteem is bound to group status, physically and symbolically. Sacrifice and risk employed on behalf of the group become valuable virtues, rewarded by social status. A PFLP would be bomber told her: "You cannot win by yourself, but your sacrifice will help show the world the true nature of your sacrificial self, and of your inhuman opponent."[54] At a profoundly important—albeit symbolic level—martyrdom is the final and irrefutable statement of group worth and dignity against the oppressor. The *shahids* gain increased social status as a result of suicide bombing operations. According to Dr. Abdel Aziz Rantisi, "For Hamas, and Palestinian society in general, becoming a martyr is among the highest if not *the highest*, honor."[55]

The portraits of the bombers (photo 8) have become symbols of resistance as political groups vie in claiming responsibility for the individual martyrs. The martyrs' posters that cover the storefronts of West Bank towns pay homage to the Intifada dead. With each incident, new posters cover over the tattered remains of the previous ones, proclaiming the Qur'anic slogan: *the martyr is not dead, but lives on* and display his or her political affiliation prominently. The martyr becomes the main topic of conversation. People discuss how they were killed, assess the posters for the kinds of weaponry displayed around them and occasionally deride the political factions who vie for the right to claim the dead as members of their organizations. "Some of these guys were never political; the factions just want to bolster their popularity."[56]

George Habash answered similar allegations that he deliberately claimed the responsibility for operatives that were not PFLP members. His defense betrays the organization's competitive spirit with the other groups.

> The PFLP . . . has never tried to take credit for operations or struggles that other heroes of the resistance from different patriotic or Islamic organizations have carried out. On the contrary, all of you know of the operations of our comrades who blew themselves up in occupied Jerusalem for which we did not announce our responsibility and which were claimed at that time by another organization. We in the Abu Ali Mustafa Brigades confirm again our responsibility for the heroic operation of blowing up the Zionist tank near the Netsarim Settlement. The first communiqué of the Brigades laid out the details of the operation just minutes after it took place. This can be considered clear proof that those who carried out the operation were the same ones who issued the communiqué with such precision and detail.[57]

In the polls conducted in 2000, support for the PFLP was lagging. In 2001 the PFLP began to use suicide bombing as a strategy, and even created a separate wing devoted exclusively to martyrdom operations in the spring of 2001 called the "Abu Ali Mustafa Brigades."[58] Between 2001 and 2002, the PFLP conducted 3 percent of all the attacks, and within months of its first attack (May 27, 2001) and days after the PFLP exploded two car bombs, the JMCC poll of October 2001 placed PFLP support at 4.3 percent. The PFLP seemingly resuscitated its popularity by using suicide bombing as a tactic. The Al 'Aqsa Martyrs' Brigades have also hinted at the competition between the various groups:

> We announce with pride and dignity to you the martyrdom of Mo-
> hammed Hashaika from Tallouza village. This martyr who proved to
> all that there won't be peace, security or solution as long as . . . Sharon
> insists on keeping occupation and commits all kinds of ugly and atro-
> cious crimes against our people. Martyr Hashaika, member of al-'Aqsa
> Martyrs' Brigades, *proved that our Brigades are leading the path of Jihad*
> [emphasis added] and resistance and martyrdom until the Zionist oc-
> cupation leaves our homeland forever.[59]

ORGANIZATIONAL BACKGROUNDS

Hamas is the Arabic acronym for the "Harakat al Muqawamah al Islamiyya" (Islamic Resistance Movement), formed in 1987 by Sheikh Ahmed Yassin (assassinated by Israeli helicopter gun ships on March 22, 2004) as an out-growth of the Muslim Brotherhood and the *Mujamma al Islami,* and estab-lished in 1974 to provide much needed social services to Palestinians under occupation. It operated out of the Gaza Strip and eventually spread to the West Bank.

Until the first Intifada (1987), the Israeli Authorities avoided interfering with the organization as part of a strategy of divide and rule as a legitimate al-ternative to Yasir Arafat's Palestinian Liberation Organization (PLO). Mishal and Sela note that the Israelis did not block the organization nor did they ar-rest any of its members, and in turn the organization did not perpetrate any attacks against Israel for the first two years of its existence.[60] These two years of relative quiescence led to allegations from the mainstream PLO that Israel and Hamas were in collusion. Arafat subscribed to this conspiracy theory saying: "We must remember that these organizations were created by Israel, which also distributes arms to them."[61] When they did turn to violent protest, Hamas effectively augmented its reputation with rank-and-file Palestinians.

> By its participation in street violence and murder during the first Inti-
> fada, [Hamas] boosted its appeal in the eyes of the Palestinians, further

enhancing its growth potential and enabling it to play a central role in the Intifada. As a result of its subversive activity, Hamas was outlawed in September 1989.[62]

Hamas' popularity threatened PLO hegemony, as it became the leading terrorist organization throughout the Territories as well as inside Israel. In 1991, Zaccaria Walid Akel, the head of the terrorist section of Hamas in Gaza, set up the first squads of the militant Izz Eddin al Qassam Battalions which squads operated throughout the West Bank and Gaza. In its first stages, they kidnapped and executed Palestinian collaborators and routinely threatened Arafat.[63]

However, in December 1991 the squads changed their modus operandi and began targeting Israelis. Hamas' leadership realized that militant activities and terror would not bring about their long-term goals and so they devised long-term strategies and tactics. Earlier analysts stated that: "If suicide attacks, or the Israeli reaction to them, become harmful to the general Palestinian public and cause it to show qualms about them, Hamas might be forced to reconsider their value. For Hamas' leaders, the social and public meaning of their activity is no less important than its religious legitimacy."[64] In fact, the reverse happened, once Palestinians became convinced that military operations were their only option against hard handed Israeli counter terror responses, support for suicide operations increased exponentially. According to the head of the organization in Damascus, Khalid Mish'al, Hamas recognized its limitations and need to adjust its approach strategically:

> We know that the current balance of power in the region does not allow us to achieve a decisive victory against the Zionists; however, we confidently believe that we are moving along the right path—the path of resistance. This choice will provide us with success in view of our accumulated achievements, our substantial ability to hold out, our will and strategic depth.[65]

Hamas' charitable associations have had a dual function. On the one hand they helped to channel funds into the region. While a portion of the funds was for charity, it was not always possible to distinguish between the charities and the funding of terrorist activities. The association pays fines and assists the families of operatives who have been arrested. Such donations are defined as *charity* but are directed only to the hard-core members. Hamas founds hospitals, pays for medical care, dentistry, prenatal care within the Territories as well as multiple social services that the occupation does not provide. The benevolent associations have helped the organization gain credibility and support throughout all of Palestine. The fund pays $10,000–$25,000 per martyr and so there is economic remuneration to underscore the institutionalization of suicide bombing.[66] Hamas appears to have several goals: to destroy Israel, to enhance its prestige among the Palestinians vis-à-vis the PA or other groups, increase its appearance as a legitimate opposition, promote ties with the Islamic world, derail the peace process when it exists, and defy the "Zionist entity."[67]

The Palestinian Islamic Jihad (*Harakat al Jihad al Islami al Filastini*) was founded in 1979–1980 by Fathi Shiqaqi (assassinated by Israeli agents in 1995 in Malta), 'Abd al Aziz 'Odah and Bashir Musa. It is a series of loosely affiliated factions rather than a cohesive group, highly influenced by the Iranian Revolutionary movement and focused exclusively on terrorism. Because of Israel's strong alliance with the United States, it also targets U.S. and moderate Arab governments that it believes are tainted by Western secularism.

In contrast to Hamas, the Islamic Jihad is much smaller and does not have a network of social services (schools, mosques, clinics). Its charter promises to work for the destruction of the State of Israel through armed struggle and to replace Arafat's government with an Islamist state on the West Bank and Gaza and raise "the banner of Allah over every inch of Palestine."[68] Competition between the Islamic Jihad and Hamas dates back to the first Intifada when, according to Ahmad Rashad:

> Jihad's spectacular acts of daring and courage in the 1980s lent credence to the Islamic movement in the occupied territories. Jihad's attacks against Israeli military targets set the stage for the Intifada . . . which spread rapidly due to the pride that Palestinians had begun to feel in the Jihad's actions. . . . Islamic Jihad's actions embarrassed Arafat and Hamas. But its brazen attacks increased the popularity of Islamic guerilla groups.[69]

The Al 'Aqsa Martyrs Brigade, the military wing of Arafat's Fatah (Harakat al Tahrir al Falistiniya) was formally given title after the September 2000 Al 'Aqsa Intifada. The Al 'Aqsa Martyrs Brigade split off from the organization when the Palestinian Authority arrested the secretary-general of the PFLP, Ahmad Sa'adat, for killing Israeli Right wing Cabinet Minister, Rechavam Ze'evi in October 2001. The PFLP claimed that Ze'evi was killed in retaliation for the killing of PFLP General Secretary Abu Ali Mustafa on August 27, 2001.[70] The Al 'Aqsa Martyrs' defection from Arafat demonstrates his growing weakness and isolation. However, in the raid of the Ramallah office of Fuad Shubeiki, head of the PA's financial apparatus, the Israel Defence Forces uncovered documents linking the PA and Fatah to the

Brigades. The smoking gun document lists the financial demands of the Al 'Aqsa Martyrs Brigade for bombings that had been carried out and the fifth article on the document lists the costs for producing explosive devices and bombs.[71]

The PFLP combines Arab Nationalism with Marxist-Leninist ideology and views the destruction of Israel as integral to ridding the Middle East of Western Influence. In the fall of 2001, the PFLP shifted its emphasis, and began using both the tactic of suicide bombing and the language of *Jihad* to attract a greater constituency to swell its ranks.[72] Palestinian support for the PFLP was lagging until the organization turned to suicide bombing, putting them back on the political radar screen. They managed to capture 3 percent of Palestinian support after their operations in the fall of 2001 and the creation of a militant wing named after Abu Ali Mustafa. Not to be left out, the DFLP claimed responsibility for a bus attack in July 2002 and yet another organization, Al Nathir (the Warning) was one of several groups that "claimed responsibility for the [July 18, 2002] Tel Aviv bombing, identified the attackers, and said they had come from the Balata refugee camp in Nablus. The group said it was linked to Yasir Arafat's Fatah movement. . . . the Islamic Jihad had previously claimed responsibility for the bombing."[73]

Since 1993 these groups have dispatched more than 250 suicide bombers. The occurrences of suicide bombings do not only correlate with the peace process or negotiations. A broad examination of the number of attacks since Ehud Barak left office and Sharon took office indicate that suicide attacks are much more closely related to periods when Arafat is weaker and rival organizations compete to fill the power vacuum.

ISRAELI COUNTER TERROR POLICIES

Faced with mounting attacks, Israeli policymakers responded with hard-line counter-terror tactics of massive retaliation, targeted assassination of militant leaders, and building demolitions to deter future bombings. Hamas and the Islamic Jihad as well as other groups target Israeli civilians in public venues for maximum effect to kill and injure as many civilians as they could. As *Jane's Defence Weekly* noted, "While some attacks are successful against military targets, most are carried out against civilians. As a Hamas training manual notes: it is foolish to hunt the tiger when there are plenty of sheep around."[74] The March 27, 2002 Passover bombing in Netanya, prompted a rapid Israeli response and reaction which they launched two days later.

"Operation Protective Shield," during which the Israelis reoccupied seven of eight major Palestinian towns in Area A, had negative consequences for Israel domestically as well as for its image abroad. Most countries rigorously condemned Israeli actions in Jenin and Qalqilya.[75] Surprisingly enough, Israelis rallied around the extreme right, under the assumption that hawkish policies would serve to deter future attacks. That policy, however, will encourage rather than deter future attacks. In essence, hard-line Israeli policy would likely backfire if its intention is to increase Israeli civilians' security over the long term. The attacks after April 2002 and daily violence during the spring of 2003 demonstrated that despite Operation Protective Shield, reoccupation might temporarily slow the pace of the bombings without eliminating the scourge. These groups will engage in greater degrees of violence for competition over legitimacy and leadership of the Palestinian people. In fact, the present policy sows the seeds for future generations to swell the ranks of terrorist organizations by increasing incentives for groups to compete and outbid each other. See figure 2.4.

MOTIVATIONS

Explanations for why the suicide bombers are motivated to sacrifice themselves abound.

> In its constant quest for an explanation of why a young man—and recently a few young women—decide to commit such an act, the Western press has mostly cited fanaticism and despair.[76]

Some people allege that the bombers suffer from low social status, few economic opportunities, or personality disorders. Bruce Bueno de Mesquita argues that the suicide bombers have a financial incentive. "They are young men with no economic prospects and little education." He adds, "There is a rational expectation on the part of suicide bombers that they are providing for their families." However, evidence shows that these explanations are not consistent with each other or with reality. Most suicide bombers are not undereducated religious zealots who blindly follow the commands of the religious leadership; rather they come from a middle or upper class background and have comparatively high levels of education.[77]

Nasra Hassan has argued that many of the bombers have suffered humiliation and persecution at the hands of Israeli forces, although she insists that they are not suffering from mental illness or personality disorders.[78] This issue of pain and personal loss features prominently in any analysis of suicide bombing, yet pain and suffering alone do not create the phenomenon; it must also be coupled with an environment where there is no outlet to express the rage and frustration to motivate someone to use suicide bombing as a weapon. The excessive use of force on Israel's part, collective punishment, check points, closures, and economic sanctions, have all contributed to the de-legitimization of the peace process and of the PA, as well as a general feeling of hopelessness.[79]

All of these factors appear to be necessary though insufficient to explain suicide bombing given that the majority of Palestinians have experienced humiliation as part of the 35-year occupation and that the number of suicide bombers remained statistically irrelevant compared to the Palestinian population as a whole, until very recently. Customary media depictions of the average suicide bomber driven to self-destruction by despair fail to convince most Palestinians. All Palestinians living under occupation, they say, are desperate. Humiliation and persecution are a "constant" under the occupation and cannot account for why there has been an upsurge in this phenomenon or why public opinion shifts in favor of suicide attacks at different times. Many Palestinians view this portrayal as a way of denuding the attacks of their political aim: striking back at the Israeli occupation.[80]

Martyrdom reinforces the Palestinian self-image as an oppressed people since this tactic is the "weapon of the weak." Terrorists make a number of moral claims that they are using such strategies only as a last resort—that only after peaceful means have failed or peace agreements have been abrogated have they turned to violence. The Palestinians know that they could not win a shooting war against the Israelis' overwhelming military superiority. The bombings may be intended to invite reprisals causing the Israelis to massively retaliate, overreact, and cause an outside intervention for which Arafat has been calling since the Al 'Aqsa Intifada broke out.[81]

Several things may motivate the individual suicide bomber,[82] whereas the leadership appears strategically minded vis-à-vis domestic rivals in the Palestinian Authority and vis-à-vis its international rival—Israel. Islamic extremist groups sending out suicide bombers are participating in a two-level game. Their attacks are intended to hurt Israel while at the same time they undermine the legitimacy of the Palestinian Authority. Suicide bombing is an effort to punish and deter Israeli actions and to create a "balance of terror." The Palestinians seek to persuade Israelis that they will pay a high price for the occupation and force them to pressure their government to withdraw from the Territories and, thus end the occupation. The extension of the front to inside "green-line" Israel is an attempt to bring the war to the heart of Israel, creating a condition under which Israelis can no longer ignore the realities of the occupation. Through these attacks, they seek to wear down Israeli morale.[83]

This strategy has proven effective, as Israelis fear going to public places, going shopping, or going out to eat; the suicide bombings have changed Israelis' lifestyles and assurance of security. During periods of deadlock, when most Israelis are comfortable with the existing status quo, Palestinian extremists know that something is required to tip the balance and change it. At the same time, with Arafat's leadership in crisis, several groups and individuals vie for control of a future Palestinian state and seek to place their imprimatur on what kind of state (e.g. Islamic Fundamentalist) will emerge.

CYCLES OF VIOLENCE

The unprecedented Israeli siege of the occupied territories constituted a turning point for Palestinian public opinion. The hermetic closure of the West Bank and Gaza Strip, and the policy of "separation" removed any remaining ambiguities about the nature of post-Oslo Israeli-Palestinian relations.

The defection of Fatah loyalists swelled the ranks of the Al 'Aqsa Martyrs' Brigade, the Jihad Amarin cell—named after a militant killed by the Israel Defense Forces in the early days of the Intifada—operating in the Gaza Strip, and ideologically close to the Palestinian Islamic Jihad, as well as Al Nathir. The violence has increasingly assumed a pattern of attrition. Although seemingly irrational because the attacks and counter measures only generated more victims, Israel answers Palestinian suicide bombing by assassinating Hamas and Islamic Jihad leaders, the Palestinians respond with more bombings, and the Israelis respond with yet more assassinations.[84] The Israelis and Palestinians appeared to be in a deadlocked battle of assassination-suicide bombing-assassination-suicide bombing in an unending causal loop. This call and response blood bath has radicalized the Palestinians, encouraging yet more "martyrs".

> Since Israel's first assassinations in 1995–1996, which reached a climax with the killing of Hamas' Yahiyeh Ayyash ("The Engineer") and the Islamic Jihad's leader Fathi Shiqaqi, all of the assassinations have generated acts of revenge that have cost the lives of dozens of Israelis … the policy of assassination is a boomerang that hurts Israel badly.[85]

However, many Israeli policymakers refute the idea of a boomerang effect, among them Shimon Peres:

> In my opinion it's [the boomerang effect] nonsense, since we know that the Engineer was about to launch more attacks. Let's say that we hadn't hit him, and he had carried out the attacks, what would have been said then? You could have prevented them. After all, it is only journalistic theories. I know the truth, I know he was about to carry out more attacks.[86]

Israeli tactics make a perverted kind of sense. Targeted Assassination, renounced by almost every other democratic government and by international law, has been a standard operating procedure for Israel since the Black September Organization massacred eleven Israeli athletes at the 1972 Munich Olympics.[87] Israel has assassinated dozens of Hamas and Islamic Jihad operatives. The logic of targeted assassination is that murdering their operatives saps the effectiveness of Hamas and the Islamic Jihad. The targeting not only neutralizes the dead men, but also forces other terrorists to go underground. Since they know that Israel will kill them, the terrorists spend much of their time running or hiding and less time plotting future terrorist attacks. Without skilled bomb-makers and planners, Hamas and the Islamic Jihad would theoretically have more difficulty infiltrating Israel and carrying out their missions. Israel's logic however proved fallible. Although several Palestinians were caught before their bombs could detonate or they have been killed or wounded while making bombs,[88] the events of March 2002 demonstrated that the extremists' organizations are fully capable of replacing operatives as fast as Israeli targeted assassinations eliminate them. The suicide bombers have metamorphosed into a hydra, for every one killed by Sharon's policies, another two appear to take his (and potentially her) place.

Targeted assassinations have a political utility for the Israelis and are more media friendly—unlike the negative effect that shooting stone-throwing children had during the first Intifada. The most important benefit to Israelis might have been a psychological one. Assassination showed that the government was being proactive, counteracting the chaos brought about by the bombings and bringing precision and order back to the conflict. According to public opinion polls in Israel, this policy was widely supported.

Thus, suicide bombings and targeted assassinations may be considered case studies in the law of comparative advantage. Israel, where labor is expensive and capital cheap, invests in assassinations, a high tech strategy that requires lots of equipment but does not risk Israeli lives. By comparison, Palestinians possess neither tanks nor Apache helicopters. Thus the Palestinians have adopted a labor-intensive strategy—literally throwing bodies at the problem. Advocates have described the attacks as the most important "strategic weapon" of Palestinian resistance. And while religious justification for the attacks is important for Muslims, secular groups have resorted to similar tactics.[89] George Habash, leader of the PFLP substantiated this as a deliberate strategy:

> The losses in manpower that the Israelis are sustaining are very high. The Zionist entity has not witnessed the likes of this high rate of loses in any period of battle in any of the past decades. According to the latest figures, the rate is one Israeli killed for every three Palestinian

martyrs. This is despite the great differential or the great imbalance of power and the minimal fighting means and equipment available to the Palestinian people.[90]

Suicide bombings exact no significant cost on Hamas, the Islamic Jihad, or any of the secular groups. Though each bombing episode sacrifices one supporter, it recruits many more. More people are willing to become suicide bombers now than in the past. In response to the upsurge of bombings, Ariel Sharon initiated counter-terror policies which further enraged Palestinians and swelled the ranks of militant organizations. This tactic has been proven unsuccessful because they underestimated Palestinian resolve against the occupation and outrage at Israeli reprisals, which has swelled the ranks rather than drawn down the number of suicide bombers.

Conclusions

An Israeli reserve soldier discussed the difficulty of winning the war on terror against Palestinians and of defeating the phenomenon of suicide bombings by making reference to the role of hearts and minds:

> There's no way to break the system of terror in the West Bank, because the system is now in the minds of the people, in the minds of the teenagers, and what we're doing by this operation [Defensive Shield] is giving them more reasons to build that system. The government talks about how many guns and bomb factories and suicide belts it's capturing in the offensive, of how we are going to break the terrorist infrastructure. But what infrastructure? I think the most terrifying thing here—and maybe it's something that a lot of people don't want to see—is that there's very little of an infrastructure to break.[91]

The key is to reduce the Palestinian motivations for suicide bombing rather than their capabilities to carry them out. Suicide attacks serve multiple purposes besides inflicting damage on Israelis. They generate a huge amount of publicity for the cause. The emergence of the "CNN factor" has enabled global awareness much like airliner hijackings did for the Palestinian cause in the late 1960s and 1970s. The perpetration of these acts has become bound to concepts of self and honor in the community.

In settings where the power disparities are as great as between the Israelis and Palestinians, the question is: which insurgent tactics are appropriate? Disparities in relation to power and force are further accentuated by the degree to which the media portrays Israeli victimization as humanized, while

Palestinian victimization is reduced to statistical abstraction and treated as an unintended byproduct of legitimate Israeli counter-terrorism enforcement actions. Palestinian violence is viewed as an extreme form of terrorism, while Israeli responses, even when directed at civilian targets, are at most criticized as "excessive force."[92]

There is a sense that terrorism is the weapon of the weak, that if groups had the ability to, they would refrain from using terror instrumentally. To avoid charges of terrorism, Palestinians must find ways to resist that do not rely on violence directed at Israeli civilians. Such a burden may be difficult given the harshness of the occupation, but it can only be lifted by Palestinian ingenuity. However, there is little moral concern over civilian immunity. For most Palestinians, there is no civilian immunity in Israel due to the universal conscription of men and women. Any civilian is either a current, past, or future soldier. From this perspective, all Israelis are complicit in the immoral and illegal occupation of the West Bank and Gaza, moreover these very same civilians willingly twice elected a hawkish government which pursues maximalist goals.

Finally, terrorists use suicide bombing and violent strategies to delegitimize the state. Part of the Palestinian goal has been to force Israel's hand, drive it to massively retaliate, betray its democratic principles and force it to rip off the mask of legal justice—to show it to be the ravening beast that the Palestinians claim.

> A more far-reaching success [for suicide terrorists] is that Israel's leaders, in retaliating, have behaved so harshly, putting three million people under siege, with recurring curfews for unlimited periods of time, all in front of the world press and television, with the result that Israel may now be the most hated country in the world. This is hugely damaging to Israel, since the difference between being hated and losing legitimacy is dangerously narrow. Throughout the world, moreover, the suicide bombings have often been taken more as a sign of the desperation of the Palestinians than as acts of terror.[93]

There are no military solutions to terrorism; the challenge is to preserve the state's legitimacy and, even in the face of atrocious acts, to hold its high ground. The failure to do so is to hand the terrorists an absolute victory. However, there is a failed state in Palestine. The systematic destruction of the political, administrative, and social apparatus of the Palestinian Authority—in Israel's campaign to weed out the terrorists—has crushed the Palestinian Authority as an authority. Without a legitimate authority in Palestine, there can be no real security for the state of Israel. President Arafat's death on November 11, 2004 leaves questions as to who would replace him. According to the Palestinian Basic Law of 2003, once Arafat died, he was to be temporarily replaced by the speaker of the Palestinian Legislative Council, the PA's parliament. The speaker, Rawhi Fattouh, is a little known politician. Elections for Arafat's replacement have to take place within 60 days of his death. As Arafat has never groomed a successor nor shared any real power with any other Palestinian leader, there is no one of any reputation or standing in the wings prepared to take over. It appears that Abu Mazen (Mahmoud Abbas) the former prime minister who resigned after only a few months, has taken over the PLO although he does not have the same standing and popularity among the younger generation. It is also likely that Abu Ala (Ahmed Qurei) will continue to be the prime minister which creates an opportunity for rivalry between the two leaders. The next most popular Palestinian politician is Fatah's Marwan Barghouti, currently serving two life sentences in an Israeli jail. Finally, the major challenge to Fatah's dominance comes from Hamas. According to press reports, Ismail Haniyeh, the leader of Hamas in Gaza, called on October 29, 2004 for the "formation of a united national leadership" and to prepare for a general election in the event of Arafat's death and there have even been discussions that Barghouti would run as a candidate from an Israeli jail.[94] The danger of violence between Palestinians and Israelis in clashes or within the Palestinian community in a power struggle remains high. Thus prospects for the future are dim although in such flux it is exceedingly difficult to predict any outcomes. Suffice it to say, any struggle for power will benefit Israel in the short term but will unleash increasing cycles of violence over the long term.

Destroying the Palestinian Authority can only result in increased lawlessness and create windows of opportunity for more violence and new groups who will use martyrdom operations to increase their popularity. This has been increasingly the case with Israeli hard line policies under the second Sharon administration thus decreasing any hopes that the conflict can be resolved peacefully rather than imposed separation by building a wall. Discussing whether a wall could ever prevent terrorism in Iraq and the importance of winning over the hearts and minds of the Arab Street, Senator Hillary Rodham Clinton has argued: "It is very hard to build a fence to keep a terrorist out. That is certainly the tragic lesson of Israel's effort against terrorism over all these years . . . we have to convince Iraqis that their future lies with us."[95] One way of doing so is to create economic incentives and opportunities for greater collaboration between the two communities. Unfortunately, the al 'Aqsa Intifada has decreased any joint ventures.

The toll on the two communities has been all encompassing. The rates of casualty have been high for both sides. According to local human rights organizations, more than 2,289 Palestinians and 440 Israelis have been killed (some statistics place the number at 572 Israeli civilians), including hundreds of children and 90 suicide bombers. Approximately 24,407 Palestinians were injured between September 2000 and January 2004.[96]

The crisis has devastated the Palestinian economy. Israel's policy of closures and internal sieges kept poverty and unemployment hovering just below 50 percent. There were 120,000 Palestinian workers, over 40 percent of the Palestinian work force, employed in Israel in 1993. The suicide bombings of 1995 and 1996 then led to the decision of the government to close off the territories and drastically reduce the numbers of Palestinians working in Israel. Many were eventually replaced by foreign workers from Thailand, Romania, and various African countries. By 2000 the Palestinian workers were back at work in Israel, many of them as illegal workers. Their number is estimated to have reached about 130,000, which by then was a lower percentage of the Palestinian work force than it was in 1993. The second Intifada stopped the flow of goods and services to and from Israel, the only serious market for Palestinian exports. The result has been devastating for the Palestinian economy. The Palestinian Authority, which subsists on donations from abroad, is the only remaining employer.[97]

A UNSCO report put the initial cost of the Al 'Aqsa Intifada at between $2.4 and $3.2 billion for the first year. The Palestinian Authority's revenues plummeted by 57 percent and real income decreased by an average of 37 percent, resulting in 46 percent of Palestinians living below the poverty line— twice as many as before.[98]

Closures and curfews began in tandem after the Oslo process. Palestinian Purchasing power—which often came from day labor in Israel, atrophied their domestic market—and affected the lives of poorly- to moderately-educated citizens.[99] Nichole Argo adds that:

> University graduates emerged from school with the promise of a future they couldn't create domestically, and were unable to [enter] flooded Israeli markets. Relatively speaking, those with the most promise were stuck with the least opportunity, and few political channels for pursuing change.[100]

In this environment, few Palestinians are prepared to disavow terror and more attacks will follow regardless of Israeli counter measures—no matter how severe. It is only when Israeli policymakers conclude that force is not the solution and when the majority of the Palestinian polity feels a moral outrage against the martyrdom operations that suicide terrorism will cease to be a viable policy option for the groups employing the tactic.[101]

In the short term mass arrests,[102] deportations, house demolitions, and targeted assassinations might have a nominal effect on the number of attacks inside Israel. According to Israeli counter-terrorist expert Boaz Ganor:

> The Israeli offensive activity was successful at times, as it caused short- and medium-term damage to the terror organizations and their leaders, forcing them to invest time and resources in repairing the damages. But in most cases the Israeli offensive activity did not deter the leaders and activists of the organizations and didn't bring about the cancellation of terror attacks. In any case the Israeli offensive activity did not solve the terror problem.[103]

This research predicts that the number of attacks will increase as groups vying to lead the Palestinians will use violence as their main source of recruitment and mobilization. According to polls conducted by Khalil Shiqaqi support for Martyrdom operations against Israeli civilian and military targets remains high, although there is a willingness to resume negotiations if Israel were willing to fulfill the commitments made in Oslo. Consider Prime Minister Yitzhak Rabin's explanation to the Knesset on April 18, 1994 about why Israel should withdraw from Gaza and its war on terror:

> For 27 years we have been dominating another people against its will. For 27 years Palestinians in the territories ... [have gotten] up in the morning harboring a fierce hatred for us, as Israelis and Jews ... for which we are also, but not solely, responsible. We cannot deny that our continuing control over a foreign people who do not want us exacts a painful price: the price of continuing confrontation between us and them. . . . Hamas and Islamic Jihad ... carried out most of the terrorist attacks, some on suicide missions. For two or three years, we have been facing a phenomenon of extremist Islamic terrorism, reminiscent of Hizbullah, which emerged in Lebanon and carried out terrorist attacks including suicide attacks ... There is no end to the targets. . . . Each Israeli, in the territories and inside sovereign Israel, including united Jerusalem, every bus and every home, is a target for their murderous intentions. With nothing separating the two populations, the current situation creates endless possibilities for Hamas and the other organizations ... [but] more acts of terrorism will not halt the peace convoy. We may not succeed in completely preventing terrorist attacks. But peace will be victorious.[104]

Rabin operated under the motto: The Palestinian peace process will continue as if there were no terrorism, while the war against terrorism will be fought as if there were no peace process.[105] The experience of the past and Rabin's clear eyed assessment gives us additional evidence to recognize that Israeli policy must change before the violence will end. It is difficult to expect a country under siege to reward violence and yet the current policy is a prescription for an intensification of attacks in the long term. In as much as Israel can alter Palestinian perceptions of the conflict, they can control the environment and backdrop against which the attacks occur. The only solution is to negotiate with the secular groups and provide the Palestinians with a hopeful future so that the bombings cease to resonate positively with the majority of Palestinian public opinion. Once the public ceases to support these attacks, they will fail to mobilize the new generation and the nonaligned voter.

CHAPTER THREE

ETHNIC CONFLICT, STATE TERROR,
AND SUICIDE BOMBING IN SRI LANKA[1]

In Sri Lanka, suicide bombing has made both sides war weary, had an impact on external donors' support, moderated both sides' demands to calls for devolution (rather than for independence), and was a factor in bringing both to the negotiating tables.[2] Extremist groups who use violence to spoil the peace have plagued similar kinds of civil war negotiations in the past. In an article by Barbara Walter and Andrew Kydd, suicide terror in particular is to be expected on the eve of negotiated settlements.[3] Finally, in an op-ed piece in August 2002, Thomas Friedman asked the following question, why is Sri Lanka inching towards resolution while the Palestinian-Israeli conflict rages on?[4]

This chapter examines the situation in Sri Lanka, provides a detailed background to the Tamil-Sinhalese conflict, and draws some comparisons to the Palestinian case. The main thrust of my argument is that when violence resonates positively with the civilian population (at particular moments in time), a variety of extremist groups might compete with one another for popularity, engage in outbidding, and use violence to mobilize and radicalize the polity. In Palestine, these "windows of opportunity" occurred when the peace process stalemated and Yasser Arafat no longer monopolized the legitimate force in the Palestinian authority. The process was further exacerbated by Israeli miscalculations which attributed Hamas violence to Arafat and destroyed the remaining infrastructure and institutions of the Palestinian Authority, making Arafat's ex post facto control of dissidents impossible.

In Sri Lanka, suicide bombing emerged at a time when there were several opposition groups competing for leadership of the Tamil community. Afterward, the LTTE closed ranks and eliminated all other remaining competitors for leadership, a process that they started in 1987. Once the LTTE came to the bargaining tables in September 2002, there were no other groups left to spoil the peace.

Moreover, the LTTE represented the most extreme Tamil nationalist group, whereas in the Palestinian case, the PLO under Arafat represents a more moderate voice compared to religious fundamentalist organizations like Hamas and the Palestinian Islamic Jihad. In the Middle East, extremism is framed in religious terms. In Sri Lanka, the LTTE has never made the conflict about religion and so the conflict has never contained the ideology of war *of all against all* as it has in Palestine.

Finally, the source of funding for the organization shifted from external donors to internal extraction once LTTE funding ran dry because of legal and financial limits placed on their Diaspora contributions in North America, Australia, and Europe. The LTTE now collects money from the local civilian population through taxation, extortion, tolls, and transport levies in the north and east of Sri Lanka.[5]

This shift in funding sources resulted in a degree of war weariness not observed in the Palestinian case, whose funding for suicide operations largely derives from abroad. Charles Tilly argues that taxation brings with it a degree of responsibility to heed the wishes of the populace.[6] The LTTE's ability to continue fighting and hold out for the all of the Eelam homeland is constrained by the fact that the people paying for the war are also those suffering most from its perpetuation. We can question how supportive of suicide terror rank-and-file Palestinians would be if funding came out of their own meager pockets rather than from Arab "confrontation" states and monarchies in the Gulf.[7]

History of the Conflict

The contemporary geographic distribution of ethnic groups in Sri Lanka (Tamils vs. Sinhalese and Tamils vs. Muslims) is relevant for assessing conflict. The Tamils "traditional homelands" are in Jaffna, Vavuniya, Batticaloa, and Trincomalee. "Estate" or Indian Tamils are noticeably present in the central highlands of Nuwara Eliya and Badulla districts. In the capitol of Colombo and surrounding areas, the presence of both Estate and Sri Lankan Tamils reaches over 11 percent of the population.[8] The populations break down in the following manner: 74 per cent Sinhalese, 16 percent Tamils—divided between the Estate or Indian Tamils (6 percent) and Sri Lankan Tamils (10 percent)—and almost 10 percent Muslims. Tamils are the majority in the north and east[9] while there is significant intermixing of populations in Colombo and parts of the south.

Social and economic developments during the early colonial period under the Portuguese and then the Dutch—the commercialization of agriculture, the registration of title to land,[10] registration of births and deaths, and proselytization—all contributed toward a freezing of ethnic boundaries. As in many others parts of the globe, ethnicity had been malleable, often following patron-client like relationships (evident in parts of Africa) prior to the colonial penetration and freezing of ethnic definitions through designating identity or group membership.

> Ethnic boundaries in the pre-modern period were indistinct and permeable. There was considerable ethnic accommodation and intermingling. Ancient Sinhala cities reveal significant Tamil artistic and architectural influences, and the monarchy was not rigidly determined by ethnicity.[11]

SJ Tambiah argues that the Sinhalese and Tamil identities are *constructions*—both Tamils and Sinhalese originated from northern and southern India and the Sinhalese Kandyan kings historically married women from Southern India resulting in significant degrees of ethnic intermixing between the two communities.[12]

> Tamils are known to have ruled, often converting to Buddhism, even in Sinhala bastions like the city of Kandy. . . . Ethnic, religious, and linguistic differences were not used as the bases for exclusion from the polity. At various times, groups would speak alternative languages, adhere to alternative religions, and claim alternative identities.[13]

Further, the two terms reify more complex communities in which Tamils are subdivided between Indian Estate and Sri Lankan Tamils as well as discreet differences between regions (Jaffna vs. Batticaloa) low country and highland Tamils, as well as caste differences.[14] The same can be said of the Sinhalese differences between those in Kandy, Matara, and Kotte.[15]

From the outset, Tamil nationalists tried to bring all Tamil speakers under the umbrella of Tamil politics on the assumption that they were linked by a common language, despite their religious differences.[16] There are Christian Tamils as well as Christian Sinhalese and so religious differences cannot explain the division within the community. Finally, the Muslims are Tamil speakers yet do not consider themselves Tamil.[17]

One of the main arguments of Tambiah's thesis is that:

> Sinhalese-Tamil tensions and conflicts are of relatively recent manufacture—a truly twentieth century phenomenon. We can see them as exhibiting over the last three decades a trend toward an increasing *ethnic* [emphasis added] mobilization and polarization previously unknown.[18]

The Portuguese and the Dutch encouraged religious intolerance by favoring certain groups and disadvantaging others—sometimes alternating nepotism between the two. This effectively meant the consolidation of a 'Sinhala community' in the central and southwestern parts of the island and of a 'Tamil community' in the north and on the eastern shore. Economic developments during the British occupation of the island gave rise to two other phenomena that made the ethnic picture in Sri Lanka even more complex.

The Estate Tamils descended from the indentured and migrant workers who emigrated from India. The coffee plantations established by the British in the nineteenth century brought to Sri Lanka, as plantation labor, more than one million Tamil workers from southern India. These were at first seasonal migrants but with the development of the tea plantations the majority became permanent residents. The question of their citizenship rights became an issue that subsequently soured relations between India and Sri Lanka.[19]

Economic development under British Colonialism focused on the central and western areas of the island. This left the Tamil community in a disadvantaged position vis-à-vis the rest of the country. Because of agricultural limitations of the Tamil areas, more Tamils than Sinhalese took advantage of educational opportunities afforded by missionary and British education which consequently allowed them greater access to civil service and other high paying jobs. Tamils moved, in large numbers, to state service employment, the private sector, and entered into the medical, legal, and banking professions. This movement was helped by the growth of educational facilities in English in the Tamil regions, and particularly in the Jaffna peninsula. This also meant that large numbers of Tamils migrated to the southern and central regions for the purposes of employment and that the Tamil traders established themselves in these regions.[20]

The British enlarged the Tamil population by bringing in Indian Tamils to work the plantations, and the growth of the plantations transformed the economy of Sri Lanka and created opportunities for Tamil and Muslim entrepreneurs to make large fortunes. Some of these Tamils converted to Christianity and sent their children to Britain for education. These émigrés returned and filled the expanding needs of the state services as well as staffing the ranks of hospitals, law firms, engineering firms etc. The local bourgeoisie that resulted spoke in English and was multi-ethnic. However, Burghers (the ethnic group of Portuguese/Sri Lankan mixed marriages) and Tamils entered the professions and the state services disproportionately to their population size.

Sinhala traders could not break into the import and export trades, which were dominated by the British and Indians or the retail trade, dominated by Muslim and Chettiar traders, because of a lack of access to finance, controlled by British bankers or South Indian Chettiars (who were Tamil). The Sinhalese professionals and the educated petit-bourgeoisie had to vie with Burghers and Tamils for state and private employment. Workers at their own level found themselves confronted with migrant workers from Kerala and Tamil Nadu (India) as well as with workers from the Muslim minority groups.[21]

Barriers to their advancement were perceived by the Sinhalese at all levels and as being caused by the non-Sinhalese elements. Anagarika Dharmapala, an early Buddhist revivalist leader, agitated against the Muslims. In 1915 just before rioting began he stated:

> The Mohammedan, an alien people by Shylockian method, became prosperous like the Jews. The Sinhalese sons of the soil, whose ancestors for 2358 years had shed rivers of blood to keep this country free from alien invaders . . . the result is that the Mohammedan thrives and the son of the soil goes to the wall.[22]

To understand why economic antagonisms should be perceived in ethnic terms, we must examine the ways in which the Sinhalese asserted national identity as the basis for winning political reforms to give them more power.[23] In asserting a Sinhalese identity and in legitimizing their control, Sinhalese revivalist leaders reconstructed an image of the past using many elements of the "origin" mythology. They claimed that the Sinhalese descended from Aryan migrants from Bengal in the fifth century BC; the arrival of their leader, Prince Vijaya, in Sri Lanka coincided with the death of the Buddha, whose doctrine would be preserved for 2,500 years in Sri Lanka by these immigrants and their descendents. Buddha had visited the island three times, consecrated it to his doctrine, and on his deathbed instructed Sakra, the chief of the Gods, to safeguard Vijaya to ensure his supremacy in the land.

Thus Sri Lanka became the land of Sinhala and Dharma—Buddhist doctrine. The belief was that the survival of the Buddhist religion depended on the survival of the Sinhalese people who espoused the doctrine and controlled the land consecrated to the religion. Thus the religion, the people, and the land were bound together in an indissoluble unity. The stories in the Buddhist tract, the *Mahamvasa*, with its accounts of repeated invasions and conquests by Tamils from Southern India, exacerbated and fed nationalist fears.

Discrimination against the Tamil population began soon after the peaceful transition from Colonial rule to independence on February 4, 1948. Nationalist ideology denied the multiethnic and multireligious character of Sri Lankan society and refused to accept the collective rights of minority groups. This consciousness was counterposed against the British imperial state, which was seen as foreign and Christian; the revival was thus more anti-Western than anti-imperialist, asserting a Sinhalese Buddhist identity against all foreigners and minorities. Over 100 years, this ideology was asserted against Muslims, Christians, Tamil plantation workers, Malayalis, and Sri Lankan Tamils.[24]

The Tamils (and the Burghers to a lesser extent) allegedly benefited disproportionately from the British presence and the issue of official language became one of paramount importance. In the 1950s, Sinhalese nationalism dominated the island seeking to redress the imbalances created by colonialism. In 1956, Solomon West Ridgeway Dias Bandaranaike, leader of the Sri Lanka Freedom Party (SFLP), was elected to power on a *swabasha* "Sinhala only" platform.[25] Sinhalese soon became the only official language of the country dethroning English as the language of administration and education for higher employment.

At the ideological level, the response to Sinhalese nationalism was the emergence of Tamil chauvinism and extreme forms of nationalist mythmaking. According to Radhika Coomaraswamy, these included the myth that the Tamils were the pure Dravidian race, that they were the original inhabitants of Sri Lanka and heirs to the Mohenjadaro and Harappa civilizations of northern India. That the Tamil language in its purest forms is spoken only in Sri Lanka and that the "Saiva Siddhanta" form of Hinduism has a special homeland in Sri Lanka.[26] Many of the Tamil militant groups were sustained by such ideologies, and expressions like "Dravidian Drive" and "Chola Charisma"[27] were used in to mobilize support for armed struggle. The Muslim community reacted defensively to the increased exclusivity and paranoid ideology emanating from both ethnic groups, including the emergence of an Islamic Jihad organization in Trincomalee.

Discrimination against Tamils continued throughout the 1960s as Buddhism was given primacy as the state religion by Mrs. Bandaranaike in Chapter Two of the new Constitution, which disenfranchised Tamils from government and other positions of authority. For example in the state sector, in 1949, 41 percent of government recruits Tamil and 54 percent were Sinhalese. By 1963 the proportion was 7 percent were Tamil and 92 percent Sinhalese.[28] A quota system was imposed on Tamils in the universities.

During this period, the Tamils responded politically, mediated by the Federal Party (FP) representing Tamil interests through a nonviolent protest movement called *Satyagraha*. However, the 1970s gave rise to an increasing trend of Tamil calls for separation and increased militancy. The manifesto of the United National Party (UNP), during the general elections of 1977 which brought Junius Richard Jayewardene to power, finally acknowledged Tamils.[29] Although Tamils had supported Jayewardene's campaign promises of improved ethnic relations, his election in 1977 witnessed the outbreak of ferocious communal violence, which spread throughout the island.[30] The

Grant of Citizenship to Stateless persons act of 1986 addressed issues of statelessness and the Grant of Citizenship (Special provisions) act of 1988 provided Estate Tamils with a degree of rights[31] but discrimination remained palpable during this whole period.

Four Tamil political groups: the Tamil Federal Party (TFP), the All Ceylon Tamil Congress (ACTC), the Tamil Progressive Front, and the Ceylon Worker's congress joined forces in 1972 to form the Tamil United Front (TUF), to campaign for parity status for the Tamil language. In May 1973 the TUF decided to work for an independent state, "Tamil Eelam," the Tamil Homeland. Not all the member groups endorsed this position. The Tamil United Liberation Front (TULF) political party, also established in 1972, began calling for a separate Tamil state in 1976 to be achieved constitutionally.

A proliferation of Tamil groups, known as the Tamil Five, emerged in this period. The Tamil Five included the Tamil Eelam Liberation Organization (TELO) formed in 1974 under S. Thangathurai, the Eelam Revolutionary Organisation of Students (EROS) formed in 1975 under V. Balakumar, the People's Liberation Organisation for Tamil Eelam (PLOTE) formed in 1979 under Uma Mahaswaran, the Eelam People's Revolutionary Liberation Front (EPRLF) formed in 1980 under K. Padmanabha, and the more radical Tamil National Tigers (TNT) which emerged in 1973 under Vellupillai Prabhakaran, was renamed the Liberation Tigers of Tamil Eelam (LTTE) in May 1976 and split from the TULF in 1978 with greater calls for secession and independence.[32]

VIOLENCE UNLEASHED

Separatist agitation went through several phases according to KM de Silva. In the 1950s it was peaceful, moving to civil disobedience in the 1960s, to individual violence in the 1970s[33] until it became a dangerous threat in the 1980s.[34] In 1979 the government promulgated the Prevention of Terrorism Act (PTA), which permitted the army and the police to hold prisoners incommunicado for up to eighteen months without trial. It defined certain acts as:

Unlawful including speaking or writing words intended to cause religious, social, or communal disharmony or feelings of ill will or hostility between communities or racial or religious groups. It also undermined an existing British law that no confession made in police custody was admissible unless made in the presence of a magistrate. The PTA allowed for confessions, made under duress or torture to become admissible.[35]

The PTA was made retroactive. The police and army interpreted the law as carte blanche to arrest without warrant, search and seize, and long-term detention without trial or communication with family. Over the years increasing numbers of Tamil civilians were rounded up and detained without access to lawyers or family for prolonged periods of time.[36]

Rather than mitigate the occurrences of violence, the PTA escalated Tamil violence in the 1980s, and additional repressive counter measures of the government led to a spiral of increasing brutality and tit for tat violence. The PTA has never been repealed, although it was suspended by parliament. The use of torture declined significantly in the late 1990s, though the damage was done and the seeds of violence sown.

By the early 1980s, parliamentarians of the TULF lost out to a younger, more radical generation of fighters. Although the LTTE had started out as the foot soldiers of the TUF and the TULF, they proclaimed a preference for violent tactics and resorted to terrorism. In July of 1983, the government declared emergency regulations (martial law) in the Tamil districts of Jaffna, Vavuniya, and Mannar. [37] Tambiah writes,

> The last straw for the Sinhalese was the adoption of the old Chola tiger symbol and their mounting attacks on the security forces and police—acts which they interpret as calculated to make Sinhalese security forces and extremist politicians react with violence, thereby reducing the island to such disorder that foreign intervention (both by India and Western powers) might ensue and become the channel for a just settlement.[38]

The riots of July 24–August 5, 1983 were part of a series dating from 1956. Major outbreaks of ethnic violence had occurred in 1958, 1977, and 1981 escalating into the severe riots by July and August 1983.[39] "Localized violence in 1977 ripened into the widespread and destructive riots of 1983 that marked the beginning of the civil war."[40] However, according to Neelan Tiruchelvam: "There was a qualitative difference in the intensity, brutality, and organized nature of the violence in July 1983. No other event is so deeply etched in the collective memories of the victims and the survivors."[41]

The trigger for the 1983 rioting was the ambush of thirteen Sinhalese soldiers[42] at Tinneveli in the Jaffna district that had been under occupation for quite some time. Anita Pratap alleges that the 1983 attack at Tinneveli was retaliation for the murder of Charles Anthony, Prabhakaran's right-hand man, in July 1983 by Sri Lankan forces.[43] Colombo's population was outraged when the military returned the bodies of the slain soldiers, which had been mutilated, and displayed them publicly in Colombo's Kanatte Cemetery in Borella.

This led to a three-day wave of anti-Tamil violence against civilians during which time Sinhalese burned homes, destroyed Tamil-owned factories and businesses, and engaged in widespread looting, pillaging, and rape. The degree of state involvement was unclear. It appeared to be disorganized mob violence yet the government admitted to 360 deaths[44] and the "mobs were armed with voters' lists, and detailed addresses of every Tamil owned shop, house or factory, and their attacks were very precise."[45] The mob allegedly had detailed lists of personal belongings and knew what to look for.

In Colombo, protesters burned most of Wellwatte and parts of Dehiwela and Bambalapitiya. President Jayewardene admitted that some of the armed forces had participated in the riots, and that Sinhalese people had taken part, but he pointed to a Communist conspiracy (external and internal), and a Naxalite[46] plot blaming Indian expansionism.[47] On July 31, 1983, the Minister of Tourism, Broadcasting and Information, Ananda Tissa de Alwis, stated: "The unrest is the work of unnamed foreigners who hatched a deep plot to overthrow the government."[48] Neelan Tiruchelvam counters, "It was widely believed that elements within the state or the ruling party had either orchestrated the violence or encouraged the perpetrators." [49] Jayewardene and his government's reaction to the violence did not help matters:

> Implicit in all [these] statements is the fundamental premise that "Sri Lanka is inherently and rightfully a Sinhalese state . . . and it must be accepted as such, not a matter of opinion to be debated. For attempting to challenge this premise, Tamils have brought the wrath of Sinhalese on their own heads; they have themselves to blame."[50]

The president was helpless to do anything and was sealed in his residence out of fear of reprisals and the breakdown of law and order. Between July 25 and 28 fifty-three Tamil "terrorists" who were incarcerated at the Welikade top security prison died in police custody[51] and the army ran rampant in the Jaffna area, torturing and killing hundreds of civilians. The result was the introduction of Emergency Regulation 15A which allowed the security forces to bury and/or cremate people they shot without revealing their identities or carrying out inquests.[52]

The Tamil Tigers were few in number and limited in scope. They targeted Tamil moderates and police collaborators and operated exclusively in Jaffna. Support for the LTTE increased sharply after the 1983 attacks. Coomaraswamy puts the pre-1983 figures at 600 LTTE members, "by March 1983 after the 'pogrom' LTTE support exceeded 10,000."[53] As recruitment increased, the Tamils extended the target lists to include the security forces while they funded their actions through bank robberies.[54] The rural poor were largely ambivalent and most local Tamils did not support the LTTE, although they might have been sympathetic to its goals if not its methods.[55] After 1983, the LTTE drew its support from marginalized Tamils who resented their second-class citizenship status and from the growing number of internally displaced people (IDPs). The majority of the Tigers came from the lower castes—exacerbating splits between the masses and elites.

In the immediate aftermath of the 1983 riots the government declared emergency rule and passed the Sixth Amendment to the Constitution, which effectively excluded and banned the TULF (the main opposition party) from Parliament. This amendment outlawed any party from advocating secession or irredentism within Sri Lanka. Violating the law could have dire consequences including the forfeiture of property, loss of passport, and the loss of any professional license. All members of parliament were required to take an oath to uphold the Constitution and all of its amendments. Thus the TULF's formal commitment to a separate state effectively meant the end of constitutional solutions and left none other than violence as a possible response.

Civilians who had been targeted by the government forces had little choice but to support the LTTE. The army blamed them for LTTE attacks and randomly retaliated against the civilian Tamil population. Membership in the LTTE afforded minimal protection. The most significant base of support came from expatriate Tamils who fled the country in the 1970s and 1980s to Britain, Malaysia, India, France, Germany, Canada, Italy, Australia, and the United States. The LTTE and international terrorist groups such as the Baader-Meinhof Gang, the PLO, ANC and the IRA were linked.[56] Edgar O'Ballance writes that all five Tamil insurgent groups sent their cadres to Palestinian Resistance Camps in Lebanon.[57]

The attacks against Tamils in July 1983 and the ensuing clashes had two very important demographic consequences for the island. One was the exodus of more than 150,000 refugees from the northern regions of Sri Lanka to Tamil Nadu in southern India. Many of the refugees were repatriated to Sri Lanka over the course of two cease-fires in the 1990s. It is thought that more than 100,000 Tamils still reside in refugee camps today. The Sri Lankan security forces had often turned against Tamil civilians in their attempt to flush out LTTE militants. This exodus consisted primarily of those civilians who had become the victims of the government's drive against Tamil *militants*.[58]

The second consequence was an exodus of Tamils living among the Sinhalese in the Southern parts of the island to their traditional homes in the north and east. The violence of July 1983 convinced many Tamils that they could be safe and secure only in their own areas, despite the presence and operations of the army. These moves immediately strengthened the notion of a homeland (Eelam) in which Tamils would have their own state, and it established a close link between the Tamils of Sri Lanka and the Tamils of India, resulting in the Sri Lankan Tamil issue becoming the major issue in Tamil Nadu and Indian politics.[59]

Tamil Nadu was conscious of its cultural heritage and its role vis-à-vis Tamil communities in the other parts of the world. It had also been the scene of separatist demands for an independent state in the 1960s. Although these demands died down, the embers of Tamil nationalism were kept alive by the Dravida Munnetra Kazhagam (DMK), which held power between 1967 and 1977.[60]

After July 1983, the DMK, which was by then in opposition, took up the cause of Sri Lankan Tamils. It described the 1983 Sri Lankan riots as genocide against the Tamils and called on the Indian government to send its armed forces to Sri Lanka in order to save their beleaguered brethren. The ruling party in Tamil Nadu was the All-India Anna Dravida Munnetra Kashagam (AIADMK), a split from the DM; its leader, M.G. Ramachandran, spoke out on the behalf of Sri Lankan Tamils. The party mobilized public opinion by protesting against the Sinhalese oppression of Tamils. They passed a resolution in October 1983 in the Tamil Nadu State Assembly condemning the violence and urging the United Nations to intervene. The Sri Lankan Tamil issue became a focal point in the internal politics of Tamil Nadu itself though the AIADMK's support stopped short of espousing Tamil independence.[61]

Many attempts in 1986 to solve the conflict proved abortive. The militants employed several strategies designed to wear down the morale of the government forces including conventional guerrilla tactics, terror against civilians, assassination of political leaders, assassination of local Tamil (non-LTTE) leaders (e.g., Neelan Tiruchelvam), bombing symbolic and military targets, and "almost anything that could help impress its supporters and antagonists."[62]

Beginning in August of 1986, officials of the two governments held talks in Delhi to draft the terms of an accord. These terms envisaged a system of devolution at three levels: divisional, district, and provincial. Powers at the provincial level were defined, allowing for devolution with respect, for example, to law and order, agriculture, and land settlement.

A car bomb exploded at a bus station in Colombo at the end of April 1987, killing 113 people. The government, faced with popular outrage, launched an "all-out offensive" on the Jaffna Peninsula and, by the end of May, captured a large part of it at great cost in terms of life, property, and the massive dislocation of the area's inhabitants. It was at this stage that the Indian government intervened directly and decisively. Arguing that the army offensive had rendered the people of Jaffna completely destitute, India decided to send in "humanitarian relief." When a flotilla of boats carrying relief supplies was turned back by the Sri Lankan navy, India dropped relief supplies by air—in violation of Sri Lankan airspace—and then negotiated with the government for the further deliveries.

There were intermittent but short-lived efforts at negotiating peace over the years with India playing an important role in brokering the Indo-Lanka Peace accord in July 1987. Sri Lanka was under great pressure from donor countries to solve the conflict—especially in view of the economic devastation caused by the war and the increase in military expenditure. The Indian government enforced willingness from both the Sri Lankan government and from the LTTE. Indian Prime Minister Rajiv Gandhi and President JR Jayewardene signed the Indo-Sri Lankan Accord on July 29, 1987.[63]

"The accord endeavored to provide a conceptual framework for the resolution of the ethnic conflict and to outline the institutional arrangements for the sharing of power between the Sinhala and Tamil communities. It declared that Sri Lanka was a multiethnic and multilingual plural society" consisting of four ethnic groups; Sinhalese, Tamils, Muslims, and Burghers. The accord further recognized that the Northern Province and the eastern province "had been areas of historical habitation of the Tamil speaking population. Thus without conceding the claim that the northeast constituted part of the traditional homelands of the Tamils, the accord provided cautious acknowledgement of the distinct character of the region." Both of these statements had important ideological significance in framing the policy of bilingualism, the provincial council scheme, and the temporary merger of the northern and eastern provinces as the unit of devolution.[64]

India moved from the position of mediator to that of direct participant, one with separate and specific interests of its own because of the Punjab conflict and concerns over Khalistani secession and Tamil separatism in southern India.[65] The pressure emanating from Tamil Nadu forced the Indian central government to intervene in the matter. The Tamil Nadu government was no doubt concerned to see the issue settled, but the central government of India was motivated by reasons of national security as much as the pressure from Tamil Nadu.

The agreement had three components. First, the modalities of settling the ethnic conflict through the devolution of power to a Tamil region combined the northern and eastern provinces. Second, there were Indian guarantees and obligations with regard to the implementation of the accord. Third, (in letters exchanged along with the agreement), the actions by the Sri Lankan government vis-à-vis India which were not related to the ethnic conflict but concerned India's regional security interests were stipulated.

The other conditions mentioned in the accord included assurances that Sri Lankan territory would not be used for "activities prejudicial to Indian interests," -- implying the port of Trincomalee; and Sri Lanka was to reconsider the use of Israeli and Pakistani military advisors and the presence of the Voice of America radio station which beamed its broadcasts all over South Asia. Finally, the oil installations at Trincomalee would be restored and operated by a joint Indian-Sri Lankan company.[66]

The framers of the accord hoped that they could present political groups in the northeast and the south with a *fait accompli*. However, the Indian intervention sparked Sinhala chauvinism in the south. Both the LTTE and the JVP radical youth movement repudiated the accord.[67] Prabhakaran had only agreed to the accord because he was under house arrest in the Ashoka hotel in New Delhi and prophesized that the accord would not bring the end of the conflict but merely open a new chapter.[68] The controversy surrounding the IPKF Intervention eventually led to an armed confrontation between the LTTE and the IPKF, which tried to control security in the northeast for three years, resulting in ever increasing antagonism between the LTTE and IPKF. Riots in the south led the government to arm the LTTE as a counter weight to the Sinhala People's Liberation Front, Janata Vimukti Peramuna (JVP) and to attack the Indian peace enforcers. "As part and parcel of "military/ geopolitical strategy," the government supplied a consignment of firearms to the LTTE with the objective of enhancing its capacity for guerrilla attacks on the Indian Peace-Keeping Force, and thus hastening the withdrawal of the Indian army units from Sri Lanka."[69]

When Ranasingha Premadasa (UNP) took office as President of Sri Lanka in January 1989 he "faced all three major categories of threats any state could face: a threat to national independence and sovereignty; a threat to its territorial integrity; and a threat to the state apparatus and to state power itself."[70] His initial approach was one of conciliation which derived from a position of strength given his capacity to match violence with yet more violence. Once the LTTE began negotiations with President Premadasa in April 1989, the IPKF was no longer welcome. This led to the withdrawal of forces on March 31, 1990, although the LTTE never forgave India for the behavior of the IPKF troops. Relations between Sri Lankan Tamils and Indian (Estate) Tamils suffered when a female "Black Tigress" named Dhanu (a.k.a Gayatri) assassinated Indian Prime Minister Rajiv Gandhi on May 21, 1991.[71]

The LTTE's ability to resist the IPFK as well as the Sri Lankan army had a great deal to do with its tactics. In addition to the use of suicide terror and the willingness of its operative to die (and take a cyanide pill to evade capture), the LTTE made great use of the strategic position of the Jaffna peninsula and the ability to escape from there to Tamil Nadu if the enemy pressure was too strong.

From the outset, the LTTE made optimum use of its access to the sea. First of all, it served as a means of transporting narcotics from the Golden

Crescent and the Golden Triangle to Europe. This began as early as 1984. Narcotics provided the main source of income until it was superseded by external donor support and now by infrastructural taxes, highway tolls and other levies. Access to both sides of the Indian Ocean made smuggling weapons easier. The weapons came from India (before the 1987 Accord) and then South East Asia—Myanmar, Thailand, and Cambodia. The LTTE ferried wounded cadres across the straits to Tamil Nadu for treatment, even when they were wounded by the IPKF. LTTE also appears unique in its development of a separate merchant marine, which combines the smuggling of weapons and drugs with the transport of commercial items.[72]

The Indian withdrawal left the LTTE in de facto control of the north and the east. Premadasa kept the military barracks closed for three months during which time peace negotiations appeared to progress. Devolution discussions were short-lived and fell apart over the issue of secession and the LTTE declared the Eelam War part II on June 10, 1990 and the Tigers took over Jaffna on September 26.[73]

THE ONLY GAME IN TOWN

Would be competitors and the Sri Lankan government financed anti-LTTE groups: the People's Liberation Organization of Tamil Eelam (PLOTE),[74] the Tamil Eelam Liberation Organization (TELO), the Eelam People's Democratic Party (EPDP), and the Rafik group: their membership—predominantly youths— was bankrolled by the Sri Lankan government but remained outside the authority of the armed forces. The paramilitary cadres had freer reign to terrorize people, torture them, and extort money at gunpoint.[75] Their leaders have frequently been installed as members of parliament and support government policies. Those paramilitary groups in competition with the Tigers have been virtually eliminated in many parts of Sri Lanka by the LTTE through a campaign of harassment and political assassination.

At the outset, guerrilla groups in the north and the east jostled each other for territory, recruits, and weapons. Apart from the Tamil Five group, there were at least twenty others in the Jaffna Peninsula, all locally based. EROS bandwagoned onto urban terrorism, mainly in Colombo, to increase its organizational profile. Some assumed that EROS collaborated with the LTTE, although this remains unconfirmed.

> [EROS] was taking this course to compensate for its comparatively small number of rural guerrillas in the field, in order to bolster its prestige in insurgent counsels. On May 1 a bomb exploded on board an

Air Lanka airliner at Colombo International Airport. . . . EROS claimed responsibility.[76]

The Tamil Tigers had become the strongest and most aggressive of the groups. They began by pushing aside the People's Liberation Army of Tamil Eelam (PLATE), the military arm of PLOTE. Then the Tigers came into conflict with TELO, which had suffered a loss of leadership during the Welikade Prison massacres, and they set about getting rid of those who survived. This internecine strife benefited the security forces, which concentrated on capturing leaders, offered cash rewards for information as to their whereabouts, and encouraged rival groups to inform on one another.

Sometime in 1985, Prabakharan decided to eliminate the other four major resistance groups. He had always seen himself as president of an independent Tamil Eelam in Sri Lanka. He began with PLOTE, and there was a shootout in Madras, when a Tamil Tiger attempted to kill Maheswaram, the PLOTE leader and former right-hand of Prabhakaran.[77]

In a joint press release on April 11, 1985 the groups announced the formation of what became known as the April Alliance of the Eelam National Liberation Front (ENLF), between the LTTE, EPRLF, TELO, and EROS (but excluding PLOTE) to coordinate their revolutionary activities. This merging had been prompted by "the escalation of State violence and genocide against the Tamils in Sri Lanka."[78]

Nevertheless, Prabhakaran sent coded messages detailing how TELO members (based in Jaffna) should be eliminated. The government did not intervene and was content to sit back and let the groups kill each other off. The process by which Prabhakaran's rivals were eliminated occurred over the span of fifteen years. The LTTE rendered its former political mentors, as well as rivals and opponents within the Tamil community, peripheral and dispensable while it posed a security threat to the integrity of the Sri Lankan state.

One by one their rivals and opponents among the Tamil separatist groups succumbed to the relentless violence of the LTTE. An essential feature of the process was the physical elimination of the leadership of several important Tamil separatist groups, rivals and one-time associates of the LTTE. At its foundation . . . the LTTE was only one of several separatist groups operating in the Jaffna peninsula . . . between 1977 and 1986 the TULF consistently lost ground to the LTTE which dominated public life in Jaffna and Tamils in the Peninsula. The LTTE seized the leadership of the movement and was soon strong enough to engage in a struggle on two fronts, against the security forces of the Sri Lankan state, and in internecine warfare in which it systematically eliminated all rival groups, culminating in the brutal massacre of the Tamil Eelam Liberation Organization (TELO) and the killing of its leader, Sri Sabaratnam, between 1 and 3 May, 1986 in Jaffna.[79]

Piecemeal all of the LTTE's rivals were eliminated or went underground in Tamil Nadu, across the Palk Strait. Their influence and control of Tamil separatism was extremely limited as a result. Rural groups attempted to capture public imagination by staging massive terror attacks. For April 11–20, the government declared an official cease-fire to cover the festive religious holidays. This cease-fire was broken on April 17, when three buses and two trucks were ambushed in a heavy rain storm by LTTE fighters near the village of Althoya, near Trincomalee. In all 127 passengers and 21 servicemen were massacred and another 60 wounded. The incident became known as the "Good Friday Massacre."

Four days later, a huge bomb exploded during rush hour at the main bus station in Colombo killing 100 people and injuring another 200. The LTTE denied any involvement and the government blamed the attack on EROS. EROS initially denied involvement but later admitted its responsibility. EROS had denied responsibility so as not to embarrass its sponsor, India. Nevertheless it was believed that the LTTE had conspired with EROS in the attack.[80]

THE LTTE AND SUICIDE TERROR

The LTTE effectively used suicide terror from 1987 until 2001. In fact, they perpetrated the most suicide bombings of any single organization and more than those of the twelve other organizations using this tactic put together, until bypassed by Palestinian groups in 2003.

The LTTE is internally divided according to specialization, like a professional military. The general umbrella organization is the Tamil Tigers, but the organization is further subdivided between the Black Tigers (suicide bombing division), Sea Tigers (Naval attack unit), Baby Tigers (child soldier division), Air Tigers (Air Force division) and the "Women's Military Units of the LTTE."[81] There are both Hindu as well as Christian Tigers[82] and so there is no particular religious element to the organization although the majority of Tamils are Hindu. Any leader that wishes to split off from the organization is simply killed.

Over the years, the LTTE's use of suicide bombing adapted to political circumstances. In addition to attacking Sinhalese targets, the LTTE has used suicide terror against its moderate Tamil opposition. At various points in time, the LTTE perpetrated suicide terror against military targets, civilian infrastructure, indiscriminate attacks against Sinhalese civilians, while targeting specific politicians for assassination.

Vicious infighting between the Tamil liberation groups was the norm in the initial phase of suicide terror. PLOTE suffered heavy casualties at the hands of the Tigers, and the Tigers attacked its members even after the groups officially ceased their military operations. According to the *Voice of Tamil Eelam*, a radio station run by the Communist Party of Tamil Eelam (CPTE), the LTTE killed a PLOTE military commander on January 11, 1987. The following month 57 EPRLF insurgents were killed as the result of the infighting between the groups.

> Due to successful counter insurgency tactics by the STF, almost 2,000 strong and operating in the Eastern province, numerous Tamil informers were persuaded to come forward and give details about rival groups which resulted in many deaths (while resisting capture or from taking cyanide suicide pills).[83]

Between 1991 and 1994 the LTTE eliminated the core of the UNP's political leadership. In October 1994 a suicide bomber killed Gamini Dissanayake, the UNP's presidential candidate and more than fifty people including several former current cabinet members and appointees, the general secretary of the party, all but eliminating the UNP from the running.

Chandrika Bandaranaike Kumaratunga of the People's Alliance party (PA) was elected president in 1994 on a platform of peace and constitutional reform.[84] Within two months of her coming to power a ceasefire was declared with the first round of peace talks beginning in 1995. The devolutionary proposals put forth in 1997 only touched upon autonomy and stopped short of separation (and even shorter of what many Tamils wanted). More significantly, the LTTE had not been consulted about devolution and it used the ceasefire to regroup and rearm. The negotiations fell apart after only three months when the violence, and notably suicide bombings, resumed.

Subsequently, the government's strategy was to weaken the LTTE through continued war while at the same time plan to devolve power into regional councils. The policy was ironically called the "War for Peace." As a result of LTTE victories,[85] the president called for another state of emergency throughout the island on August 4, 1998.[86]

The December 1999 presidential election gave the LTTE the opportunity to attack President Kumaratunga. On December 18, 1999 the LTTE dispatched a female suicide terrorist who detonated herself after a political rally near the Town Hall. The President lost an eye, but survived the attack, which killed her security guards and bystanders. On the same night, another LTTE suicide bomber, a male, chose an election rally in the Ja-Ela township near Colombo to kill a former general who was expected to get a cabinet position in the UNP government had they succeeded in the election.[87] In July 1999 the LTTE killed moderate TULF Member of Parliament Neelan Tiruchelvam and in June 2000, a senior cabinet Minister, CV Gunaratne.

The LTTE likewise had a firm grip over the civilian population because the penalty for refusal to obey or comply is usually death. "Their principal targets, among the Tamils, were the cadres of rival separatist organizations and defectors from their own ranks, who were pursued relentlessly and killed by scores and often by hundreds."[88]

Kumaratunga responded to a series of bomb attacks, military reversals (see photo 12) and the deepening political crisis by lashing out at the minority Tamil population with a wave of police harassment and repression. Both the government and the Colombo media held a racist premise that all Tamils were responsible for the actions of the LTTE.

The government's campaign began after a suicide bomb attack outside the Prime Minister's office in Colombo on January 5 [2000]. Security forces imposed a 14-hour total curfew on the capital, deployed nearly 5,000 troops and police and rounded up thousands in the predominantly Tamil areas of the capital for interrogation. Since then the army and police have engaged in numerous "search operations" in Tamil areas, towns and villages, all in the name of apprehending "LTTE suspects."[89]

DOMESTIC POLITICS MATTER

The National Security Council (NSC) required all residents in the Batticaloa District obtain a security clearance and carry a special identity card to prevent the LTTE from using Batticaloa to infiltrate into southern Sri Lanka, including Colombo. The decision affected 600,000 people. Police harassment and intimidation also intensified in the plantation areas of Kandy, Hatton, Maskeliya, Nuwara Eliya, Badulla, Bandarawela, Passara, Matugama—which are in the hill country of central Sri Lanka where the majority are Estate Tamils.

The government responded with scorched earth tactics they had honed and perfected against the JVP in the South, destroying homes and farms and employing overwhelming force.[90] They utilized official death squads and show killings and public executions to terrorize the populace. There were massive human rights abuses in the north and east as well as assaults by air and sea.[91]

According to Darini Rajasingham-Senanyake, the government organized and routinized violence through a systematic campaign of "disappearances," while turning a blind eye toward the use of rape. It used check point searches in order to dehumanize Tamils, as well as widespread torture. Entire villages were razed in remote areas.[92] Rajasingham-Senanyake adds that, "check point rape and murder were well documented in Sri Lanka, in this context militant groups who infiltrate camps have little difficulty in recruiting new cadres from deeply frustrated and resentful youth, men and women, girls and boys."[93]

The government tactics, which were not mindful of differentiating between civilians and combatants, only emboldened the LTTE and solidified their control of Jaffna.[94] Civilian deaths caused by the government made the LTTE stronger in these areas and soured the Tamil population on government assurances of devolution and equal rights.

Individual Motives

The LTTE and the Tamils generally feel that they had little choice but to use violence against the Sri Lankan government. The Tamil progression from peaceful opposition to violence demonstrates how the government cut off other avenues of negotiations for years.

> Ask Vasantha why he is prepared to contemplate such a drastic action and the boy replies simply: "This is the most supreme sacrifice I can make. The only way we can get our Eelam [homeland] is through arms. That is the only way anybody will listen to us. Even if we die."[95]

The government began to employ heavy handed tactics, among them the targeting of specific villages and alienating its population who would then become enthusiastic supporters of the LTTE and joined the Black Tigers in droves.

> [Villagers of Kokkurill] say that during a 1990 crackdown on the Tigers, the Sri Lankan army arbitrarily arrested 183 people from the village, including women and children. In the years since . . . the village has sacrificed more lives for the cause than any other in Sri Lanka: A hundred men from this village of 500 have already left to fight for the rebels, never to return.[96]

The individual motives for the bombers vary between the personal desire for revenge and reactions to the domestic policies of the Sri Lankan government. All however, were inspired by an extreme ethnic nationalism and complete dedication to the leader of the LTTE, Villupilai Prabhakaran.

The personal sense of outrage is often expressed through violence. For individual bombers, the connection between personal loss and the willingness to become martyrs is clear: "The harassment that I and my parents have suffered at the hands of the army makes me want to take revenge.... It is a question of Tamil pride, especially after so much sacrifice. There is no escape."[97]

It is precisely this sense of ethnic pride that the Tigers tap into. Every individual bomber for the LTTE joins a "pantheon of martyrs ... [in which each] boy's picture will be framed, garlanded and hung on the wall of his training camp, to be revered by hundreds of other teenagers willing to sign their lives away for the cause."[98]

The pictures of martyrs are evident throughout the Tamil areas; everyone knows their names, which are printed up in pamphlets and distributed at Heroes' Day celebrations all over the Vanni, and in the Tamil Diaspora. The booklets include the name, date of birth, age, time of the attack, where the attack occurred, and include the martyr's picture. Young Tamils know the names of the martyrs the way young American kids know the names of sports stars. They look up to them, and want to emulate what they have done.

One of the ways that the LTTE is able to persuade young men and young women to become bombers is grounded in a complete dedication to Prabhakaran, who fosters this sense of community and one of the highlights for an individual bomber is that they enjoy a last meal with the LTTE leader himself prior to an operation.

Prabhakaran is mindful of his impact on the individual foot soldiers. In his 1993 Black Tiger Day speech he stressed that:

I have groomed my weak brethren into a strong weapon called Black Tigers. They possess an iron will, yet their hearts are so very soft. They have deep human characteristics of perceiving the advancement of the interest of the people through their own annihilation.... Death has surrendered to them. They keep eagerly waiting for the day they would die. They just don't bother about death. This is the era of the Black Tigers. No force on earth today can suppress the fierce uprising of Tamils who seek freedom.[99]

The LTTE has a preference for young recruits and women to fill the ranks of their suicide squads (Black Tigers for the men and the Birds of Freedom for female suicide bombers) because they—and especially the women—are better able to avoid detection and pass through security because of the ease with which they can penetrate crowds and reach their targets. (See photo 13.)

The LTTE's strategy of deliberately using the civilian population, particularly the exploitation of child soldiers for use as spies, couriers, and suppliers as well as front line soldiers is in direct violation of international law.[100] Many of its operatives are between the ages of 14 and 17, in violation of UN resolutions governing the prohibition of child soldiers, and yet the young people in the uncleared areas where the LTTE reigns supreme find the idea of joining glamorous and an expression of dedication to the cause and the leadership. Since April 1995, 60 percent of casualties have been under the age of 18.[101]

Many parents worry that their rations will be cut if they do not allow their children to be recruited. Once recruited, child soldiers benefit from a rapid elevation in social status. One critic of the organization emphasized to me that Prabhakaran is better able to manipulate young people or those who have suffered from a personal grievance.

Recruiting (and kidnapping) in schools has led many Tamil families to remove their children from them. This is yet another clear signal of the war weariness. Parent groups, like the "Mothers of Stolen Children," voice their anger toward the LTTE with leaflets and graffiti across the north and east. These groups surfaced in 2000 and sent the LTTE, who believe their own rhetoric of being the "rightful and true" leaders of the Tamil population, a shocking message.[102]

There is an argument that there is a caste system within the LTTE. It is significant that every leader of the LTTE except one in the east originates from Jaffna, whereas a large portion of its recruits come from lower castes in Ampara, Mannar, and Batticaloa. For those who espouse this argument, the LTTE is using the lower castes as cannon fodder for their war.[103]

Caste remains a highly sensitive topic among Tamils. During the course of my research and interviews, Jaffna Tamils indicated which caste they belonged to, whereas many of the people I polled in the east left that part of the questionnaire blank or wrote *Tamil* when that was clearly not the question I had asked. Colonel Karuna's 2004 split was based on caste difference between the LTTE leadership and the cadres.

The perpetuation of the war in Sri Lanka over a period of nineteen years has created additional economic incentives for young Tamils to join the LTTE. The Sri Lankan economy was devastated, opportunities dwindled as a result, and even educated Tamils had few professional prospects outside of working for the international community, aid organizations, and NGOs. Since 56 percent of the working population currently holds a government paid position, disenfranchising Tamils cuts off more than half the possible job opportunities. "There is rank discrimination against Tamils in the most practical forms, at check points, at job interviews . . . The harsh reality is that a Tamil in Sri Lanka is and will remain a second-class citizen to the Sinhalese."[104]

The years of civil war reduced the possibility of farming as a source of employment and income. The Sinhalese land distribution schemes in the north and east (especially in Trincomalee, Batticaloa, and Ampara) of the 1990s set the stage for massive land and property rights conflicts.

For young Tamils who do make it out of high school, jobs are scarce and movement to other parts of the country (like the Urban areas in the south) is restricted. The lack of opportunity and work in regions that have exhibited no visible signs of development for a decade is often cited to explain Batticaloa's high contribution to the Tigers.

This sentiment was echoed by the people I encountered at St. Michael's College in Batticaloa and other schools throughout Malavi and Trincomalee. The students and their teachers demonstrated a love of learning and yet were cognizant of how few opportunities were available to them—even with an education.[105] Many of the key programs by various international organizations like CARE, have centered on transforming educational opportunities and career placement for a population that has only experienced war for a whole generation. Many young people are shockingly ill prepared for peacetime, and the international organizations have made this a priority in their efforts to build peace.

The LTTE claims that educating this generation is their priority and computer science training is exploding all over the Vanni and uncleared areas as the LTTE identifies the best way to prepare Tamil Youth for a peaceful future.[106] The provision of social services allows the LTTE to mobilize the Tamil population very effectively. However, the LTTE has not actually expended its own resources to provide such services and public goods. Cleverly, the organization has managed to piggyback onto the programs initiated by the international community, which require a local middleman—who is inevitably linked to the LTTE. Thus, the LTTE is able to ingratiate itself to the civilian community, winning the hearts and minds of the people while maximizing its resources. This way, the LTTE claims any social services provided by the NGO or IO community while reserving the majority of its resources to procure weapons and train operatives.[107]

TAMIL PUBLIC ATTITUDES ABOUT SUICIDE TERROR

Unlike the two-thirds Palestinian support for suicide terror in the Israeli-Palestinian conflict, Tamils attitudes about violence are varied and nuanced and constrain what the organization can and cannot do and who they can target.

Unlike in the Palestinian case, establishing Tamil public attitudes is challenging given the absence of comparable research institutions which have collected data for twelve years on a regular basis, polling thousands of Palestinians, which result in our ability to observe attitudinal shifts over time. In Sri Lanka no such polling data exists; although there is some data available for Tamil support of the LTTE, questions regarding suicide terror and civilian casualties remain taboo subjects which people are hesitant to discuss.

The Center for Policy Alternatives (CPA) Social Indicator, *Perspectives on Peace from Jaffna,* and the Social Science Association (SSA) measured Tamil attitudes about the peace process and support for the LTTE. They have not, however, asked questions about suicide operations. Thus, I conducted research to establish a baseline of attitudes from which to measure future changes. My findings are preliminary and limited, although highly illuminating. Over three months in 2002, I interviewed or polled hundreds of Tamils all over Sri Lanka, in the north, in the east, in mixed ethnic urban and mixed ethnic rural areas. The size of the polling sample limits the definitive nature of my findings although they provide insight; and in two questions where there was overlap with existing polling data (support for the LTTE and attitudes about the peace process) my results mirrored those of the established research institutions exactly though they had significantly larger samples.

Tamils with whom I spoke generally were optimistic about the peace process and were hopeful for the future. People were extremely war weary and anticipated a significant peace dividend in the near future. See figure 3.1 in the appendix.

This degree of optimism contrasts with the Palestinian case in which most Palestinians have no confidence in the peace process and thus suicide terror appears to be the only way to achieve their goals. Many Tamils polled thought that armed confrontation and non traditional methods which had been effective in the past were no longer necessary although people acknowledged that it had been necessary in the past. See figure 3.2 in the appendix.

Another significant difference in Sri Lanka concerned the attitudes toward terror. The Tamils with whom I spoke differentiated between attacking civilians and attacking military personnel or politicians. There was virtually no support for attacking civilians regardless of whether they were in Sinhalese territory or in the Tamil regions. The attitudes regarding attacking military targets (Sri Lankan soldiers occupying Jaffna for instance) were more varied.

The survey duplicated the questions asked of Palestinians by the JMCC and the Palestinian Center for Public Opinion and attempted find the "equivalents" of Green Line Israel, the Occupied Territories, and ethnically mixed urban centers. Figure 3.2 in the appendix demonstrates that regardless of where the civilians are there is little or no support for killing innocent bystanders. The majority clearly opposes (or strongly opposes) such attacks. However support for attacks against soldiers in Jaffna was split evenly across the board. See figure 3.3 in the appendix.

As clear as people's opposition to civilian attacks, the attitudes about killing soldiers varied by region and by age group. I separated out the responses of those said they supported or strongly supported civilian casualties to ascertain whether gender, age or level of education had any impact. Similar to the Palestinian-Israeli Conflict, men supported violence much more often than women. See figure 3.4 in the appendix.

The data indicates that those who supported violence tended to be under 30 and were high school graduates. What is significant about these observations is that Tamils with a university education were less supportive of violence as a tactic. This contrasts markedly with the Palestinian case in which we see a direct correlation between more education and support for militant organizations. See figure 3.5 in the appendix.

The LTTE appears aware of people's attitudes regarding civilian immunity. When asked what was the key difference separating the LTTE from groups like Hamas and the Islamic Jihad, LTTE spokesperson S. Puleedevan acknowledged that the LTTE did not deliberately target children at the Pizza Hut, a reference to Hamas' bombing of the Sbarro Pizzeria in Jerusalem.[108]

Intercommunal Violence

As enlightened as the LTTE might appear for an insurgent organization, the treatment of minorities who live or have lived in their midst has been brutal at times. The LTTE attacked Muslims in the northern and eastern provinces at regular intervals between 1984 and 1990 killing more than 300 people. The Sinhalese population of Jaffna was ethnically cleansed after the LTTE took over in 1990. The idea was to force the Muslims out of some strategic villages, which separated Tamil settlements on the east coast. Although the LTTE failed to secure the villages, they held the north and northwest of the island, the Jaffna Peninsula, and the Mannar district.[109] Notable among the clashes was the August 1990 massacre of 120 Muslims at a mosque in Kattankudy in Batticaloa during evening prayers.[110]

Muslim-LTTE rivalry focused on Muslim claims for a provincial council centering on the Ampara district of the eastern province and with cantons covering major Muslim centers like Batticaloa and Trincomalee and more worrisome for the LTTE than parts of the Jaffna Peninsula and the Mannar district. To the LTTE, this impinged on their concept of the traditional homeland and posed a serious threat to their control and the prospect of a united Eelam.[111]

Having failed in their attempt to expel Muslims from strategic villages in the eastern province, the LTTE turned against the more vulnerable civilian population. In October 1990 approximately 75,000 people—the entire Muslim population of Jaffna—were driven from their homes at gunpoint. Dr. SH Hasbullah writes: "The mass expulsion of the Muslims from the north was carried out in the following manner:"

> On 22 October 1990, quite unexpectedly, the LTTE announced over loudspeakers in the streets of the Muslim settlements in the Northern Province that the Muslims must leave their homes, villages, and towns, leaving all their valuables behind or face death. The ultimatum was that Muslims should leave the region within 48 hours from the 22nd of October. In Jaffna town the time given was only two hours.[112]

In addition to attacking Muslims at prayer, the LTTE struck at two of the most sacred sites of Buddhism. The precincts of the Bodi tree, one of the oldest trees in the world and alleged to have been the tree under which Buddha attained enlightenment at Gaya in India and the ancient city of Anaradhapura. In July 1987 a group of LTTE assassination squad killed 32 *samaneras* (*bhikku* priests in training) at Arantalawa and on January 25, 1998 an LTTE truck bomb blew up a large section of the Dalada Maligawa (Temple of the Tooth) in Kandy although the tooth was unharmed the building suffered extensive damage and the loss of several precious frescoes.[113]

Yet the major conflict in Sri Lanka remains secular and religion is incidental. This is not the case with the Muslim community which poses an increasing danger. In the eastern provinces, the main thrust of competition comes not from other Tamils but from Muslims who are Tamil speakers. Within the Muslim community there is no consensus about leadership. It is a fragmented and competitive environment with a multiplicity of actors competing to represent Muslim concerns in Trincomalee over representation in an emerging Sri Lanka and including specific issues about land rights. In this context, the outbidding model succeeds in explaining the radicalization of young Muslims in the east and the emergence of new groups like the Islamic Jihad who are attempting to play a spoiler role to the peace process by rioting in Muttu and Wellewatte.[114]

Beginning in late October 2002, the rioting spilled over into Colombo ostensibly over the rebuilding an Islamic school (madrasa) in Maradana.[115] Muslim *hartals* (street violence/riots) of June 2002 occurred after the Catholic Church erected fourteen crosses on a hillside in Trincomalee. The crosses were destroyed and a Muslim three wheel driver was blamed and attacked outside of the LTTE offices.

Muslim extremists rioted outside the LTTE offices and attacked again. Muslim concerns, despite the Hakeem-Prabhakaran Agreement,[116] have been heightened by the talks in Thailand, which, by definition, devolve powers in the East to the Tamil majority and do not split the powers between the two populations. Thus a peace agreement between Tamils and Sinhalese threatens the Muslims of the east. The Muslims are unsympathetic toward a division of the country along ethnic lines. The fact that the Muslims have been largely left out of the peace talks in Thailand contributes to the possibility that they will try to act as a spoiler to the process.[117]

The multiplicity of parties to represent Muslim concerns has led to a radicalization of the Muslim position and radical groups competing with one another for Muslim "market share." While bitter memories exist on both sides,[118] the real danger is that Muslim violence will cause instability in the Sri Lankan government and decrease its willingness to give the east autonomy, a necessary part of the LTTE's demands.

There are two other areas of Muslim concern regarding the LTTE.

Trade: The Muslim ability to continue their involvement in the trade industry is vital—and seriously threatened by the LTTE. The LTTE and Tamils are jealous of the Muslim community's success in business and industry. They seek to remove ALL Muslim businesspersons from Trincomalee, Batticaloa, Valaichchenai, Jaffna, and Akkaraipattu. That is a prime motivator for Muslims to turn to militancy.

Religion: Muslims in the East have been marginalized by both sides because of their beliefs. The LTTE regards them as different from "normal" Christian/Hindu Tamils and not dedicated to the cause of Tamil nationalism. Extreme Sinhala Buddhist culture views all other religions as alien and troublesome.[119] This has made the Muslims more insular and involved with their faith.[120]

When I interviewed Muslims during Ramadan 2002, most were fasting and many had started to study Arabic. Several people admitted to me that they had become religious after having been raised secular, and largely in response to their expulsion from Jaffna by the LTTE. Many women have donned the veil and burqa in the east, something that was not observable two or three years ago, and support for radical Islamic organizations has continued to rise.

CONCLUSIONS

The LTTE is not defeated but neither is it victorious. The civil war lasted for nineteen years, with grave human rights abuses committed by both sides. Since 1983 more than 64,000 lives were lost and over a million people have been internally displaced from their homes.[121] After the government's losses in the Jaffna Peninsula in 2001, both sides came to the peace talks because of war weariness and a realization that the status quo was untenable. When peace talks had fallen apart in 1998, those within the LTTE who opposed the negotiations were able to mobilize large numbers of people. By December 2001 this had all changed with the shift in government policy and willingness to negotiate with the LTTE. In December 2004 the dynamic was equally affected by the December 26 tsunami which killed over thirty thousand people on the island, especially in the east.

There are doubts as to whether a consociational arrangement would work in Sri Lanka. The social cleavages within the state are intense and cumulative. Most Sinhalese and Tamils are differentiated by both language and religion. With regard to the Estate Tamils, there is a coincidence similarity of class, caste, and ethnicity, as most were denied citizenship until very recently and constitute a distinct economic and social underclass.

The coming to the negotiating tables of the most extreme Tamil opposition group boded well for the resolution of suicide terrorism in the Sri Lankan case. The key difference between Sri Lanka and the Palestinian-Israeli conflict is the lack of competing groups to radicalize the polity.

John Burns once wrote about the LTTE's firm control in the *New York Times*:

> [Prabhakaran] has established a rule of terror in the city of Jaffna. According to scores of accounts from defectors and others who have escaped Tiger tyranny, many of his own lieutenants have been murdered; Tamils who have criticized him, even mildly or in jest have been picked up for years in dungeons, half starved, hauled out periodically for battering by their guards.[122]

Thus there has been little opportunity until recently for competition or outbidding between Tamil groups since the LTTE eliminated most of its domestic rivals; wherever the LTTE reigns supreme no opposition whatsoever is permitted.[123] In March 2004, a rebel colonel on the East coast formally broke with the LTTE complaining that the east was not being represented by the organization's northern-based leaders. Colonel Karuna, whose real name is

Vinayagamoorthy Muralitharan, was once Prabhakaran's bodyguard. Prabhakaran had promoted him to the rank of special commander for the eastern Batticaloa-Amparai districts in 2003. He replaced special commander Karikalan, who was ousted following his remarks over the communal situation in the district. Prabhakaran later made Colonel Karuna part of the team that negotiated with the government during several rounds of peace talks in Bangkok, Oslo and Tokyo. Karuna took 6,000 troops of the 15,000-strong rebel movement with him when he left. The Tamil leadership at first sought to play down the split, but their tone changed dramatically when Karuna posed a real challenge to their supremacy.

> To safeguard our nation and our people, it has been decided to get rid of Karuna from our soil. Our cadres should comprehend Karuna's treachery and keep away from him," said the Liberation Tigers of Tamil Eelam on the Tamilnet website. Further, anybody who opposes disciplinary action against Karuna, will be considered as a traitor to the Tamil National cause.[124]

The group offered those cadres who left with Karuna an amnesty to return to the fold. Karuna's defection wasn't tolerated and he went into hiding—surviving only with the assistance of the Sri Lankan Army.

According to reports:

> The peace process has been deadlocked since April (2003) when the Tigers walked out of talks, complaining that the government had not honored pledges for the rebels' stronghold in the north and east. Relations between the Tigers and the government deteriorated further over the case of renegade rebel leader Colonel Karuna, [who] tried to set up a separate rebel group in the east but was crushed by the mainstream Tigers and disappeared in April. The government admitted some elements in the army may have helped him but denied it had sanctioned the assistance.[125]

Karuna was quickly marginalized and went into hiding, surviving only with Kumaratunga's help. The Tigers rule with terror and complete control.[126] This makes negotiating with the LTTE simpler. Further, the most extreme elements of the Tamil Liberation movement are the ones negotiating the peace rather than the moderates (as in the Palestinian case). In contrast to the Palestinians, the majority of suicide bombings targeted a particular individual with the remaining victims as collateral damage. In contrast, Palestinian suicide bombs are intended to create a form of mass terror and general panic. When suicide terror first began, there existed a multiplicity of groups vying for public support; suicide terrorism increased the LTTE's popularity both inside the country and with outside expatriate donors. Once the LTTE reigned supreme, and competition was absent, their willingness to negotiate and compromise increased accordingly. Karuna's split threatened this balance of power.

Unlike Israel, when a terror attack occurs or one side is found to have violated the terms of the agreement by smuggling in weapons, the Sri Lankan government under Wickremesinghe did not use this as an excuse to stop negotiating and resume violent confrontation. This was observed by both sides. On November 1, 2002, a boat-load of illegal stinger mines was discovered by the Sri Lankan navy. The Sea Tigers had violated the terms of the ceasefire by trying to smuggle in the weapons and yet the talks in Thailand continued. On November 2, 2002 the Sri Lankan High Court sentenced LTTE leader Prabhakaran to 200 years imprisonment because of the attack on the Central bank which killed 91 and wounded more than 1,400 people.[127] The LTTE did not use this as an opportunity to break off negotiations with the government. Even when there have been isolated incidents of violence and tension, neither side has resumed the conflict.

For example, a young female cadre exploded in Kollupitya Police Station in July 2004 (only days after Black Tiger Day which celebrates suicide bombers) killing six police officers during a botched assassination attempt on the Tamil politician, Douglas Devananda, minister for Hindu Cultural Affairs. A statement from the LTTE immediately condemned the attack saying such acts caused "severe damage to the peace process" and denied any involvement in the bombing. Tamil Tiger spokesman, SP Thamilselvan, alleged "[That] this act of violence could be the work of anti-peace elements."[128] However, there is little doubt the Tigers were responsible and meant to warn the government. Since the ceasefire was signed between the rebels and the government in February 2002, the Tigers have eschewed using suicide bombing tactics although there have been a handful of incidents when cadres have exploded to avoid capture or prosecution. Both the Tigers and the government played down the impact of the July 2004 suicide bombing because the Tigers do not want to incur international condemnation for resorting to such tactics again, and the government faces local elections and does not want to lose votes by talking up the prospects for war. Prime Minister Mahinda Rajapakse said that this would not change the government's commitment to bring a negotiated settlement. "Isolated incidents like this attack can be expected but they should not be made a reason to hinder peace efforts."[129] The present deadlocked peace process, the return of government policies to hard line tactics, and the plummeting hopes for a better future point to a potentially worsening situation. The lessons learned from the Palestinian case may not be sufficient to deter the Tigers from initiating another round of violence.

In November 2003, Sri Lankan President Kumaratunga sacked three government ministers (defense, information, and interior) who supported the peace negotiations, suspended parliament, and reoccupied the capitol. All of the policies that had exacerbated conflict in the past were making a return and diplomatic activity kicked in to defuse the tense political situation. In an interesting contrast to other cases where the terrorists might try to spoil the peace, Kumaratunga's move was designed to halt government concessions to the Tigers and curtail the negotiations. The Parliament judged Kumaratunga's actions illegal and voted to disregard any future attempts to disrupt the legislature. One cannot predict what the outcome of this current crisis will be.

Finally the issue that separates the two cases is one of external and financial support. Throughout the 1990s and even up until September 11, 2001, much of the LTTE financial support came from expatriate groups living abroad in democratic countries. The most significant communities existed in the UK, Northern Australia, and Canada. The Tamil population in Toronto equals (some say exceeds) the Tamil population of Jaffna.

A 1995 U.S. Department of State report, *Pattern of Global Terrorism*, noted the LTTE's "significant overseas support structure for fundraising, weapons procurement, and propaganda activities" that involved "lobbying foreign governments and the United Nations." The report noted the LTTE's use of "international contacts to procure weapons, communications and bomb making equipment." To do so it exploited "Tamil communities in North America, Europe, and Asia to obtain funds and supplies for its fighters in Sri Lanka."[130]

In 1997 the United States banned the LTTE and branded it as a terrorist group thus making it illegal to transfer funds to the LTTE. The Canadian government began to curtail its open door immigration policy. After September 11, 2001 it became clear that no Western government could support the LTTE without fear of sanction and severe costs to its reputation. This is understood to be one of the reasons that led the LTTE to the negotiating table.

De Silva describes the LTTE's intractability during their ill-fated negotiations with President Premadasa between 1989 and 1990 and President Kumaratunga between 1994 and 1995 when they attempted to extract concessions from the Sri Lankan government to buy time and regroup their forces. For its part, the LTTE showed no desire to compromise, never deviated from its principal objective, the establishment of a separate state of Eelam, encompassing the Northern and Eastern Provinces. Until 2002. Now a large portion of LTTE money comes from internal taxation, levies, and tolls. The Tamils living in the north endure very high taxation and the LTTE is the only terrorist organization that issues speeding tickets (on the A9 highway). Unlike in previous iterations of conflict resolution, the majority of the mass public is exceptionally war weary.

The financial aspect is underscored by LTTE demands during the peace negotiations in 2002 and the reason for its pulling out the talks in 2003. In the proposed Interim Administration, the LTTE demanded full control over international donor aid and the collection of taxes in the north and east of the island. In addition, their demands included the expulsion of all police and military personnel. The LTTE broke off peace talks because the international community would not allow funds to be directly controlled by them. The first three frameworks for peace included provisions for the funds to be controlled either by the government or directly by multilateral actors.[131]

A three-pronged approach to conflict resolution is needed, which would include financial limits to the funding of terrorism, consolidation of extremist groups, and the elimination of rivals who might try to spoil the peace; along with it must come the ability to convince the larger public that peace, rather than continued war, is the best chance for success in the future. The government however, needs to play by the rules of the game in order to ensure that their policies do not inflame the LTTE and force it to return to the violence of the past.

In essence, both sides in the Sri Lankan case really want an end to hostilities. While there are Buddhist Fundamentalists in the JVP who would prefer to fight on, many of them have been co-opted into the government; they have thirteen seats in parliament and now seemingly play by the rules of the game. There might also be elements within the Tigers who would prefer to hold out for greater concessions than devolution and yet they are stifled by a strong leadership that is firmly in control of the negotiating process and a civilian population eager for peace. This is the most significant fact differentiating the two cases. One hopes that the deadlocked peace process does not have the same effect that it did among Palestinians. The popular perceptions of the violence and support for extremist tactics in Sri Lanka are low while support for Palestinian extremism is on the rise. In Sri Lanka, the civilians in the north and east are tired of conflict and want an end to the Eelam War III.

CHAPTER FOUR

DEVISING A THEORY OF SUICIDE TERROR

Why has suicide bombing been effective in some conflicts while in others terrorist organizations have rejected or abandoned it? What motivates organizations to employ this tactic, and how does suicide terrorism inflame or respond to public opinion? By understanding the dynamics of suicide bombing, we are better able to devise strategies to combat it.

We can define suicide bombing as a violent, politically motivated attack, carried out in a deliberate state of awareness by a person who blows himself or herself up together with a chosen target. The premeditated certain death of the perpetrator is the precondition for the success of the attack.[1] Suicide bombing is not, however, a uniform phenomenon,[2] but rather a subset of terrorism addressing issues relevant to the study of ethnic conflict and asymmetric warfare. Thus, its study provides insight into the larger theoretical issues of ethnic conflict, international security, and contentious politics.

Suicide bombing is unique in the sense that the organizations which use this tactic reap multiple benefits on various levels without incurring significant costs. On the one hand, the perpetration of the act signals operatives' complete dedication to the group and its cause. This adds a degree of legitimacy to the organization, which can claim the operative as its own, and use his or her dedication to inspire others. Each operation sacrifices one supporter and yet enables the organization to recruit many more people. The perpetrator is dead and so can never recant his or her decision. Finally, any potential negative costs associated with an attack (like the deaths of civilians) are mitigated by the logic which argues that the brutal state is so horrendous that its victims (the perpetrators of violence) have no other means of expressing their anger and no other avenues to channel their grievances than this ultimate sacrifice. These people willfully die spectacularly for one another and for what is perceived as the common good of alleviating the community's onerous political and social realities.[3]

Suicide bombing has an additional value: that of making yourself the victim of your own act, and thereby putting your tormentors to moral shame. The idea of the suicide bombing, unlike that of an ordinary attack, is, perversely, a moral idea in which the killers, in acting out the drama of being the ultimate victim, claim for their cause the moral high ground.[4]

> Suicide bombing as a tactic encompasses attacks of military targets that are immune via ordinary insurgent strategies, the assassination of prominent leaders (who would ordinarily not be accessible by any other means), and the attack of large numbers of civilians—mimicking indiscrimination—in order to create generalized fear.

There are two audiences for suicide terror, one domestic and one international.

> Although a suicide attack aims to physically destroy an initial target, its primary use is typically as a weapon of psychological warfare intended to affect a larger public audience. The primary target is not those actually killed or injured in the attack, but those made to witness it. . . . Through indoctrination and training and under charismatic leaders, self contained suicide cells canalize disparate religious or political sentiments of individuals into an emotionally bonded group.[5]

To a lesser extent there is a third audience, an international community of potential donors and supporters scrutinizing the terrorist groups. Using violence has a potential financial and public relations payoff from this third audience which I describe below.

It is important to classify which groups employ suicide terror. These may include states or non-state actors—although the majority of real-world examples of suicide bombing as a tactic tend to be perpetrated by insurgents/terrorists competing with an established state for predominance and/or control. Insurgent groups utilizing suicide bombing tend to alternate between different strategies and vary these tactics with more conventional strategies of warfare.

In order to survive, succeed, and achieve political power, insurgent terrorist groups need to mobilize supporters and maintain their support bases (constituencies) over time. To use Varshney's theory of ethnic mobilization:

> Mobilization cannot proceed [without] necessary strategies; coalitions must be formed; the response of the adversary—the state, the opposed ethnic group, the in-group dissenters—must be anticipated. And many

would join such mobilization, when it has acquired some momentum and chance of success.... The *origins* of ... mobilization are thus rational, and its *evolution* may contain a lot of strategic behavior.[6]

Constituencies' support for terrorist organizations comes in several forms. Supporters are needed to provide food, safe houses, recruits, and ultimately political power (hence the significance of public opinion). Financial support is needed to buy guns and weapons, remunerate the families of martyrs, engage in philanthropic activities to increase the organizations' influence, or to pay operatives. In order to raise funds, the insurgents may require the support of external communities, their Diaspora, or foreign patrons.

Insurgent groups that are not financially independent must search for funds either internally or externally.[7] They have two options; extract money from the broader local population or raise it from a small segment of foreign donors. Extraction, derived largely through taxation or levies, will require the terrorist group to function as a "state in the making," and will circumscribe what can and cannot be done and who can and cannot be killed. The insurgents provide social services or other benefits to the members of their society to shore up their popularity and increase support. The provision of social services is especially salient when there is little external funding, few weapons from the outside, and the insurgents need to convince the larger population that their cause is just. If the insurgent group is forced to search for money externally from a Diaspora or foreign patron, it will chose tactics that maximize publicity, while garnering greater attention to its cause and to the group employing the tactic. Thus, there are different incentives to resort to suicide bombing, depending from where the bulk of funding comes.

Suicide bombing works when it pays. In the war for public support, when the bombings resonate positively with the population that insurgent groups purport to represent, they help the organization mobilize support. If suicide bombing does not resonate among the larger population the tactic will fail. If it is applauded, it will flourish. The pattern that emerges from the case studies is that militant groups are more likely to adopt suicide bombing as a strategy, and the tactic is more likely to resonate positively with the population, after other strategies have been tried and failed.[8] Roger Petersen refers to this phenomenon as the bias of tactical victories amid strategic losses.[9]

If multiple insurgent groups are competing for public support, bombings will intensify in both scope and number as they become both the litmus test of militancy and the way to mobilize greater numbers of people within their community. When competition is especially intense, multiple organizations have occasionally vied with one another to claim responsibility for a particular bombing and identify the bomber as *their* operative. Such spectacular "heroic" attacks garner increased media attention and organizations vie to claim responsibility for martyrs. The more spectacular and daring the attacks, the more the insurgent organization is able to reap a public relations advantage over its rivals and/or enemies. According to Scott Atran:

> Like the best Madison Avenue advertisers, but to ghastlier effect, the charismatic leaders of terrorist groups turn ordinary desires for family and religion into cravings for what they're pitching to the benefit of the manipulating organization rather than the individual being manipulated. . . . this suggests that the key to understanding and parrying suicide terrorism is to concentrate more on the organizational structure, indoctrination methods, and ideological appeal of recruiting organizations.[10]

This process of outbidding between the groups depends on the domestic politics of the minority group and the state counter-terror strategies and responses to the insurgents' violence. The bombings do not occur in a vacuum. In fact, all suicide bombing campaigns co-exist with regular insurgent tactics (nonsuicidal bombings, shooting ambushes, stabbings, assassinations, etc). The organizations that adopt suicide terror do not give up the other tactics but use it as part of a range of strategies in their arsenal against their (real or perceived) enemies. In fact, even in the most extreme example of a country under virtual siege (Israel), the other traditional tactics are far more numerous than suicide terror yet it is this type of attack that garners the most press and public attention.

Suicide terror plays a greater role in disputes when the perpetrators and victims belong to different groups. Targeting the other side is easier when its members are of a different race, ethnicity, religion, or nation. This follows from some of the theoretical claims made by Chaim Kaufmann who contends that ethnic wars tend to have significantly more violence and atrocities directed against civilians than ideological contests since the key issues revolve around the control of territory rather than political or party affiliation. Success under such conditions does not rely on winning the "hearts and minds" of the people on the other side to convince the audience that your cause is just.[11]

It is a mistake to assume that only religious groups use suicide terror. Many of the groups engaged in equivalently lethal campaigns are decidedly secular. The differences between the insurgents and the state may be an amalgamation of ethnicity, language and religion. Under conditions of hyper segregation, ideas of *otherness* are easier to promote by the insurgents.[12] It becomes simpler to dehumanize people on the other side and perceive them as legitimate targets and appropriate for suicidal attacks.[13]

Suicide terror is less common in ideological wars in which the conflict revolves around party membership or ideological affiliation. Suicide terror, like other forms of atrocity, is successful against civilians when the group employing this tactic is not trying to win over members of the same civilian populace to their ideology or beliefs.

The organizations do cost-benefit analyses. Their own community provides needed material and support—money, safe houses, recruits—and the terrorist organizations require a hospitable environment in order to survive. There are potential negative *rebound effects* from killing members of your own group. The density of connections between the people and the members of the terrorist groups are more complex within this boundary than across it. This puts constraints on the insurgents as to who should be killed and who should not. The attacks by al Qaeda in Riyadh and Istanbul in 2003, in which there were significant Muslim casualties, and against children in Beslan in September 2004, demonstrate that such "collateral damage" is unacceptable to the larger Muslim community; al Qaeda's credibility and reputation suffered and the attacks were repudiated. Beslan caused a self-examination and reconsideration of violence throughout the Muslim world.

The attacks might have been perpetrated by local individuals but they were funded from abroad, thus limiting the degree to which terrorist organizations might consider the impact of public opinion. Nevertheless, rather than reap the benefits of this campaign with increased popularity and mobilization, a backlash resulted instead. In general, a wider audience may find violence unacceptable if not directed against a military occupying power.

One exception to the *unacceptability* of killing co-ethnics or co-religionists is when suicide attacks are used against the moderate opposition who challenge the dominance of the terrorist/insurgent group or appear more willing to negotiate with the established "enemy" state.[14] Such victims of collateral damage are not necessarily "innocent" in the eyes of the people whose favor the terrorists are trying to win. They may be seen as collaborators if they work in government offices, security posts, or for the occupying power. Indeed, one reason for bombing such places may be to coerce people into quitting such jobs. This is most apparent with former regime elements (FREs) in Iraq and now insurgent elements attacking other Iraqis who worked for the coalition provisional authority, L. Paul Bremer, or who work for the Iraqi government. Another example would include the Muslims killed at the World Trade Center because of their presence in the buildings on 9/11. Their deaths had little negative effect on Bin Laden's reputation. In fact, their deaths were framed as a necessary "sacrifice" if they were mentioned at all in the Islamic press. Muslim casualties played a greater role in the Western media as part of the war on terror as an example of Bin Laden's antagonism toward his own people. For some analysts of Islamic militancy, the issue of "collateral damage" is necessarily a complicated one that possibly follows the "omelet" logic. "If the omelet is spectacular enough, for instance, the embassy bombings in East Africa, breaking a few eggs doesn't seem as heinous as if the innocents seem to have died in vain."[15]

In the cases of Riyadh and Istanbul in November and December 2003, moderate oppositions or collaborators were not the target of the attacks, rather the violence was used indiscriminately against whatever civilians were in the vicinity of the bombings in order to create a sense of generalized panic among the population and attack symbolic foreign targets. The Muslim casualties were collateral damage. According to intelligence sources, al Qaeda loses the war of public opinion in the Islamic world by targeting Muslim women and children in this fashion.[16] This is borne out by the strong condemnation that followed the attack in Chechnya.

The public response to the tactical use of suicide bombing depends on the how the tactic is used, against whom, and for what purpose. If suicide terror does not resonate and the domestic environment is antagonistic to it, it will be rejected. Consequently, violence will fail to win over the "hearts and minds" of the public, the insurgent group's goal. If martyrdom is considered a proper response, the larger audience will support suicide terror and it will flourish. If the opposite is true and environment is antagonistic, acts of suicide terror will only deepen the gap between the insurgents and the masses.[17] Even the militants themselves differentiate among targets and acknowledge the difference between civilian and military targets. According to one failed suicide bomber: "From our side . . . innocent women and children are being killed. I don't intend to kill innocents, and I take precautions. I left the vegetable market and didn't detonate because of the presence of women and children."[18]

In cases where suicide attacks are considered to be a legitimate military tactic, but the organization targets civilians indiscriminately, the public's response may not be supportive of the organization. In such circumstances insurgent organizations are highly adaptable and will refocus actions on military (hard) targets which tend to be more acceptable to a wider audience.

However, if the domestic environment is extremely hospitable to violence, suicide terror may be championed because the hatred for the other side is very high. In such cases, the organization's use of violence will be unrestrained and the insurgents will not make a distinction between civilian and military targets. In fact, the insurgents will choose targets that have the largest impact and are the easiest to reach. This often means civilian targets.

Why does the general population accept or reject the violence? The explanation is somewhat endogenous to the cases and results from a variety of personal, economic, structural, and organizational issues. Suicide terrorism fosters a sense of powerlessness within the targeted society. Shimon Peres, in explaining the complexity of the battle against suicide terrorism, listed the two challenges in order to cope with terrorism as follows:

> The first, military-operational—how to fight the suicide terrorists. The second is broader—how to prevent public support for them. The correct way to fight against suicide terrorists is to discover them before they do anything, and this requires receiving intelligence both from our services and from the Palestinians. But the problem cannot be solved only through weaponry. We must produce an economic situation that will divert support for the Hamas to the alternative regime.[19]

The interplay of domestic politics and external factors like the ongoing conflict, a "hurting stalemate" or the counter-terror strategies employed by the opposing side all affect the extent to which suicide terror resonates positively.

The cases under review in this book suggest that heavy handed counter-terror strategies might appear effective in the short term, however over time such strategies will inculcate a greater sense of outrage and anger, making a formerly inhospitable environment accepting and approving of mounting violence against civilians. This appears to be the trend in Israel and in Chechnya.

We can contrast short-term and long-term successful strategies. The Israeli counter terror measures appear to have stemmed suicide terror in the short term, forced many of the most militant operatives underground, and caused them to spend more time eluding capture than perpetrating acts of terror. However, because terrorists live and work among civilians, attacks on terrorist capabilities can be nearly impossible to execute without significant civilian casualties. In the long term, Israel's heavy handed tactics, of targeted assassination, "preemptive attacks" to root out the terrorists, and destruction of their infrastructure tend to inflame Palestinian public opinion and supply continual recruits for Hamas and the Islamic Jihad.[20] The outrage caused by anger for personal losses as well as the symbolic humiliation of their "representatives" can be detrimental.

Until the autumn of 2000, Palestinian support for suicide terror never exceeded one-third of the population. Within a few short months, support for suicide terror, including acts against Israeli civilians, increased dramatically. There is empirical evidence that there is a connection between support for violence and domestic politics since the espousal of suicide violence varies over time in different countries. Significantly, the trajectory of support is not fixed as support can decrease (Sri Lanka, Turkey) as well as increase (Chechnya, Palestine) over time.

A growing number of authors are now making an attempt to explain suicide terrorism via theories of insurgency, offensive realism, as an extreme example of social solidarity, or by using econometric approaches of rational choice game modeling. Only a few theorists have cogently synthesized terrorism with political science theory, arguing that it follows a logical process of collective rationality.[21]

Martha Crenshaw measures the rationality of terrorist organizations by examining whether they were effective in achieving their goals as compared to other strategies of war. She states that, "efficacy is the primary standard by which terrorism is compared with other methods of achieving political goals."[22] It appears that suicide terror is rarely, if ever, the strategy of first choice but tends to follow other strategies deemed less effective through the process of trial and error. Crenshaw continues, "Organizations arrive at collective judgments about the relative effectiveness of different strategies ... on the basis of observation and experience, as much as on the basis of abstract strategic conceptions derived from ideological assumptions—allowing for social learning."[23]

Consistent with Crenshaw's argument, suicide terror often makes its appearance in the second iteration of conflict. Thus, it was not present during the first Chechen War, nor was it present in the first Palestinian Intifada, or in the first Kurdish rebellion, or in the first Gulf War even though suicide terror as a strategy predates many of these conflicts and its modern manifestation as a tactic of insurgent groups has existed since 1983. Thus, it is not unreasonable to have expected terrorist organizations engaged in conflict after 1983 to use suicide bombing as part of their arsenal of terror after it had been so successful in expelling the Americans and French from Lebanon.

As Crenshaw notes, there is a deliberate imitation of tactics through social learning. Terrorist organizations, often because of the high degree of publicity and media attention engendered by the more spectacular attacks, become familiar with what has worked and what has failed in other circumstances. However, Crenshaw's focus does not take into consideration the role of public opinion and domestic politics in shaping the use of violence or the ensuing competitive atmosphere that can result—something that I emphasize.

Robert Pape has argued that suicide terror is a coercive strategy directed externally (against a more powerful enemy) to coerce democratic governments to change their policies and evacuate a *homeland* territory under their control. Pape argues that liberal democracies can be coerced through the use of sufficient violence and the expectation of future violence when the attacks

occur in organized campaigns. Although Pape's explanation is useful for understanding how suicide bombing is directed against the external enemy,
it glosses over the domestic political dynamics and organizational motivations for outbidding. Pape's model correctly identifies the motivations of
nationalist-inspired suicide terrorists; however it does not fully explain why
religious groups (with goals beyond territorial demands) might use it.

Pape's focus on democratic countries should be problematized. He argues that suicide bombings work best against democratic regimes (because
of their access to the media, freedom of movement, and the shock value of
casualties), although his theory cannot be adequately verified. While there
are cases of terrorists in democracies that have not employed this tactic, his
argument is hard to assess empirically since most nondemocratic regimes
do not permit opposition, let alone violent opposition, that would use suicide terror. In instances when illiberal authoritarian regimes have gone head
to head against opposition groups (before their strategies have advanced to
include suicide terror,) the groups are eliminated. For example, when the
Muslim Brotherhood in Hama voiced opposition and mobilized against the
Ba'ath regime in Syria, the government's response was to eliminate the Islamic opposition and its geographic base of support.[24]

There are definitional issues that emerge with Pape's focus on democracies. There have been instances where al Qaeda has attacked targets in non
democracies like Saudi Arabia and Morocco, Pape's interpretation is that the
ultimate and real target was the U.S. although there is discussion about the
validity of this claim. The suspension of democratic freedoms and norms in
many of the cases, the questionable label of Sri Lanka in the 1980s, Israel in the
Occupied Territories, and Russians in Chechnya as liberal democratic societies forces us to rethink some of these propositions regarding regime type.

Lastly, Pape's model cannot explain why moderates who share the same
ethnicity as the terrorists are targeted because this approach reifies the opposition engaged in suicide terror and cannot explain the competitive environment that emerges in some cases and not in others—all of which requires
an analysis of domestic level variables.

Suicide bombing should be disaggregated into two levels of analysis—the
individual bombers who blow themselves up and the organizations that send
them. To varying degrees, both parties (individuals and organizations) are
acting rationally in the strictest sense of the term since they are pursuing
goals consistent with picking the option they think is best suited to achieve
their goals.[25]

According to Varshney's understanding of the rationality of ethnic conflict, these goals are a combination of *value rationality* and *instrumental rationality*.

Instrumental rationality entails a strict cost-benefit calculus with respect to goals, necessitating the abandonment or adjustment of goals if the costs of realizing them are too high. Value-rational behavior is produced by a conscious "ethical, aesthetic, religious or other" belief, "independently of its prospects of success." Behavior, when driven by such values, can consciously embrace great personal sacrifices.[26]

Thus the perpetrators of suicide terror and the organizations that send them are both acting according to two variants of rational calculations and on two levels.[27] The organizations strategically adapt to changing circumstances to maximize their popularity and their ability to influence the "electorate" is based on resonance; specific tactics are either applauded or rejected. This underscores a significant rational calculation—those terrorist groups that are not rational, and do not adjust to circumstances, can lose support and may cease to exist.[28]

My focus on the organizations fits the available empirical evidence from the Japanese Kamikazes of World War II to most of the Palestinian and other suicide bombers of today. All of the bombers are first and foremost members of organizations that train them, select their targets, buy their explosives, issue orders for when to launch an attack and try to convince the larger population that their cause is just.

MOTIVATIONS FOR SUICIDE TERROR

INDIVIDUALS

In the terrorists' society, a necessary precondition for suicide terror is the existence of a population that believes in violence or thinks that other (more peaceful) strategies have failed. Thus, there needs to be some pre-existing level of violence, which has become institutionalized and taken on life of its own. The individuals who perpetrate suicide attacks have social, cultural, religious, and material incentives. These include spiritual rewards in the afterlife, the guarantee of a place with God for the attackers' families, celebrity, and even cash bonuses. Although some have argued that suicide bombers are coerced, this is not borne out by the evidence. The individuals may be subject to intense group pressure to sacrifice for the greater good.

"You can't let it happen that you feel shame—that you are always talking of the struggle but don't make anything of it."

—Hamas supporter, Gaza, July 2003.[29]

Individuals most easily manipulated for such purposes also tend to be young and impressionable.

> The kamikaze ("divine wind") first used in the battle of the Philippines (November 1944) were young, fairly well educated pilots who understood that pursuing conventional warfare would likely end in defeat.... Few believed they were dying for the emperor as a war leader or for military purposes. Rather, the state was apparently able ... to convince the pilots that it was their honor to "die like beautiful falling cherry petals."[30]

Some individuals appear to be driven by a sense of humiliation or injustice.[31] Some argue, for example, that perceptions regarding the plight of the Palestinian people influence the willingness of young Egyptians, Saudis, Iraqis, and others to participate in suicide attacks.[32] Others appear to be driven by the desire for personal revenge because they have suffered the loss of a loved one. Nichole Argo's interviews of failed suicide bombers in Israeli prisons elucidate the connection between loss and revenge: When asked why they became martyrs or *shahids*, her interviewees responded:

> Pictures of dead kids had a major affect on me. Many were killed [right] before me, like my friend [whose body] I had to carry in my own arms.... [A]fter the *istishhad* (martyrdom) of a friend of mine, and after the murder of a baby.... These two cases made me think that human life is threatened every moment without good cause ... without distinction between those [of us] who are soldiers, civilians, adults, or kids.[33]

Walid Daka, an imprisoned PFLP activist, interviewed preempted bombers to ascertain what motivated them:

> The truth is that beforehand I saw pictures of dead and wounded children on television.... One day my cousin came and told me: "What do you say to us doing an *Istish'had* [martyrdom] operation?" ... the next day we went into town, to a restaurant ... with another guy, and then I went with him and I put on the explosive belt and he said it would be in the name of Fatah.[34]

Some of the motivations for engaging in this activity are the result of the personal loss of loved ones. Suicide attackers have often been drawn from widows or bereaved siblings who wish to take vengeance for their loved one's violent death. There is an empirical regularity in Chechnya, Palestine, and

Sri Lanka wherein suicide bombers have lost a family member to the "unjust state" and feel that their only meaningful response to express their outrage is to perpetrate an act of suicide terror.

The insurgent organization might also suppose that people who have lost relatives are potential recruits because they are unlikely to change their minds at the last minute or defect.[35] David Laitin has identified defection as the principal strategic problem that the insurgents must guard against:

> "Clubs" of a certain type (most easily formed through religious membership) are able to deal with defection . . . and to use suicide attacks effectively. Radical religious sects should have an advantage in recruiting suicide attackers if they can design signals of commitment that will distinguish members who have the "right" beliefs from those that will pull out or even defect.[36]

In Chechnya, the Black Widows are female suicide bombers who have often lost a loved one. Widowhood may sever the woman from productive society and/or leave her with a sense of hopelessness, especially in traditional societies. The surviving family members of people tortured to death by the security apparatuses have also filled the ranks of suicide bomber volunteers, and human rights abuses by the state only serve to shore up the justifications for violence made by the most extreme organizations. There have been allegations that Tamil women raped by the Sinhalese security services and Sinhalese military at check points join the LTTE as the "Birds of Paradise" unit of female suicide bombers.

However for Argo, the personal connection to the person killed might be a distant one if any connection existed at all. For some would-be Palestinian suicide bombers, watching the deaths of children from other villages or towns was particularly poignant and crucial to their mobilization. The images broadcast from Jenin or Nablus made personal and real every casualty of the Al 'Aqsa Intifada.

There have been other less altruistic reasons to become a suicide bomber. From the perspective of the individual attacker, the act of martyrdom in the pursuit of honor may offer an opportunity to impress a wider audience and be remembered.

> Sacrifice and risk—when employed on behalf of the group—become valuable virtues, rewarded by social status. Thus, the culture . . . transforms individual risk and loss into group status and benefit, ultimately cycling that status back onto the individual. The higher the risk, the higher the status.[37]

This symbolic act may be a powerful incentive for individuals who perceive that their lives have little significance otherwise.[38] Jessica Stern has argued that engaging in such activities affords a way out of a life of boredom, poverty, despair and likens becoming a suicide martyr to a sort of "Outward Bound" for radicalized Muslims (a program of adventure education for young adults that emphasizes growth through foreign experiences and challenges.)[39]

Bruce Bueno de Mesquita and Alan B. Krueger have examined whether financial incentives might motivate Palestinian bombers,[40] whereas other authors have discussed how Islam and the heavenly reward awaiting the martyrs in the afterlife explain the phenomenon and enthusiasm for martyrdom.[41]

A longing for religious purity and/or a strong commitment to the welfare of the group may drive individuals to engage in suicide terror. Religious ideology or political culture can be crucial. Suicide attacks in some contexts inspire a self-perpetuating subculture of martyrdom.[42] Children who grow up in such settings may be subtly indoctrinated into a culture glorifying ultimate sacrifice in the service of the cause against the enemy people or in the service of a cult-like leader such as Villupilai Prabhakaran or Abdullah Öcalan. According to Victor, Palestinian children as young as six (both male and female) report that they want to grow up and become *Istishhadis*—often not yet understanding the full impact of what that means. By the age of twelve, they are fully committed and appreciate what becoming a martyr entails.[43]

There are two kinds of individuals who become suicide bombers, those people produced by an organization under this subculture and educated outsiders who flock to the organization to volunteer because of personal motivation. These two groups are often comprised of very different kinds of individuals, with varying educational backgrounds, abilities, and profiles. Clearly different would-be suicide bombers have different motivations, some rational and others irrational, and may be provoked by any number of overlapping incentives for their actions all of which resist mono causal explanations.

ORGANIZATIONS

Regardless of the motivations and calculus of the individual bomber, the terrorist organizations coordinate the attacks and aim to gain the attention of a target audience. The terrorist organizations adapt to changing political circumstances and are sensitive to the public reactions to suicide operations. In each of the cases, the organizations that perpetrated the violence increased or decreased operations in response to the reactions of the larger population.

Flexibility to changing circumstances is far from a handicap since a sustained consistency in the organizations' ideology that use suicide terror is not required. Hamas committed itself at the start of the 1990s not to kill civilians: when the organization reneged on its commitment in 1994, it found ample reasons for justifying the shift.[44] The PFLP initially eschewed the tactic and switched gears in 2001. Should Palestinian public support for suicide terror return to the pre-2000 levels, the PFLP and Hamas would likely modify their tactics again.

According to one senior intelligence analyst, "Despite its rhetoric, Hamas' primary interest is having and keeping political power. It won't relinquish this for 'ideology'. Most Hamas leaders know very well that they will never push Israel into the sea."[45] Thus, even the most religious organization that employs suicide terror is pragmatic and power seeking. Their political survival is ultimately more important than any ideology.

As part of their propaganda, suicide terrorists are trying to portray themselves as fanatical, and irrational, because they want their potential victims to believe that there is nothing can be done against such an adversary. Terrorist organizations overwhelmingly claim that violence is a tool of last resort and is a sign of desperation, and this appears to be the case when state actors engage in suicide terror. From anecdotal evidence (and the number of states that have engaged in the tactic is too small for the claim to be statistically verified), states that use suicide terror appear to do so only when they are losing military conflicts decisively (e.g., the Kamikaze or the Iranian shock troops during the first Gulf War). Most suicide terrorism, however, is perpetrated by insurgent opposition groups struggling against an established and much more powerful state. It is used after other strategies have been tried and found wanting but it is rarely the last ditch attempt in the face of certain defeat. Thomas Friedman has argued, "Let's be very clear: Palestinians have adopted suicide bombing as a strategic choice, [and] not out of desperation."[46]

In several cases, insurgent organizations tend toward the use of atrocities when the military conflict has reached a deadlock or there is a hurting stalemate and something shocking is needed to tip the balance between forces. Crenshaw confirms this when she writes, "extremists seek a radical change in the status quo."[47]

At first blush this might appear contradictory since terrorism is the quintessential "weapon of the weak" and the terrorists claim they are using terror as a last resort, not to end a deadlock. This seeming inconsistency can be summed up as follows: non-state actors tend to resort to atrocities in the second iteration (or more) of conflict after the other strategies have failed to yield the desired results, and when faced with a hurting stalemate. At this juncture, atrocities will appear to be a good idea.

Ehud Sprinzak summarized the organizational logic of using suicide terror in the following manner: "Our enemy possesses the most sophisticated weapons in the world and its army is trained to a very high standard. . . . We have nothing with which to repel killing and thuggery against us except the weapon of martyrdom. It is easy and costs us only our lives. . . . [H]uman bombs cannot be defeated, not even by nuclear bombs."[48]

However, much of the success of this strategy—whether it will take root or be rejected—will depend on the existing domestic political backdrop against which these actions take place. Sprinzak argues that the institutionalization of suicide terrorism is temporary and conditional: "Leaders who opt for this type of terrorism are usually moved by an intense sense of crisis, a conviction in the effectiveness of this new tactic, endorsement by the religious or ideological establishment, and the enthusiastic support of their community."[49]

Ultimately there is a complexity of motivation behind this particular form of violence. But regardless of objectives, it is a form of "contingent violence." That is to say, the next iteration of violence is shaped by both the reactions of the state and the behavior of the target audiences during the previous iteration.[50]

> The highly publicized attacks engaged in by Chechens against Russian civilians have been designed to draw attention to their cause. They have also played a crucial role in shaping the timing and form of the state response. What is less commonly recognized is that the state's response to terrorism is also targeted at an audience. The actions of the Russian government demonstrate that state counterterrorism can be as consciously directed toward shaping perceptions as are the terrorist attacks to which it responds.[51]

This pattern is repeated among Palestinians who admit that violence can be used to force the state's hand and demonstrate that they are the real victims of the conflict. An art history graduate student preparing for a suicide bombing admitted that:

> At the moment of executing my mission, it will not be purely to kill Israelis, The killing is not my ultimate goal. . . . My act will carry a message beyond to those responsible and the world at large that the ugliest thing for a human being is to be forced to live without freedom.[52]

This explains both how suicide terror becomes popular in some cases and why it is rejected or repudiated in others. This logic can be extended to explain the counterfactual cases in which organizations did not resort to suicide bombing (although they did engage in insurgency) by examining public reactions to civilian casualties that resulted from conventional bombing campaigns. If the public repudiated civilian casualties, the organizations learned that increasing violence against civilians would not be a welcome tactical shift as was the case for the Basque ETA in Spain and the Provisional IRA in Ireland.[53]

DOMESTIC POLITICS AND PUBLIC SUPPORT

Popular support for suicide bombing depends on who is targeted. Suicide Operations vary along a spectrum that encompasses the targeting of civilians, military personnel and bases, infrastructure and, recently, international organizations and other NGOs.

The rejection or acceptance of such violence by the larger population (of Palestinians, Kurds, Tamils, Irish Catholics, etc.) depends on what strategies and counter-terror moves are made by the opposing side. The larger population will either support the tactic of suicide terror or reject it and make distinctions between the targets: civilian versus military targets, settlers versus civilians located in the area not part of the disputed homeland, men of military age versus women and children.

> I do not intend to kill innocent women and children, but to kill Israeli soldiers and all that support them in their mission to: take our lands, to kill us, to plant settlements. These people carry the responsibility for these crimes exactly like the soldier that executes [them]. Therefore we don't kill innocents. But when a kid is being killed, here [in Palestine] or there [in Israel], this is distressing. He is killed incidentally [sic] with no intent. I do not intend to kill children.
>
> — Preempted bomber, Shikma prison, May 2003[54]

Interestingly enough, in several cases, public support shifted in favor of suicide terror (including when used against civilian targets) when the targeted state engaged in specific counter-insurgency tactics. Thus relying on "targeted assassinations" by using helicopter gun-ships increases the chances that civilians will be killed because such tactics are less effective in distinguishing the combatants from noncombatants. If one side's civilians are fair game, the targeted community will believe that civilians on the other side are not sacrosanct.

A thorough study of whether the use of helicopter gunships and other airpower instigates terrorist groups to bring the fighting and death back to the oppressor's doorstep—to make the war real for them again—would be illuminating (and useful with regard to U.S. foreign policy in Iraq.)[55] There is a supplementary psychological factor for the terrorists: if the enemy state feels safe attacking from high above, suicide terror against the enemies' civilians increases the intimacy of the violence. In both Chechnya and among the Palestinians, the Russian and Israeli switch to heavy-handed tactics using aerial bombardment and helicopter gun ships in the second Intifada or the second Chechen war correlates with the rise of suicide terror and support for suicide operations among the general Palestinian or Chechen mass public.

After a Palestinian mob lynched two Israeli reserve soldiers who had mistakenly entered Ramallah, Israel used helicopter gunships to carry out aerial attacks on targets in Gaza and Ramallah, the first time they had used this tactic in many years.[56] During the same period, the IDF carried out targeted assassinations against Tanzim activists in Fatah, in addition to Hamas and Palestinian Islamic Jihad operatives. Israel once again began to raze the houses of those suspected of carrying out attacks.[57] In Chechnya, the shift toward a more offensive approach to counter-terrorism was equally apparent.

> The second Chechen war accompanied with total air bombing and barbarous mop-ups is producing thousands of suicide bombers.... After the Nord-Ost ordeal ... we should be glad that [suicide attacks] do not happen every day.... Since the Khasavyurt agreements, Moscow has followed only one policy—sowing death and making the people hold a referendum and elections. It is the road to a deadlock making Chechens fight in the Palestinian way.[58]

From the perspective of the Chechen, they "have a complete moral right to retribution after what Russia and the Russians have done to them. It is very difficult to expect humanism from the victims of Russia's concentration camps who have suffered torture by electric shock."[59]

In contrast to this, Turkey shifted away from its more brutal policies against Kurdish civilians in the Northeast and from its denial of Kurdish culture and language during the 1990s. After years of political and cultural repression the Turkish state softened its policies somewhat—offering carrots as well as sticks to win over Kurdish civilians. The larger Kurdish population repudiated suicide terror when it was used by the PKK in 1996. When other militant Islamic groups used violence against civilians indiscriminately, public reaction was decidedly unsupportive.

Against this backdrop, suicide bombing failed to resonate with the population and did not increase support for the PKK. This shift in state policy, in conjunction with the capture of the PKK leader Abdullah Öcalan in 1999, sealed the fate of the organization. Öcalan's death sentence was commuted to one of life imprisonment and, within a year, he renounced terror and the PKK disbanded. In contrast to this, Turkey's widely publicized (and televised) targeted assassination of Hizb'allah leader, Sheikh Huseyin Velioglu in 2000, served to energize the organization underground. It resurfaced a few years later as part of the al Qaeda network. The November 2003 attacks in Istanbul have been traced back to Bingol, the center of Hizb'allah activity. Turkey provides a good scientific experiment contrasting which tactics might have better long-term effects.

Finally, military targets become increasingly problematical to attack over time as states harden these targets and, as a result, civilians become a more obvious choice for insurgent groups. It is more difficult to breach the security of a military base or attack a soldier who can defend himself. The PKK targeted police and state representatives; the LTTE largely aimed at politicians and military targets, whereas Palestinian groups have overwhelmingly and deliberately targeted civilians by attacking shopping malls, buses, discotheques, pizzerias, and locations frequented by teenagers and children. At times, Israeli responses have exacerbated the violence.

Israel's strategy of hunting down Islamic militants, including several of the organizations' leaders (Fathi Shiqaqi, Sheikh Ahmed Yassin, and Dr. Abdel Al Rantisi) infuriate the wider Palestinian audience, increase the group's ability to mobilize popular support, decrease the ability of more moderate secular groups to rein in the terrorists, and provide "defensive" justifications for future attacks.

Rather than undermine the groups using suicide terror, such tactics have several unintended consequences that may encourage terrorism rather than demobilize it. For one theorist, Israel's use of limited coercion is a deliberate baiting strategy to force a Palestinian reaction in response to which it can escalate conflict. "The process of controlled escalation through targeted assassinations was designed to deal with what the IDF considered a key problem in the management of the conflict: the ability of the Palestinians to develop an elaborate infrastructure for the production of materials and explosives for suicide bombings in Israel."[60]

In several instances when Hamas has ostensibly shifted from targeting civilians (albeit temporarily) or has made pronouncements of its intention to do so (e.g., declaring a *Hudna* or ceasefire), Israel's targeted assassination of a Palestinian leader provided them the justification to renew attacks against Israeli civilians and certainly mobilized support for the organization.[61]

"We ha[d] a *Hudna*, but two days later they went after Rantisi. I don't like Rantisi—in the first Intifada he tried to kill my brother and I tried to kill him. But after they attempted to shoot him—in the middle of the street as people carried out their day—I can't think these bad things about him anymore." —Bomber Interview Gaza City, July 15, 2003.[62]

Thus the fashion in which the state responds to suicide terrorism will have a significant impact on whether bombers and the sponsoring organizations *win the hearts and the minds* of the larger population they purport to represent. The fashion in which a state responds to the threat will also impact international public opinion and international support for the terrorist organization and the targeted state.

> Part of the suicide bombers' strategy anywhere is to provoke the government into undertaking actions that the terrorists feel they can manipulate for propaganda purposes, which will also portray them as the victims rather than as the perpetrators. . . . for the first time in the history of terrorism, terrorists have gotten people to sympathize much more with the perpetrators of the violence than with the victims. The [Israel's] activities in the West Bank have turned large swatches of foreign public opinion against Israel in a way that nothing else has in the very long and tortured dynamic of the Israeli-Palestinian relationship.[63]

IRA Leader Tom Barry expressed this best when he said, "It would be wrong to suggest that at the beginning of the Anglo-Irish War a majority of the people supported armed action against the British. They did not, mainly because they considered such a campaign as hopeless and suicidal . . . [T]he savagery of the British and the deaths of their neighbours' children for the peoples' freedom roused them, and from the middle of 1920 they loyally supported the IRA."[64]

In sum, these domestic strategies of counter-terrorism create the backdrop (receptive or hostile) against which suicide attacks take place. The domestic environment will have an enormous impact on whether it continues to be used, whether it is abandoned, or whether there is an explosion in the number of organizations using suicide terror to mobilize the population and increase their bases of support. "Struggles won by states against terrorism may not so much involve military victories as the winning of psychological contests in which terrorists lose the support of the people in whose name they are acting."[65]

THE GOALS OF SUICIDE BOMBING, GROUP COMPETITION AND OUTBIDDING

Suicide bombing might be considered a tactic of coercive bargaining which includes the risks of outbidding because of the competition among rival organizations utilizing the tactic. Under conditions of group competition, there are incentives for further groups to jump on the "suicide bandwagon" and ramp up the violence in order to distinguish themselves from the other organizations.

Outbidding is partly the result of the structural conditions of domestic politics. How many insurgent groups are involved, is one group clearly dominant, or is there a multiplicity of groups engaged in competition to win over a future or emerging electorate? When there is a multiplicity of actors and insurgent groups, outbidding becomes more likely. In cases where one group is clearly dominant, there are fewer incentives to outbid. Suicide bombing is less likely to proliferate and will not become the litmus test against which the organizations and individuals measure themselves. However, even when one group is clearly dominant, defection of smaller organizations from the main group pose the danger of outbidding and thus defection may have dangerous unintended consequences.

Historically, we can observe that suicide terror was adopted when multiple organizations ramped up insurgent violence with increasing degrees of lethality. Where there are multiple groups, violence is a technique to gain credibility and win the public relations competition.

In such circumstances, outbidding will result as groups try to distinguish themselves from one another to establish or increase a domestic constituent base. If the domestic popularity of the organization using suicide terror increases we observe an increase in bombings. If the domestic environment supports the use of suicide terror and an insurgent group does not use the tactic, they tend to lose market share and popularity. A 21-year-old bomber described his experience in this way.

> The first time I attempted *istash'had* I didn't go to [through] organization, but did it on my own initiative. Second time, I went to the Islamic Jihad—where my brother was in charge.... Myself, I belong to Fatah [But] Fatah in that time would not do *istash'had*.... I didn't join the Islamic Jihad, but the mission was under its name.[66]

Thus, when and if the group alters its tactics and adopts suicide terror, its popularity can sometimes be resuscitated. The case of the PFLP is illustrative. PFLP leader George Habash repudiated suicide terror for years and refused to engage in such tactics. Support for the PFLP declined significantly and, in 2001, the PFLP began to use suicide terror and the language of Jihad and martyrdom. By the time next public opinion poll was taken (within three months), support for the PFLP returned to its former percentage. Since the groups are motivated to win the public relations game, and to win over as many adherents as possible, the tactics that garner them the most support win out.

The question revolves around whether there is a dominant political opposition or whether there is a diffusion of support because no one group has captured the imagination of the people. This reflects a degree of legitimacy (Arafat and Fatah were far more popular before the corruption of the Palestinian Authority became obvious) as well as the extent of coercion used against opponents (Prabhakaran and the LTTE simply kill anyone who defects or joins a different Tamil organization).[67] In March 2004, an East coast commander named Colonel Karuna defected from the organization and tried to establish an independent support base. Karuna was quickly reined in and threatened.[68]

Coercive bargaining is directed at the enemy to force them to leave the homeland territory (as Pape rightly points out); the outbidding is directed toward the domestic population who sponsor, join, support, or "vote" for these organizations. The objectives of suicide bombing are thus multiple and may reinforce or undercut each other depending on specific conditions endogenous to each case. The goals are directed against the international opponent (get out of the "homeland"), against the domestic rivals (to achieve dominance), and/or against a negotiated settlement to which they might not be party (spoil the peace.)

There are indicators that popularity which results from violence is not ingrained and the domestic population can distinguish between killing civilians and military personnel. In some cases, military targets are acceptable whereas civilian casualties are not. Organizations recognize this and adapt their strategies accordingly. The LTTE has adapted to such limitations because of similar constraints on its behavior.

Recognizing the impact of public opinion opens up different avenues of response for counter-terrorism. Shabtai Shavit former head of Israel's intelligence apparatus, the Mossad, states that the range of decisionmaking vis-à-vis counter-terrorism is restricted by the boundaries of the consent of the public opinion of the targeted community, noting: "The main problem today when combating terror is not to exceed the limit set by public opinion which is willing or unwilling to accept means that you use against terror."[69] Public opinion not only determines the range of activity, but also affects the types of steps taken against terror, the timing of their activation, as well as their scope and frequency, both on the level of defense such as the reinforcement of the security system, the establishment of designated security units.[70]

Counterterrorist policies can be directed at thwarting successful outbidding by the terrorist organizations. The target state could favor moderate factions and not induce support for the militant insurgent groups advocating extreme violence. Thus, where there is a condition of support for suicide bombing, reacting to it harshly directly supports the outbidders' strategy (as has been the case in Israel and Russia).

The conditions of support must be analyzed carefully. A possible counter-terror strategy is to "outbid the outbidders" and engage in policies that emphasize elements of domestic politics that the suicide groups cannot. The ultimate Achilles' heel of terrorist organizations is in its overall negative empowerment dynamic (stemming from their emphasis on desperation or hopelessness). The state can undercut the despair by responses designed to empower. The state can reward the community without rewarding the terrorists themselves. Jailing the leaders rather than targeting them for assassination might prove to be a superior strategy, in that it could drain the lake in which the insurgents swim by encouraging the domestic population to turn away from them.

Algeria, for example, managed to outbid the outbidders by separating the terrorists from the larger Algerian public. "It was only then when the people turned against the terrorists that counter terror strategies were effective."[71] The targeted state can go over the heads of the terrorists and outbid them to the domestic population. This path would include, for example, Israel pulling out of Palestinian Territories and the Sri Lankan Government negotiating with the LTTE. You outbid the suicide terrorists and return the objective of a negotiated settlement to prominence by giving the public a stake in the process (i.e., giving it something to lose.)

The danger of outbidding has important ramifications for whether policies aimed at democratizing previously authoritarian structures and regimes will have unintended negative consequences. A case in point has been the attempts to democratize Iraq under the American and British occupation. This theory would predict that Iraq is potentially ripe for outbidding. If a central Iraqi authority does not emerge with control over patronage and legitimizing functions, weaker factions will find incentives to outbid and use violence (killing Americans) to gain credibility and popularity. There might be an outbidding dynamic already at play in Iraq as groups vie to become the major opposition faction. Indeed, there has been a proliferation of suicide bombings since the declared end of the U.S.-led war in Iraq in 2003.

RELIGIOUS VERSUS NATIONALIST SUICIDE BOMBERS

It is important to distinguish whether the nature of the organizations engaged in suicide terror are religious or nationalistic. Nationalist groups tend to be vying for the control of territory. As Pape points out, their goal is to recapture the *homeland* and rid the area of what it perceives as a foreign occupation. Territory is often divisible although sacred areas are difficult to divide and the extent to which an area is designated as hallowed will complicate a negotiated settlement. Having said that in the secular contest for power, far less territory is viewed as *terra sancta*. In religious conflicts, these areas might be the focus of the dispute for both sides whether it is Najaf, Karbala, Kosovo, Jerusalem, or the Hedjaz.

In the game of "outbidding the outbidders," it is possible to offer the insurgents a negotiated settlement and give the larger community a stake in the process. In Sri Lanka the government finally concluded that the north and east coast of Sri Lanka was divisible under a devolution of central powers. The LTTE accepted the model of a negotiated settlement and agreed to autonomy although they had previously assassinated moderate Tamils willing to accept such schemes. Devolution and autonomy were less than the complete independence they initially fought for and yet the LTTE reduced its violence, stopped perpetrating suicide terror and sat down to negotiate with the government.[72]

Religiously oriented groups are more complicated and dangerous negotiating partners. Their ultimate goal may include the spread of religious holy war, to end Evil as interpreted by them, or the pursuit of some heavenly millenarian reward. Religious purity as an ideological goal is not divisible and it is thus more difficult to create incentives to deter the terrorists by appealing to the public. Additionally, it appears easier for religious groups to mobilize operatives to commit suicidal violence than it is for secular nationalist groups, and a growing number of groups are adapting their strategies and techniques accordingly. According to a Rand survey, religious groups have been far more successful in killing large numbers of people than nationalistic ones.[73]

Barbara Victor argues that some of the secular groups in Palestine had great difficulty mobilizing suicide bombers. Logically, before the Nationalist and Marxist groups switched to suicide bombing tactics, anyone predisposed towards martyrdom already belonged to a religious militant group like Hamas or the Islamic Jihad or aligned with them to volunteer for martyrdom.[74]

The Islamic groups prohibited women's participation and so this became the pool from which the secular groups drew their new operatives. Victor alleges that this explains why women were finally permitted to participate in martyrdom operations (rather than simply play a supportive role) and the Al Aqsa Martyrs' Brigades were able to emerge onto the scene as a contender by tapping a previously unexploited constituency. However, the groups in question appear highly adaptable. In 2003 the Palestinian Islamic Jihad claimed responsibility for two women bombers and Hamas initial ideological rejection of women *shuhada'a* (martyrs) shifted over a period of two years. Sheikh Yassin finally claimed responsibility for a female martyr Reem Riashi on January 14, 2004.[75] (See photo 10).

Finally, the issue of capabilities and resources come into play. Terrorist groups that can fund suicide bombing and reward their operatives accordingly can generate financial incentives to become martyrs. Organizations that are resource poor might be induced by powerful external actors to jump on the suicide bombing bandwagon if there are financial rewards attached to perpetrating acts of suicide bombing (conventional bombing campaigns do not garner the same degree of external support from Hizb'allah or al Qaeda as suicide terrorism). Scott Atran writes that after Ayat Akras bombed the Supersol in Jerusalem, a Saudi telethon raised more than 100 million dollars for the Al 'Aqsa Intifada.[76] For example, see figure 4.1 in the appendix.

When the non-state actor or insurgent group must raise money for operations from within its own ranks, a different dynamic comes into play. When the group suffering from the perpetuation of conflict is also subsidizing the struggle, there is a greater likelihood that the larger population will grow war weary and may exert pressures on the terrorists to abandon military operations and negotiate a settlement.

In cases where the money to support the organizations comes from outside the conflict zone, almost as a form of rent, the terrorist group is less beholden to the will of the people. This war weariness was a crucial element bringing all sides to the negotiating table in Sri Lanka—partly because the LTTE has resorted to domestic taxation, levies, and tolls of the Tamils who reside in Sri Lanka once expatriate financial contributions were precluded by anti-terror laws promulgated after 9/11. Following from Charles Tilly, the LTTE's reliance upon taxation increasingly transforms the organization into a "state in the making" responsible to its constituency rather than a terrorist organization operating above the population.[77] The LTTE must be more responsive to the will of the people, their desire for a peace dividend, and their opposition to the targeting to civilians. In response, the LTTE has also become more pragmatic and amenable to negotiation.

From the perspective of the terrorists themselves, taxation plays a role in justifying why civilians are not sacrosanct. According to the Chechens: It is precisely the people of Russia who, by supporting the authorities and their taxes, are sponsoring this war and this genocide. The people of Russia say nothing, they know nothing and they want to know nothing of the truth about Chechnya, their brains have been reliably washed by the propaganda. . . . Silent complicity with the genocide, refusal to protest actively, from a civic position, from conscience and truth—this is what the "civilians" of Moscow are dying for. The submissiveness of the slave goes hand in hand with the aggressiveness of the invader.[78]

This final element sheds greater light on potentially more productive counter-terror strategies than the heavy-handed approaches preferred by the Russians, Israelis, and, previously, the Turks. If terrorist organizations are severely handicapped by the loss of financial support from abroad, and they are forced to rely on internal financial resources which limit their ability to carry on the fight, there is an opportunity for the targeted state to outbid the outbidders by providing the civilian population with the material benefits, infrastructure, and autonomy that would erode the insurgents' support base. If the terrorist leader can be captured, imprisoned, and made to denounce his/her organization this is a proven effective strategy. The loss of leadership in this fashion takes the steam out of the organization, (e.g. Abdullah Öcalan of the PKK in Turkey, Abimael Guzman of Peru's Shining Path, and Michael (Mickey) McKevitt of the Real IRA.) Capturing the LTTE's leader alive has been elusive for the Sri Lankan Security Service, the STF, because Vilupillai Prabhakaran wears a cyanide capsule around his neck to prevent this from happening.[79]

In contrast to this, killing terrorist leaders appears to serve the purposes of the outbidders, creates nationalist myths, martyrs, and cults of personality. Among the Palestinians, Israel has tended to prefer a policy of targeted assassination, since they rightly assume that to capture their targets alive would be very costly in terms of Israeli life. In Turkey, the assassination of Hizb'allah Sheikh Huseyin Velioglu might have been a factor in the rise of suicide terror in Turkey in 2003. The strategy of killing a leader, rather than imprisoning him and making him renounce violence, has yet to be proven productive in the long term since new groups or units emerge among the terrorists named after the slain martyr—who becomes a symbol and source of inspiration and emulation. Targeted killing further reduces moderates ability to control the extremists (or self police)[80] since they lose credibility among the larger audience and undermine them overall.

There are no easy solutions to the problem of suicide terror. To paraphrase Scott Atran, policies aimed at empowering moderates from within, supporting certain values (like the respect for life), and similar behavior may produce emotional dissatisfaction with the existing terrorist leaders which could lead to lasting change from within. However, some of the more heavy-handed counter-terrorist tactics of certain states, such as the preemptive attack on the supporters of terrorism, is likely to backfire and mobilize greater support for terror. An alternative counter-terrorist strategy is to change the targeted state's behavior by addressing and lessening the minorities' grievance and humiliation, especially in asymmetric ethno-nationalist conflicts. There is little evidence (historical or otherwise) to indicate that support for suicide terrorism evaporates without the realization of some of the fundamental goals that suicide bombers and their supporting communities share.[81] Thus it is imperative to understand the complexity of motivations, processes, and the inner workings of the organizations to suggest alternative policies to combating suicide terror—making it less effective and less popular.

1. Japanese Suicide Pilots © *Hulton-Deutsch Collection/Corbis*

2. USS Bunker Hill Hit by Kamikazes © *Corbis*

3. Marine Stands Guard at Bombed U.S. Embassy in Beirut © *Bettman/Corbis*

4 Nairobi Embassy Bombing © *Reuters/Corbis*

5. One World Trade Center Collapsing on September 11, 2001 © *Reuters/Corbis*

6. Spanish Policeman Walks Past Wreckage After Train Explosion in Madrid on March 11, 2004 © *Reuters/Corbis*

7. Memorial Rally for Bombmaker "The Engineer" © *Ricki Rosen/Corbis SABA*

8. A Ramallah Street with Posters Celebrating Hamas Bomber
© *Ricki Rosen/Corbis SABA*

9. Bus Burns Where a Car Bomb Exploded in Central Israel ©*Reuters/Corbis*

10. Reem Riyashi, Hamas' First Female Martyr in Gaza City
©*Handout/Reuters Newmedia Inc./Corbis*

11. Rome Demonstration Against PKK Leader Öcalan's Extradition © *Corbis*

12. LTTE Attacks in Colombo © *Corbis*

13. Two Female Tamil Tiger Rebels Stand Attention at a "Black Tigers Day" Ceremony in Kilinochi Sri Lanka ©*Reuters/Corbis*

14. Palestinian Boy Holds a Toy Machine Gun in Front of Iraqi Flag During a March in Gaza © *Reuters/Corbis*

15. Insurgent Holds Up Wanted Poster © *Reuters/Corbis*

16. Muslims Protest in Lebanon During Iraq War © *Reuters/Corbis*

CHAPTER FIVE

HALTING SUICIDE TERROR FROM WITHIN:
THE PKK IN TURKEY

In some instances terrorist groups may themselves cease and desist from using suicide bombing although they may still persist in using conventional strategies of insurgency. Perhaps they have achieved their perceived goals; perhaps the organization's use of the tactic has backfired, and the group finds it is losing public support. Two groups within the Middle East voluntarily halted the use of suicide terror but for very different reasons.

In Turkey, the Kurdish Worker's Party, the *Partia Karkaren Kurdistan*, (PKK) abandoned the tactic after it seemingly failed to win adherents to the cause and in fact began to lose more support than it gained. This was complicated by the loss of their leader, Abdullah Öcalan, who, as was Abimael Guzman of the Shining Path in Peru in 1992, was captured alive in 1999. In Lebanon, the Hizb'allah, the group that made famous the strategy in 1983, eventually became a "legitimate" player in Lebanese politics, ceasing its suicide attacks against Western targets after having achieved the stated goal of ending the Israeli occupation of southern Lebanon.

For many analysts, the Hizb'allah remains a terrorist organization even though it is formally cloaked in the respectability of Lebanese Parliamentary politics and offically plays by the rules of the game. Hizb'allah continues to fund and support other terrorist groups within Israel proper, its military wing sends Katyushka rockets into Northern Israel, and there remain lingering issues of Israeli prisoners of war. Nevertheless, regardless of where one stands regarding Hizb'allah's *legitimacy*, their systematic use of suicide terror appears to be a thing of the past. (Chapter 6 contains a full discussion of Hizb'allah's influence on other terrorist organizations.)

In this chapter I will examine how the PKK in Turkey launched its use of suicide terror and why it abandoned the tactic. I contrast the PKK's terror with that of one of its domestic Islamic rivals, the Turkish Hizb'allah.

The PKK and Suicide Terror

Although Turkey is overwhelmingly a Muslim country, the PKK adopted suicide terror as a manifestation of nationalism, not Jihad or martyrdom. As can be demonstrated in terms of gender. Turkey provides a distinctive manifestation of suicide terror in the Middle East because of the role played by young, female bombers. Eleven of the fifteen PKK suicide attacks were carried out by women. Unlike the case of Palestine and Sri Lanka,

The women activists in Turkey were unmarried, between the ages of 17 and 27. They were largely uneducated, from poor families, had no professional skills, and no great prospects.

Some analysts have made great issue of the girls' youth and impressionability. "They may not have been aware of the nature of the reaction their action would draw. But their elders, their mentors, definitely are. They are doing this deliberately to escalate tension. The more people become tense and alarmed, the more ground terrorism would cover towards its goal."[1]

Suicide bombing occurred for a very brief period in Turkey and failed to resonate positively with the Kurdish population. After the loss of its leadership, the PKK began to disintegrate, transforming itself into a political party before it finally dissolved in 2003. After Abdullah Öcalan's capture, there was a series of bombings to protest the government's plans to execute him. (See photo 11.) The government, with an eye directed toward its desire to join the European Union, reversed its original position and commuted the sentence to life imprisonment. However, to understand why the PKK initially became popular and why suicide terror did not catch on it is important to understand the linkages among all of these factors.

Domestic Political Factors

Demographically, Turkey consists of a number of ethnic and religious groups and has a long history of religious tolerance; yet it has an equally problematic history with ethnic minority groups that have challenged the state, demanded autonomy, or rebelled against the central authority in Istanbul and, after independence, Ankara.

After a rather brutal suppression of Armenian nationalism on the eve and end of World War One, Turkey faced yet another ethnic challenge from within. The Kurds, a beleaguered minority group that straddled several mountainous regions of Turkey, Syria, Iraq, and Iran opted to secede. The Kurds were divided along ethnic, tribal, religious and linguistic lines. Even in Turkey proper, there are Sunni and Alevi Kurds, and the Kurds speak various dialects like Sorani, Kurmanji, and Zaza. However, in each of the countries in which the Kurds resided, there has been a tenuous relationship with the central authorities because of their irredentism.

The problems with the Kurdish minority existed at independence in 1923. And though Attatürk (Mustapha Kemal) brutally suppressed Kurdish rebellions in the 1920s and the 1930s, which included the Koçgiri in 1920, the Shaykh Said Rebellion in 1924, revolts in Agri (1930), and in Dersim (Tunceli) in 1937–1938, there has been an on-going guerrilla campaign for Kurdish independence in southeast Turkey since 1984. The PKK's origins can be traced to the Revolutionary Youth (Dev Gençö) branch of Kurdish students from the Tuzlucayir district of Ankara in 1974. Since then, Turkey has faced a separatist organization that had a sizable membership fighting for autonomy and independence. It is one that has received political and logistic support and weapons from other countries (training camps existed in the Beka'a Valley and the Syrian government provided arms and finances) and growing popularity among the rank and file.[2] Approximately 30,000 people died since the conflict began.

The insurgency in Turkey has gone through many phases: Abdullah Öcalan formed the PKK in 1977, when he was a student in the faculty of Political Science at Ankara University. Öcalan and some of his closest associates escaped to Syria ahead of the 1980 military coup and thus eluded the government's dragnet to capture him, and began armed activities in 1984.

The PKK, although it had originated as a Marxist-Leninist organization in continuation of the violent student movements of the 1970s, placed its emphasis on its Kurdish identity. Nevertheless, its ideological Marxism served several functions. First, it was the dominant discourse in the Turkish universities during the 1970s. Second, it helped distinguish the PKK from other Kurdish groups, especially the more conservative, tribal, and Iraqi-associated organizations that flourished in the southeast. Third, it provided the ideological means to indoctrinate recruits and maintain control over the organization.[3]

From the outset, the PKK favored of a separate Kurdish state with pan-Kurdish aspirations. "Its objectives changed with the fortunes of the insurgency; initially in favor of non-compromising stand against the Turkish state, the PKK changed its tune with first the end of the Cold War and then when it lost the initiative on the ground. It begun to downplay the Marxist-Leninist roots of its ideology and then sought to define its aims for the Kurds in the form of successive federations, Arab-Kurdish in Iraq, Turkish-Kurdish in Turkey and Persian-Kurdish in Iran."[4] After his capture, Abdullah Öcalan went so far as to denounce some of his former associates, claimed that he had been duped by foreign powers and paid his respects to the Turkish people.[5]

The major bone of contention between the PKK and the government has historically revolved around issues of cultural autonomy, language rights, political representation and the government's human rights abuses. For decades, the official government position refused to recognize the distinctiveness or existence of the Kurdish people. Turkey refused to acknowledge a distinct Kurdish ethnic minority with minority rights. The official Turkish government's position was that "we have no ethnic minorities."[6]

In May 1990, Fugan Ok of the Foreign Ministry told the Helsinki Human Rights Committee that, "the Kurds are not a minority, since according to the Lausanne Treaty of 1923 only religious minorities are recognized."[7] Kurds were not considered a minority under Ottoman Law because they are Muslims; Islamic Law only recognized non-Muslims as constituting legitimate minorities. Government policies aimed toward assimilating the Kurds had the reverse effect and set in motion a process of constructing or reconstructing a militant Kurdish identity.

Denials of a Kurdish existence provoked a zealous response as well as international condemnation of Turkish policy. This condemnation had a negative influence on Turkey's relations with Europe and jeopardized its prospective membership in the European Union. According to one analyst, the insurgency never posed a strategic threat to Turkey; the Kurds had no chance of defeating one of NATO's largest armies, and thus prospect of secession was a fantasy. However, the ferocity of the struggle meant that Ankara had to commit a large number of soldiers to fighting it, "a costly proposition for a country continuously mired in economic troubles, and it sullied Turkey's relations with neighbors, the U.S., the European Union, friends and foes alike. It also undermined the rule of law in Turkey and gave rise to wide abuses of power."[8]

There was a contagion and diffusion of Kurdish terror and violence to Europe. Some of the more heavy-handed Turkish anti-insurgent policies have affected the EU proper as the conflict was exported to Western Europe in various forms. There are 2.5 million Turks living in Germany, half a million of whom are Kurdish, who migrated there as a response to the Turkish government's poor record of human rights abuses and brought terror and violence with them.

The Kurdish Diaspora in Europe was a crucial source of PKK support, including the recruitment of would-be combatants, financing for their operations, and providing a constituency to lobby European governments. The PKK relied on financial donations from the community as well as intimidation to raise funds. They also (allegedly) funded their activities through the drug trade in Germany, France, Belgium, and Denmark. According to The Spectator, "The PKK financed its war against Turkey by extortion and the sale of heroin, and, according to British security service sources, it is responsible for 40 percent of the heroin sold in the European Union."[9]

In addition to the drug trade and arms purchases, the PKK operated a satellite television station called Med-TV (later renamed Medya-TV). This television station proved to be an important consciousness-raising instrument. In the absence of any broadcast in Kurdish, a large number of Kurds, many of whom did not support the PKK, would watch its programs. Over time as the PKK became more popular, it modified its tactics from sheer terrorism to more conventional guerrilla tactics, such as targeting the Turkish security forces. As increasing numbers of recruits joined the organization, the PKK upgraded its fighting techniques, created training bases in the countries surrounding Turkey, and professionalized its fighting forces. It focused its military activities largely in the southeast and east with occasional forays into other parts of the country. However, in the large urban areas of Istanbul, Ankara, and Izmir, where many Kurds had migrated to, its activities remained relatively weak. With the exception of a few spectacular terrorist events, it shied away from engaging in activities or investing too much military capability in the cities.[10]

The group's support base, once limited, expanded demographically. According to historian Martin Van Bruinessen, the PKK leader, Abdullah Öcalan, drew heavily from the lowest social classes—the uprooted, half educated village and small town youth who understood oppression and wanted action, and not ideological sophistication.[11] Van Bruinessen observed that the PKK represented "the most marginal sections of Kurdish society, the ones who feel excluded from the country's social and economic development . . . the victims of rural transformation with frustrated expectations. Öcalan offered them "a simple . . . theory, and lots of opportunities for action, heroism, and martyrdom."[12]

The PKK targeted landlords who had become increasingly unpopular.[13] The Kurdish southeast and east were particularly culturally and religiously conservative areas where these landlords who had been co-opted by Ankara "delivered votes" to political parties and helped maintain order. As a consequence, the PKK polarized the Kurdish regions; the landlords with the help of the central government organized themselves against the PKK and formed village guard units which, in turn, provoked more violence. Barkey and Fuller hypothesize that since the state co-opted the wealthier, land-owning Kurds, and the merchants, the only groups left to fill the ranks of the organization were the lowest echelons on the socioeconomic ladder.[14]

However, as the PKK increased it basis of support, it also became a more serious adversary; and support for the PKK increased as Turkish repression intensified. As support for the PKK increased, Turkish counter-terrorist policies likewise increased—creating a virtually unending cycle of violence.

The Kurdish community was outraged by the daily harassment and official Turkish government denials of their existence. The Kurds desired cultural
autonomy, the right to study their own language, to read Kurdish books, and
sing Kurdish songs. The government meanwhile would distribute pamphlets
in Turkish schools contending that Kurdish was not a distinct language but
actually a dialect of Turkish.[15] This denial of cultural distinctiveness exacerbated an already tense relationship.

HEAVY-HANDED COUNTER-TERRORIST STRATEGIES

There were multiple human rights abuses, harassment, killing, torture, and
the systematic disenfranchisement of the Kurds in the southeast.[16] The government countered with forced relocation and the evacuation of villages.
The government gave local Kurds two options, join the government and
fight the PKK as their proxies or abandon their homes. The military initiated
a policy of scorched earth tactics and the destruction of villages—turning
most of the Kurds into active opponents of the state. "Village evacuations,
a village guard system and sheer repression characterized the state's policy
until Turgut Ozal decided to seek a different approach in the aftermath of
the 1991 Gulf War."[17] The government introduced decree 413 that legalized
press censorship, justified further population transfers, and enforced exile
for anyone who "acted against the state."

The extent of Kurdish support for the PKK varied from place to place
but overall support increased partly as a response to the government's policy
of mass arrests, extra judicial killings, torture, and harassment by the security forces. From the perspective of human rights organizations, "The tactics
used by the Turkish government were counter productive—driving more
and more civilians into the arms of the PKK."[18]

> Instead of trying to win the hearts and minds of the local population,
> the security forces played into the hands of the PKK. As John Grant
> has argued, the initial reaction by the authorities was to assault the
> PKK's "fluid military infrastructure." "It took the Turks a while to learn
> that the PKK's true center of gravity was the support it received from
> the Kurdish population in the southeast and not its guerrilla army."[19]
> Although Ankara continuously increased its security presence in the
> Kurdish regions, especially in the towns the police with few friends to
> rely on tended to be on the defensive, often retreating to fortified posi-
> tions at night which suited the PKK.[20]

The political program of the second congress of the PKK (in 1982) had spelled out a three-phase plan of strategic armed struggle for Kurdistan. Öcalan's three phases included periods of strategic defense, balance of forces, and attack. The first phase was expected to last until 1995 with the balance of forces phase projected for 1995–2000. The final stage would lead to a popular uprising in the southeast after 2000.[21]

Although a proper recounting of the complex history of the Kurds cannot be done justice in this work,[22] what is relevant for our study is that in the mid 1990s the PKK diverged from the plan for armed struggle and shifted their anti-government behavior to include suicide terrorism—overwhelmingly employing female bombers to carry out these operations. "The PKK adopted a new method of using young girls as "live bombs"—sending them to their deaths after they had been allegedly brainwashed."[23] With such attacks, the PKK fanned the feelings of hate throughout the country and exacerbated the divisions within the society.

What is significant about the pattern of Kurdish violence against military and civilian targets was that they appeared to correlate in time with European intervention in Turkey concerning its human rights record. Following from Kuperman's controversial thesis, the PKK attempted to incite a devastating government response by using suicide terror. Thus, whenever Europe raised its voice on Turkey's human rights record, the PKK would instigate the Turkish security forces to massively retaliate against terrorism. Of course, this harsher stance would likely prevent Turkey's admission into the EU as a result of its poor human rights record. From one perspective, the PKK was "playing a fine tuned game."[24] This is consistent with the strategy employed by several insurgent and terrorist groups facing "democratic" governments. One of the goals of terrorism is to incite an overreaction on the part of government forces. To show how the democratic government will betray its ideals while helping to mobilize additional support from the civilian population.

> The PKK sought to provoke the state into engaging in counter insurgency tactics that were violent and indiscriminate. This had the goal of radicalizing Kurdish attitudes, forcing the Kurds to choose sides and banking on the fact that decades of ill treatment would make the PKK the natural repository of the local population's loyalties. . . . in the end, the combination of PKK operations and state violence in response contributed to precisely such a radicalization.[25]

On October 29, 1996 as the country marked its "Republic Day," two PKK militants carried out a suicide attack in Sivas, killing three policemen and one civilian.[26] The Sivas police had been alerted to the risk of suicide bombers posing as pregnant women. The policemen became suspicious of a young woman and took her in for questioning but did not frisk her once they reached police headquarters—rather they looked for another woman to conduct the search because of issues of modesty.

The police eventually decided to take the suspect to the anti-terrorism squad where she could be searched by policewomen. The operative was veiled from head to toe in the traditional garb of devout Muslim women (a black chador) in which only her eyes visible. The police demonstrated respect for women's modesty but doing so cost them their lives. The girl, a PKK operative, turned out to be a living bomb, and detonated the IED (Improvised Explosive Device) around her waist once she entered the police car. The blast killed the woman, three police officers and a civilian passerby.

One witness to the explosion reported seeing, "pieces of human body flying in the air."[27] As lethal as the attack was, the original plan would have caused many more fatalities. Police officials surmised that had the bomber detonated the device during the Republic Day parade a massacre would have resulted. No one claimed responsibility for the attack, but PKK leader Abdullah Öcalan had threatened a wave of suicide bombings and did eventually acknowledge the PKK's responsibility for the operation.

As a result of the Sivas attack, the government inaugurated new security measures. In the future, all female suspects would be frisked by policemen rather than await the arrival of a policewoman. Police would stop and search anyone suspicious if they happened to be within 200 meters of a police station. The blast in Sivas was the third suicide bombing in the summer and fall of 1996. In each of these operations, the bombers were women. In July (the first attack), ten people died in Tunceli and a PKK suicide bomber killed herself and four others in an attack on a police station in Adana, in southern Turkey. Police in the southeastern city of Diyarbakir alleged that they had arrested a Kurdish guerrilla carrying explosives who was planning to detonate a suicide bomb at a Republic Day military parade. In Yeni Yuzyil, the police reported that in 1998 approximately 243 soldiers and Jandarma, 10 police officers, 114 village guards, and 132 civilians died in such terrorist incidents.[28]

Turkish government tactics tended to inflame opposition rather than co-opt or alleviate violence. After years of massive retaliation against Kurdish separatism and multiple human rights abuses, the government altered its approach to combating terrorism. It appeared that they finally understood that the counter-terror strategies of the past exacerbated rather than mitigated conflict and had created very counterproductive consequences. Previously, the government had rarely distinguished between real PKK operatives and the larger Kurdish civilian population. By lumping together the insurgents with the larger population and punishing both equally, they had alienated the Kurds from the government and driven them into the arms of the PKK. The shift in policy effectively meant that the government was willing to grant greater cultural rights. The government added carrots to its arsenal of sticks. Bit by bit, Kurdish language was permitted and Kurdish culture was decriminalized.

However, Barkey asserts that after Ozal's death, violent responses again dominated the Turkish government's policies.

> Early signs of change in policy were abandoned after Ozal's death in 1993 and the government resumed the hard-line policy with a vengeance: this included mystery killings in the hands of state-sponsored paramilitary groups and severe restriction on the freedom of expression. The state carried the war to the Kurdish regions and also engaged in cross-border operations seeking to destroy the PKK's rear base in northern Iraq.[29]

For Barkey, the more aggressive tactics included free fire zones, village evacuations and the punishment of local villagers. The number of villages and hamlets evacuated and burned were estimated to be between 2,200 (with 500,000 villagers being relocated) and 4,000 (with in excess of a million villagers losing their homes). Diyarbakir, the Kurdish regional capital, swelled with internally displaced persons. Many Kurds migrated west to Adana, Mersin, Istanbul, and Izmir—all of which experienced a major influx of dislocated Kurds. There is no question that government's tactics eliminated the PKK's room to maneuver and reduced its ability to feed and shelter its ranks.[30]

Turkish government sources allege that there was a positive shift in policy motivated by a desire to win "the hearts and minds" of the Kurdish people. Essentially, the government began to differentiate between the real terrorists and regular Kurds. The Turkish Chief of Staff explained this tactical switch in 1996:

> We [could have] finished off terrorism totally in three months. But we do not want to hurt the people's feelings (treat the people harshly in the fight against the outlawed Kurdistan Workers' Party [PKK]). Because then the innocent could be harmed along with the culprits. We want to wage this struggle against terrorism without making any concessions from democracy, human rights and principles of the law. Because we are devoted to these we take our steps in a controlled manner. . . . But we must be patient in the fight against terrorism.[31]

The government had altered its military tactics. According to Barkey, the military command rethought its methods and strategies to learn from its previous mistakes. Its aggressive ground tactics were supplemented by better air-ground coordination. The increased mobility enabled the military to slowly take the initiative away from the PKK. Moreover, the military decided to flood the area with security forces and soldiers. As General Güres explained, the aim was to block potential escape routes and deny the fighters access to food and replenishment. "They [PKK] could not do anything in the winter. We are ready. We have clothing for minus 40 degree [centigrade] conditions. . . . In 1991 we would stop. Now we never halt operations."[32] In fact, in addition to the village guards, there were as many as 200,000 additional security personnel in the region to fight the PKK.

Government policy included the promise of economic as well as cultural inducements as well as the negative sanctions of aggressive military tactics. In 1999, Prime Minister Bulent Ecevit and eight other ministers visited Hakkari, a province in a Kurdish region of southeastern Turkey, touting a new $114 million economic development program designed to combat the Kurdish insurgency in the region. Ecevit said "We will cut off the sources of separatist terror by bringing development to our people, halting unemployment and giving everybody educational opportunities."[33] While nine previous economic development packages failed to boost the Kurdish region's economy significantly, Ecevit said this package—which included tax exemptions, low-cost loans and free state land—was different. However, the development package apparently never materialized.[34]

THE PKK'S SHIFT

At the same time, the PKK's tactics changed from what had been a moderate position from 1993 to 1996[35] to a renewed cycle of violence that marked the organization's origins before it sought legitimacy. In a pattern of self cannibalization observable in other Middle Eastern conflicts when any insurgent organization suffered losses, the PKK directed the bulk of its violence against perceived traitors from within the Kurdish community. Thus it was the PKK which ceased to differentiate between military and civilian targets and casualties—gradually alienating the civilian population upon whom they relied.

The PKK committed widespread abuses as part of its terrorism against the government and civilians, killing many Kurds in a particularly gruesome manner. Its violence was designed to spread fear among the rural Kurdish population. The PKK routinely targeted state officials: governors, police, and school teachers. "By assassinating officials, the PKK aimed at physically separating the Kurdish regions from the rest of the country and showing that it was capable of taking on the mighty state. If schoolteachers were intimidated and refused to show up for work or policemen were afraid to venture out at night, then the PKK could claim success."[36]

The PKK terrorists targeted village officials and village guards who they perceived as state representatives. In this crude way, the PKK's intention was to reduce the influence of the state, halt the spread of the Turkish language and government policies of assimilation.

The Turkish government, in a policy of divide and rule attempted to co-opt some Kurds loyal to the state and use them against the PKK. The village guard system was designed to exploit the preexisting clan rivalries. Ankara identified villages and local leaders who could contribute peasants to local militias. Sometimes, villagers were not given a choice and were forcibly recruited and at other times the monthly pay of $100, a princely sum then for anyone from that region, produced volunteers. At its peak 60,000–70,000 village guards were deployed to protect their villages from PKK attacks, provide advance intelligence to the government, and act as shock troops during anti-PKK operations. The PKK, in turn, would attack the guards mercilessly. The system contributed to both the deepening of intra-Kurdish animosities and ultimately to the region-wide refugee crisis.[37]

The PKK committed random killings in tourist areas like Antalya, in their effort to intimidate the populace. The government, human rights organizations, and the media reported that the PKK routinely kidnapped young men or threatened their families as part of its recruiting effort.[38]

> Between 1992 and 1995, the height of the conflict, Öcalan's PKK is believed to have been responsible for at least 768 extrajudicial executions, mostly of civil servants and teachers, political opponents, off-duty police officers and soldiers, and those deemed by the PKK to be "state supporters." In addition, the PKK committed numerous large-scale massacres of civilians, usually against villagers or villages that somehow were connected with the state civil defense "village guard system."[39]

The PKK intensified terrorist activity in 1994—initiating a campaign of terrorism inside and outside Turkey, while Iran offered the PKK fighters a safe-haven. It also conducted attacks on Turkish diplomatic and commercial facilities in dozens of West European cities in 1993 and in the spring of 1995. In an attempt to damage Turkey's tourist industry, the PKK bombed tourist sites and hotels and kidnapped foreign tourists. Because of the large number of expatriate Kurds in Germany, there was a serious threat to European security when the PKK threatened to target German Turks. Germany subsequently banned the organization.

In Europe, many PKK-related organizations emerged to provide Kurdish workers with a place to meet and socialize. Although the PKK was banned in many European countries, it used these front organizations to recruit and finance activities. When necessary the PKK could easily mobilize tens of thousands of Kurds in Europe for protest meetings and influence European political opinion. (See photo 11.)

PKK DECLINE AND DOMESTIC COMPETITION

In 1993, schisms emerged whereupon the PKK attempted to redress its sagging popularity by expanding its support base through the adoption of religious language and the concept of Jihad to curry favor with an untapped market of potential supporters—Islamists. According to Turkish military sources:

> The PKK brought into being an organization named "Kurdistan Islamic Movement" with the purpose of reaching larger masses. At the congress of the Kurdistan Islamic Movement in July 1993 a series of decisions were made to expand ties with other religious groups, to induct women into the war, to unite so-called Kurdistan and to revive the old Kurdish *madrassas* [Islamic religious schools] and religious complexes. . . . It is becoming increasingly evident that the separatist terror organization [PKK], whose influence in Turkey has been declining steadily, is now working behind and with the support of reactionary elements at home and abroad and that it is trying to generate new options by forming an alliance with them.[40]

By the mid to late-1990s, the PKK was, for many reasons, internally weak. On the one hand, other terrorist groups emerged who were funded by Iran and themselves engaged in anti-PKK activity. In 1995 there were more than ninety terrorist incidents and five bombings in cities throughout Turkey. Islamic terrorists targeted the PKK as much as they did the secularists and the organization found itself, in many respects, fighting on two fronts.

The relations between the PKK and some of the Islamic radical groups were marked by an ideological rivalry which competed over the same Kurdish constituency in the southeast. "One of the possible consequences of PKK's decline as a fighting organization against the Turkish state, after the demise of its guerrilla strategy and the new peace process strategy . . . could be a strengthening of the radical Islamist groups, and mainly Hizb'allah."[41]

Hizb'allah, an Islamist group not related to one in Lebanon, mobilized religious Kurds. Hizb'allah regarded the PKK as Islam's enemy and accused it of "trying to create an atheist community, supporting the communist system, trying to divide the people through chauvinist activities and directing pressure on the Muslim people."[42]

The organization's goals included the founding of an Islamic state in Turkey. They focused activities in city centers and its members tended to be made up of young people between the ages of 15 and 24, and included children as young as 10. Over 40 percent of its members were high school graduates and 22 percent had university degrees.[43]

At times, the Turkish authorities would use the more extremist Islamic elements of the Hizb'allah in their fight against the nationalist PKK.[44] One of the most controversial activities of Hizb'allah in southeast Turkey was the liquidation of dozens of pro-PKK activists, journalists, intellectuals, and politicians; and Hizb'allah allegedly stabbed hundreds of PKK members in the provinces of Bingol, Diyarbakir, Van and Batman.

In a classic move of divide and rule, Turkey allowed the two groups to eradicate each other.

> Hasan Cemal of the *Milliyet* newspaper quoted Lieutenant General Hasan Kundakci, commander at the time of the bloody clashes. "As we went after PKK with full force, they saved their power. This is the main principle of the strategy. We were aware of Hizb'allah. They first tried to seize the mosques that were in the hands of PKK. After seizing them, they became active around the mosques. But they did not try to confront us."[45]

Hizb'allah enjoyed a fair amount of immunity from the Turkish security authorities, and because it was targeting the PKK, it earned the name "Hez-bol-contra."[46] However, the rivalry between the PKK and Islamic groups was short lived according to some other sources. "This situation changed in 1993, when the two conflicting sides understood the danger of the internecine strife and arrived to an agreement of *modus-vivendi* and common struggle against the Kemalist regime."[47]

Secondly, the tide of public opinion had decidedly shifted away from violence. The public had no stomach for attacks against civilians. The October 7, 1998 attack on the Egyptian covered spice bazaar (Mısır Çarşısı) provoked widespread rebuke for killing 7 and maiming 118 civilians. Public opinion reactions to the Islamic terror were equally unsupportive. "A series of terrorist events provoked a sharp reaction from Turkish public opinion: huge street demonstrations in favor of the secular regime, a strong press campaign, and swift action by security authorities against the perpetrators and their sponsors."[48]

Thirdly, government policy had moved away from the harsh measures of the 1980s. Thus with greater opportunities to win rights legally and a more peaceful way to express their grievances, Kurds were given a stake in the state and something to lose. However, the same could not be said regarding the growing Islamist threat. On January 17, 2000, an elite Turkish police squad killed Hizb'allah's leader, Huseyin Velioglu. The operation was televised.

Finally, the PKK leadership was in disarray. First its second-in-command, Semdin Sakik, was arrested in March 1998. Then, later that year, Syria withdrew its support, under pressure as a state sponsor and benefactor. On October 28, Syria and Turkey signed an agreement six days after Turkey had threatened military action. Syria promised to end its support of the PKK, close all of the PKK training camps, and expel Öcalan, who fled to Italy, where he was arrested on November 13. Italy, however, refused to extradite him to Turkey. Although Human Rights Watch did not support Öcalan's bid for asylum they supported Italy's refusal to extradite him. "While urging accountability for these abuses, Human Rights Watch praised the decision to deny Turkey's extradition request. Turkey still has the death penalty on the books, and its use of torture has been well-documented by international and non-governmental organizations," said Holly Cartner, executive director of Human Rights Watch's Europe and Central Asia division. "But it is a shocking injustice for Italy to simply release Öcalan. In Italy or another jurisdiction where he can be assured a free and fair trial, he must be held accountable for the wanton killing of innocent civilians."[49] Öcalan was eventually arrested at the Greek embassy in Kenya (assisted by U.S. intelligence) in 1999 and remains incarcerated on the prison island of Imrali, south of Istanbul, after being sentenced to death by a state security court in June 1999. As previously stated, his sentence was commuted to life imprisonment.

Barkey and Fuller make clear that the PKK was very much a one man show with Abdullah Öcalan maintaining a firm grip on the organization. He created a personality cult reminiscent of Saddam Hussein, Kim Il Sung, or Villupilai Prabhakaran. Öcalan instilled blind devotion among his followers and the potential replacements for leadership, Cemil Bayik or his brother, Osman Öcalan, lacked the same cult of personality.

Dr. Emin Gurses of Sakarya University asserts that the PKK's disintegration began in 1999, with Öcalan's arrest. He predicted that eventually it would be replaced by an Islamic organization. Professor Umit Ozdag of Gazi University stated that it would be very difficult for the PKK to continue without Öcalan—who is single handedly responsible for European fundraising.[50]

Öcalan's arrest did not stem the tide of violence; in fact suicide terrorism temporarily increased. When Öcalan was officially captured in February 1999, the country witnessed violent street clashes and several suicide bomb attacks. Authorities cracked down on Kurdish activists, detaining more than

3,000 people, many of whom were members of the pro-Kurdish People's Democracy Party (HADEP). Turkey's constitutional court debated whether to ban HADEP candidates from the April 18, 1999 elections, amid charges that the party was a front for the PKK.[51] Abdullah's brother, Osman Öcalan, declared to the German magazine *Der Stern* that, "We are now forced to rely on a violent solution." Osman Öcalan threatened reprisal actions all over Turkey. "Popular uprisings will erupt in Turkish cities" and "the Kurds will girdle themselves with explosives and blow up together with Turkish soldiers" if any harm came to his brother.[52]

On March 4—a Kurdish suicide bomber killed herself and wounded three civilians outside a police station in southeastern Turkey to protest Öcalan's arrest. The bombing took place in Batman, the scene of a shootout between Öcalan's supporters and police two weeks previously. On March 8, 1999 the PKK Central Committee issued a statement which warned "all Turkish state officials, civilian and military, for the last time: current measures being taken against our party leader must be immediately halted and he must be addressed as the leader of our people. If the current situation persists, those responsible will be subjected to similar measures by us."[53]

In June 1999, PKK terrorists stopped a minibus near Tunceli, nine passengers were murdered and two were wounded. In July the PKK stopped 40 vehicles in Hakkari and kidnapped five people. In August the police thwarted a PKK suicide bomb attack with the arrest of a female would-be bomber in Adana. In November and December in separate incidents, three young women carried out suicide bomb attacks in public areas, leading to the deaths and injuries of scores of civilians.[54]

Suicide terror in Turkey had two purposes—to prevent the Turkish government's plans to execute Öcalan and as a last ditch attempt to bait the Turkish government into massively retaliating against civilians (i.e., a return to their former counter-terror strategies)—which would play right into the PKK's hands.

In the past, government heavy-handed policies had increased the PKK's popularity and organizational profile. Now that the PKK's popularity was sagging, Turkish government violence might help resuscitate and bolster support. However, it did not engage in indiscriminate violence against Kurdish civilians rather, the Kurds became weary of the PKK because of its violence and civilian casualties. Suicide terror was marginally successful (along with the potential threat from the European Union) in staying the hand of the government's decision to execute Öcalan but failed to elicit the overreaction that would play into the insurgents' hands.

Barkey provides a different perspective. For him, government hard-line tactics yielded positive results.

In the end, the tide turned completely against the PKK not just because of the increased sophistication of counter-insurgency operations but also because of the dire straits in which the Kurds of the region found themselves.... The coup de grace came when, the Turkish military having succeeded in containing and then reducing the size of the PKK went after its leader in Damascus by threatening Syria with war. Then President Hafez al-Assad quickly sent Öcalan packing. Once Öcalan was captured, the PKK in order to save his life decided to withdraw from Turkish territory into northern Iraq and announce a unilateral ceasefire.[55]

In August 1999, Öcalan announced a "peace initiative," denouncing violence and requesting dialogue with Ankara over the Kurdish issues. At the PKK Congress in January 2000, members supported Öcalan's initiative and claimed the group now would use only political means to achieve its new goal, improved rights for Kurds in Turkey.[56] It was then that the government commuted the death sentence.

According to the U.S. government: "The PKK/KADEK did not conduct any terrorist attacks in 2002; however, the group periodically issued veiled threats to resume violence if the conditions of its imprisoned leader are not improved, and [the PKK] continues its military training and planning."[57]

Turkish Foreign Minister Abdullah Gul said that fighting between the guerrillas and Turkish troops dropped off sharply after Öcalan's capture in 1999. In addition to the loss of their leader, most of the PKK's fighters (perhaps as many as 5,000) withdrew to northern Iraq. The PKK presence while not an immediate threat to U.S. forces nonetheless posed a delicate political problem.

Turkey has adamantly opposed first the creation of a federal state in Iraq, preferring a return to centralized rule by Baghdad and second, if a federation were to eventually emerge, any ethnically devised configuration. Ankara's fears are grounded in the demonstration effect of Kurdish federalism in Iraq on its own Kurdish minority. By hiding behind the minority Turcoman community, Turkey hopes to weaken Kurdish claims to a "Kurdistan" in Iraq. How the U.S. manages these twin problems will have a long-lasting impact on Turkey's Kurdish question.[58]

The war in Iraq and the elimination of Saddam Hussein, brought Kurdish insurgent groups face to face with the American led occupation. Since the Americans were cracking down on all insurgent and armed groups, the PKK was included on the list of groups to combat.

In April 2002 at its 8th Party Congress, the PKK changed its name to the Kurdistan Freedom and Democracy Congress (KADEK) hoping that the changing political conditions in Turkey, specifically the advent of the pro-Islamist and liberal Justice of Development Party (AKP) of Recep Tayyip Erdogan, would provide the organization with a second lease on life. KADEP proclaimed a commitment to nonviolent activities in support of Kurdish rights. A PKK/KADEK spokesman stated that its armed wing, the People's Defense Force, would not disband or surrender its weapons for reasons of self-defense; however, on November 12, 2003, the PKK formally disbanded to be replaced by a broader body, KONGRA-GEL, hoping to get recognition as a political movement twice removed from its violent past. The statement read: "KADEK is being dissolved in order to make way for a new, more democratic organizational structure that allows for broader participation and a peaceful settlement with the dominant nation states."[59]

However, the Turkish state was unlikely to allow any political space for former fighters—no matter how reformed they may profess to have become. This was evident in the restrictive amnesty law that the Turkish parliament passed designed to lure back rebels in northern Iraq.[60] Moreover, facing a superpower was far more challenging than facing the Turkish military, so that it is likely that the PKK, already in disarray, will pass from the scene completely.

METAMORPHOSIS OF SUICIDE TERROR

It appears that the PKK has in fact been supplanted by more extremist Islamic groups as Dr. Emin Gurses predicted. The series of suicide attacks in Istanbul—targeting two synagogues on November 15, and two British targets (the HSBC bank and the British Consulate five days later) were perpetrated by the Islamic Great Eastern Raiders' Front, known as IBDA-C, loosely affiliated with al Qaeda, who jointly claimed responsibility for attacks. Scores of civilians were killed, including many other Muslims.[61] The attacks killed 61 people, including the four suicide bombers, and wounded 712. Once again, violence is not resonating with Turks, giving the government a slightly freer hand to "liquidate" (their term) the perpetrators.[62]

The bombings bore the hallmarks of an al Qaeda operation, with near-simultaneous timing and the use of fertilizer-based explosives. Istanbul's deputy police chief Halil Yilmaz told a news conference, "The suicide bombers have carried out the attacks with ammonium nitrate-based explosives placed in the beds of pickup trucks."[63]

Although, the bombers were Turkish nationals who were previously affiliated with the Islamic groups in Turkey, they were probably talent-scouted by al Qaeda when they expressed dissatisfaction with the local agenda, and then sent to various training camps for further indoctrination, and finally fed back into Turkey.[64]

Suicide terror has metamorphosed in Turkey. It is no longer the exclusive realm of local, homegrown groups like the PKK or Hizb'allah. The new manifestation bears all the trademarks of internationalized terror, funding from abroad, and unlimited capabilities. The Turkish Justice Ministry investigated the attacks' connection to Hizb'allah.

According to the KADEP, the suicide bombers who carried out attacks against the two synagogues in Istanbul were not Arabs, Afghans, or Pakistanis, but Turkish citizens. "The roots of the attacks run too deep and too wide to be connected to external currents by saying they are 'barbaric attacks by al Qaeda.' Although al Qaeda has reportedly 'claimed joint responsibility,' the roots of three of the attackers were in the southeastern province of Bingol ... one of the birthplaces of Hizb'allah."[65]

Consistent with my argument regarding the importance of public acceptance or revulsion, even the Turkish religious leaders condemned the perpetrators. The Turkish Premier Recep Tayyip Erdogan, whose Islamic political party opposes Turkey's ties to the West and was forced to step down from government in 1997, voiced his rejection of the attacks.[66] Erdogan vowed to defeat the attackers, who struck during the Islamic holy month of Ramadan. "Those who bloodied this holy day and massacred innocent people will account for it in both worlds," he said. "They will be damned until eternity."[67]

It is interesting to note that the different counter-terror strategies in Turkey have yielded somewhat different results. We can almost conduct a controlled scientific experiment by contrasting the strategies used against the PKK with those used against Hizb'allah. Vis-à-vis the Kurds: After years of repression and the indiscriminate use of force against Kurdish civilians and militants alike—which inflamed Kurdish civilians—the government shifted strategies to provide carrots as well as sticks. The government successfully captured the PKK leader alive and, eventually, commuted his death sentence to one of life imprisonment. In Prison, Öcalan was encouraged to renounce the use of violence and the PKK ceased to engage in suicide terror. It transformed itself into a political organization and eventually disbanded.

Vis-à-vis Hizb'allah: the government first encouraged or turned a blind eye to the rise of Hizb'allah because it recognized in it a potential rival to the more established secular nationalist opposition of the PKK. After a few years, as Hizb'allah became more threatening, and thus the government killed its leader in a very well publicized targeted assassination. If allegations regarding Hizb'allah's role in the 2003 bombings are borne out by the investigation, Hizb'allah gravitated toward al Qaeda, emerged with a powerful foreign patron, financial support from abroad (thus it was not constrained by dis-approving domestic opinions regarding violence), and adopted increasingly violent tactics after its leader was assassinated. Turkey's experience with sui-cide terror should thus serve as a cautionary tale of what works and what may come back to haunt the state in question years later.

CHAPTER SIX

TERROR 101:
THE TRANSNATIONAL CONTAGION
EFFECTS OF SUICIDE BOMBING

In 1981, Claire Sterling linked countless terrorist organizations together—contending that they all provided each other with some level of support. Sterling demonstrated how an assortment of terrorist groups furnished one another with safe houses, funding and operational support. The Popular Front for the Liberation of Palestine (PFLP) was at the forefront of training other groups as diverse ideologically or ethnically as the IRA, Germany's Baader-Meinhof Group, the Italian Red Brigades, the Japanese Red Army, Turkish left wing revolutionaries, and various European right wing anti-government factions. Sterling highlighted how groups seemingly unconnected ideologically worked together closely, and used as an excellent example the Japanese Red Army attack at Lod Airport in Israel in support of the Palestinian cause to underscore the idea of strange bedfellows. More recently other authors, like Richard English, have substantiated international terrorist connections by explaining how the IRA received weapons from Libya, and cultivated connections in the 1970s with Lebanon, Syria, and East Germany.[1]

Leila Khaled, one of the PFLP's most notorious operatives, corroborated this link between organizations when she revealed that: "the Popular Front sen[t] instructors to Turkey in order to train Turkish youth in urban guerrilla fighting, kidnappings, plane hijackings, and other matters ... in the same way as it train[ed] Ethiopians and revolutionaries from underdeveloped countries."[2]

Bruce Hoffman documented that as many as forty different terrorist groups were trained by the PLO—who sometimes charged between $5,000 and $10,000 for a six-week program of instruction.[3] A patron-client relationship developed because of the competition between the superpowers. Under bipolarity, the Soviet Union prioritized support for insurgent organizations around the globe as long as they were steadfastly opposed to Western Imperialism and could potentially act as a thorn in the West's—especially, the

U.S. side. Sterling pointed out the degree to which Moscow participated in the global network of terrorism and ran a virtual terrorist academy in the guise of the Patrice Lamumba University, funding thousands of third world revolutionaries on full scholarship to the Soviet Union to be indoctrinated with anti-colonial sentiment and to study guerrilla tactics.[4]

Both Sterling and Hoffman date the internationalization of terror to 1968 when the PFLP hijacked an Israeli El Al flight en route from Rome to Tel Aviv.[5] This hijacking changed the genre of airline pirating wherein an airline was now symbolic to and representative of the targeted country and not simply a means to return to the homeland as many Cubans had done previously. This hijacking was particularly violent and brutal, and, for the first time, demonstrated how porous international borders were for terrorist activities. Finally the terrorists' intent was to shock and awe to gain international recognition. They were effective.

From 1968 until the mid-1980s, several Palestinian groups were at the forefront of global internationalized terrorism. In 1970, the PFLP simultaneously hijacked three planes to Dawson Field at the Al Zarqa Base in Jordan (30 miles from Amman), which triggered severe Jordanian reprisals. Their counter-terrorist actions proved disastrous for Palestinians residing in Jordan; the events led to a mini civil war and to the eventual expulsion of the PLO to Lebanon. Significantly, the Jordanian backlash against Palestinians instigated the rise of an even more militant group named "the Black September Organization" which targeted moderate Arab leaders as well as Israelis and Jews. The BSO was ultimately responsible for one of the most infamous terrorist events, the killing of 11 Israeli athletes at the Munich Olympics in 1972. The symbolism and imagery imbued by all of these events in the month of September continues to be of great significance for terrorism.[6]

Throughout the 1970s and 1980s terrorist groups proliferated with training camps in Jordan (until the PLO expulsion in 1970), Libya, Lebanon, North Korea, and the Sudan that hosted militants, left-wing revolutionaries, and "freedom fighters" from around the globe. Ideology and techniques spread among the groups—resulting in a contagion of terrorism and a diffusion of methods. In the words of Hagop Hagopian, the leader of ASALA (the Armenian Army for the Secret Liberation of Armenia), the reemergence of Armenian terrorism in Lebanon in the 1970s was ascribed to Palestinian influence. In a 1975 interview he credited the Palestinians for the inspiration to begin terror operations because of the "the failure of the policies of the traditional Armenian parties [to publicize the Armenians' cause and grievances] . . . and the fact that many Armenians since 1966 have participated in the Palestinian Arab struggle from which they learned many things."[7] ASALA claimed lineage from George Habash's PFLP. The patron-client relationship was solidified by the PFLP's provision of arms, training, and operational support.

Not only have terrorists cooperated with one another generally, but also suicide bombing, in particular, has been shown to be contagious. This kind of diffusion takes various forms: a spillover of violence to neighboring areas within the same country or to other countries, or a learning process wherein violence in one country prompts other groups to duplicate tactics. We can also discern that suicide bombing leads to escalation. So when used effectively by one group, not only will the tactic be perpetuated but it is also likely that groups will increase the levels of violence. Both escalation and diffusion/contagion can be at work simultaneously.[8] We can discern the direct (patron-client) and indirect (through observation) influences of suicide terror. In some instances, insurgent factions have been physically trained by other organizations and taught how to best use horrifying tactics to devastating effect, who subsequently import the tactic far and wide. Terrorist groups provide financing, technical, and tactical training. On other occasions, factions observe the successful operations of groups from afar—because of the publicity and media attention engendered by spectacular bombings, and then tailored the techniques to suit local circumstances. It appears that suicide terror taps into latent angers and impacts beliefs. This is especially true when the tactic demonstrates that is has had an effective performance in other contexts.[9]

SUICIDE TERROR CONTAGION:
FROM LEBANON TO PALESTINE

This diffusion or contagion can occur between rival factions within one state or among neighboring states. Joyce Davis explains how suicide terror was a nondenominational strategy first employed by Christian Lebanese militias, by means of female operatives, against the Israeli occupation and only afterward spread to the Islamic Hizb'allah.[10] Hizb'allah's success in expelling the Israeli military from a cordon sanitaire in southern Lebanon and the Beka'a Valley led to its imitation by Hamas and the Palestinian Islamic Jihad—then spreading further to secular organizations like Fatah's Tanzim, the Al 'Aqsa Martyrs' Brigade, and the Marxist PFLP. Other scholars have underscored a direct patron-client relationship between the Lebanese Hizb'allah and militant Islamic groups in the Occupied Territories.[11]

In November 1992 Hamas formed an alliance with Iran, Hizb'allah's benefactor, to support the continuation of the Intifada.[12] Significantly, we can infer the contagion effect of suicide terror from Lebanon to Palestine in December 1992, when Israel expelled 415 Hamas and Palestinian Islamic Jihad militants to Marj al Zahour (flowering pastures) in Lebanon in retaliation for the kidnapping-murder of a border guard policeman, Nissim Toledano, by Hamas, on December 17, 1992.

> Most of the deportees were affiliated with the civilian-informational and political infrastructure of Hamas—responsible for the distribution of contribution funds, and served as spokespeople and political activists; they were not necessarily members directly involved in the attacks. Rabin defined the deportation as a strike against "the top level of the Hamas," rather than the hard-core terror activists.[13] The deportation was meant to weaken the environment in which Hamas functioned and to signal the government's determination to combat terror and reassure the public.[14]

This deportation was unique not only because of its unprecedented scope, but also because of the way it was performed. The government decided to deport hundreds of Palestinians to Lebanon for a period that would not exceed two years. Refused refugee status by Lebanon and the neighboring Arab states, the Hizb'allah took them in and they remained in Marj al Zahour, a mountain slope refugee camp, for six months until international condemnation of the deportations forced Israel to agree to their return.[15] According to one expert, the Marj al Zahour expellees were far from militant terrorists, rather they were overwhelmingly university students, teachers, doctors, engineers, and Imams—the bulk of Islamic intelligentsia at the time.[16] On December 18, 1992, the UN's Security Council passed resolution 799, which condemned the deportation and demanded that Israel ensure the immediate return of the deportees. On September 9, 1993, the Marj al Zahour deportees were returned to the occupied territories. Eight of the expellees elected to remain in Lebanon, apparently fearing that they would be arrested upon their return. Many of the Marj al Zahour expellees became active in the struggle against the occupation and a few can be linked directly to suicide terror operations after their return.

As part of the Hizb'allah's sponsorship of the deportees, it provided aid and operational training including military training, and instruction in the preparation of explosive devices and attack methods. It is probable that the transfer of knowledge and training in the use of suicide terror occurred at this point.[17]

According to an October 1997 report from the JMCC, the Jerusalem Center for Media and Communication:

> The bombers, and those responsible for a previous string of attacks on Israelis, seem to have been working in small and isolated cells. . . .

The fifth bomber ... may be Mahmoud Abu Hanoud, 34, also from As-
eera [who] was a Marj al Zahour expellee, who has been in hiding and
wanted by the Palestinian Authority and Israel for two-and-a-half years.
Israel says he may have been a bomber, or may have been the ringleader,
and still be alive and in hiding somewhere in the West Bank.[18]

Yet another instance of a Marj al Zahour expellee bringing techniques
to Israel was Adnan al-Ghoul, an activist during the first Intifada. After his
expulsion to Marj al Zahour, al-Ghoul returned to Gaza City in 1996, using
forged documents, all the while maintaining close ties with Hizb'allah. In
Gaza he ran a bomb factory and his main client was Hamas, although he was
on the payroll of Arafat's Preventive Security Services according to Palestinian intelligence officials.[19]

The domestic political situation in the Palestinian Territories deteriorated in 2001, and led to outbidding among rival Palestinian organizations.
Several groups jumped on the suicide bombing bandwagon, new groups
emerged, and previously secular groups adopted the language of *Jihad* and
martyrdom. The tactical switch, as mentioned in chapter 2, rehabilitated the
PFLP's sagging popularity. In Israel, contagion and diffusion occurred at two
levels, spreading from other Arab countries to the Palestinians and spreading within the Palestinian community as various groups who competed for
popularity adopted suicide bombing as a tactic.

However, because of the competitive environment among groups, there
were multiple unintended consequences as Hizb'allah and Hamas eventually
competed with each other for leadership of the Palestinian community.

When the Aqsa *Intifada* erupted ... Hezbollah's leaders saw a chance
to boost their prestige in the West Bank and Gaza Strip and to expand
their brand of Islamic revolution to the gates of Jerusalem.... They
aren't keen to share the spotlight with Hamas. In the past few months,
Hezbollah canceled the training of Hamas operatives in Lebanon's
Beka'a Valley and in Iran. Hezbollah is still training Palestinians, but
when it sends them back to the Gaza Strip or West Bank, they work
for Hezbollah, not Hamas. A source in the Hamas military wing, Izzedine al-Qassam, claims that Hezbollah has recruited several activists
from Hamas and from the military branch of the Palestinian Islamic
Jihad—people who were frustrated by their organizations' ineffective-
ness and tempted by Hezbollah's training and weaponry.[20]

Boaz Ganor writes that Hizb'allah's influence in the Palestinian Territories exploded after Israel's unilateral withdrawal from southern Lebanon

in May 2000. The Lebanese, the Palestinians, and the rest of the Arab world interpreted the hasty withdrawal of the pressured IDF as a terrified bolt from Lebanon and served to strengthen the feeling among the Palestinians that violence pays.

> The withdrawal from Lebanon brought the Palestinians to understand that if Hizb'allah could succeed in ridding itself of Israel in Lebanon, the Palestinians could do the same in the territories. As a result, the influence of Hizb'allah increased in the territories, illustrated by the fact that Hizb'allah flags began to be raised during gatherings, parades, and demonstrations that took place there.[21]

Thus the *Hizb'allah Model* has become the dominant paradigm among Palestinian insurgent organizations. There is little incentive to moderate their position or negotiate with the enemy because of domestic pressures which support suicide terror and the Hizb'allah's appearance of victory against the Israelis by not negotiating or backing down. There is a learning curve at work and terrorist groups learn from one another's successes and failures.

Contagion also occurs as operatives pass through training camps—spreading their tactics and techniques. Israeli security forces arrested Hassan Abdel Rahman Salameh (a.k.a. Abu Ahmed) in 1992. Following his release, he fled to Jordan and, from there, traveled through the Sudan and Syria where he passed through a series of training camps. Two years later, he returned to Gaza via Egypt and joined Hamas' Izz al-Din al-Qassam Brigades. In 1996, he set up a squad of suicide attackers with Muhamed Dief. Armed with intelligence, instructions, and supplies, Salameh set up a suicide bombing cell, recruited three bombers, including a member of his family, and persuaded them to carry out attacks at Ashkelon junction and on Jerusalem's No. 18 bus in which 45 people were killed and 91 wounded in these attacks.[22] The demonstration effect and its success have been profound.

CONTAGION BEYOND THE ARAB–ISRAELI CONFLICT

Suicide terror has spread throughout the Middle East and the Islamic world. There is speculation regarding the extent of this spillover effect on North Africa and to the Algerian crisis. On Christmas Eve 1994 the hijacking of a French Airbus plane in Algiers by four Algerian terrorists was seemingly a failed suicide mission.[23] The terrorists demanded the release of two Islamic Salvation Front (FIS) leaders, Abassi Madani and Ali Belhadj, but were ignored by the Algerian authorities.[24] The hijackers initially attempted to reach Paris but as a consequence of insufficient fuel, landed at Marseilles, where French elite paratroopers stormed the plane—killing the terrorists. Charles Pasqua, the French Interior Minister, alleged that the terrorists had planned to destroy the Air France jet—either exploding it over Paris or ramming it into a building. Documents captured in London alleged that the terrorists had intended to crash the plane into the Eiffel Tower. What seemed far-fetched then, in the light of 9/11, is no longer implausible; the date of this event too, prior to the 1995 decision by GIA (Groupe Algerien Islamique) to renounce suicide terror, yields some credibility to an interpretation which is not, however, unanimous among scholars.[25]

If war is the extension of politics by other means, terrorism has become the extension of war by other means. As suicide terror has proven relatively successful in the Middle East or places like Sri Lanka, there has been an upsurge in the number of regions, countries and non-state actors that utilize it as a tactic in their nationalist struggles against (real or perceived) foreign occupations.[26]

To Chechnya and Beyond

Throughout the 1990s and increasingly since, the spread of suicide terror appears contagious in Russia's civil war in the breakaway region of Chechnya. In December 1994, Russian troops embarked on a painful and bloody campaign to wrest the capital city of Grozny from secessionist forces. Russian Intervention was met with widespread resistance from ordinary civilians and they consistently failed to win the hearts and minds of most Chechens. This was exacerbated by the aerial bombardments of civilian areas in Gekhi and Makhety. The center of Grozny was literally flattened by the joint actions of heavy artillery tank fire, missiles, and bombs launched by airplanes and helicopters. At the cost of numerous casualties and terrible damage to the city, the Russians eventually succeeded. But victory was short-lived. Five years to the day, Russian troops were once again battling rebel forces in the streets of Grozny in a second iteration of the war.

According to Oliker, the key mistake the Russian military made between the two Chechen Wars was in drawing the wrong conclusions from urban combat: not only that it should be avoided, but that it could be. When this belief proved incorrect, the Russians found themselves making the same mistakes on the very same streets from five years earlier. There was a willful refusal by the on-scene commanders and the generals at higher levels to honor Boris Yeltsin's order to halt the aerial bombardments in December 1994.[27] The tragedy of Chechnya underscored all the shortcomings of Russia's force employment repertoire by making its leaders look confused, uninformed, and unable to heed public opinion. Worse yet, the Russians did little to demonstrate much of a learning curve over time. In both iterations of conflict, Russian failings were exacerbated by Chechen advantages, among these, the fact that they knew their cities better and were prepared to defend them using any tactic necessary to shake off Russian imperialism. The Chechen resistance turned the tide of war by becoming exactly what Moscow had branded them—terrorists.[28]

Chechen rebels bombed Russian tanks during the battle of Grozny in 1994.[29] In June 1995 Shamil Besayev led a raid against the Russian town of Budennosk in retaliation for Russian massacres of Chechen civilians in Samashki two months earlier. Although the intended target of the raid was a military base, when the attack failed, Besayev seized a hospital instead. However, more than 100 civilians died when the Russians stormed the facility and Besayev emerged victorious with few casualties. The raid resulted in widespread international media attention on the Chechen cause as well as outspoken Russian public criticism of the war as Russians blamed their own government for its incompetence and heavy-handed tactics. In January 1996, after another failed attack against a military base in Kizliar, Chechen commander Raduev took a village hospital and two thousand hostages. The Russians stormed the hospital as they had done in Samashki killing 69 people, including 28 civilians.[30]

The rebels kidnapped, hijacked, extorted money, and assassinated police officers. However only during the second War in 1999, did they use suicide terror systematically. Islamic extremists of Foreign Arab origin allegedly introduced the tactic in Chechnya in mid-2000. The operations were carefully coordinated attacks on military targets by mainly male suicide bombers who used the method of exploding trucks loaded with explosives near the target. Units of Chechen fighters then followed up the attacks with conventional insurgent strategies.[31] Chechen women took part in fighting during the First Chechen War, in 1994–1996. However, they also turned to suicide attacks against civilians in the second war. Of the seven suicide attacks by Chechen separatists on Russia in 2003, six were carried out by women.[32] Virtually all of the 12 attacks on Russia in 2004 have involved women—"black widows," avenging the deaths of family members in Russia's conflict in Chechnya. Eighteen of the 50 terrorists of the three-day Dubrovka theater siege on October 23, 2002 were women, some as young as 16. The next chapter details the exploits of Chechen women suicide bombers and provides insights into their motivations.

Dmitri Trenin writes: "In January 2000, the war in Chechnya entered a new phase . . . marked by guerrilla war tactics that the Chechen rebels began to use."[33] The first bomber—a woman—exploded herself along with a Russian army truck. The Chechens instituted a campaign of terror and bombing of subway stations, trolleys, and apartment buildings in Moscow. Then they ramped up the campaign of suicide terror against Russian civilians to place the issue of Chechen independence on the front burner of international attention.[34] Suicide terror has become one of the methods of choice, evidenced by the growing number of attacks in recent years. In October 2002, a band of Chechen militants seized the Dubrovka theater in Moscow—taking the audience believed to be 711 people hostage and threatening to blow everyone up—themselves included. The rebels and 129 hostages were killed by the subsequent Russian "rescue." The Dubrovka theater siege ushered in a hostile escalation in the Chechens' ten-year fight against the Russian state.

In August 2003, Chechen rebels killed 43 people when they attacked a Russian military hospital. Although the Chechens attacked military and political targets, rebel assaults—which increasingly involve civilians—have undercut the Kremlin's effort to portray the situation in the war-shattered region as *stabilized*. According to *New York Times* reporter Stephen Myers, this may indicate desperation, a sign that the Chechens are losing the war, "unable to control territory or fight Russian forces head-on, they have increasingly resorted to suicide attacks."[35] Michael Wines agreed: "as Russian forces have largely neutralized the guerrillas' ability to wage organized battles, the bombings have become more deadly and spectacular."[36] If these assessments are correct, they suggest that for the Chechen guerrillas, the demonstration effect of spectacular suicide bombings outweigh their potentially counterproductive effects on public opinion. However another argument can be made that under specific circumstances, suicide terror will be very productive if the average Chechen perceives the tactic as an appropriate response. Like in the Palestinian territories, Russian abuses and the indiscriminate use of military force, *zachiskti*, inflame the resistance groups.

> [Diplomacy] is a dead end, since without pulling out Russian troops that loot and execute civilians it is impossible to rebuild the economy and social life in Chechnya. . . . In the meantime, it is clear that the Chechen resistance cannot be effectively eliminated. . . . If atrocities committed by federal troops against Chechen civilians come to an end it could be the first step in stabilizing Chechnya. But . . . extrajudicial kidnappings and executions by the Russian military continue. . . . In an interview with Rossia television on April 24, Dudayev said that 219 Chechen civilians were kidnapped by Russian troops since January. Seventy-nine Chechens were abducted in April alone. This approach to the Chechen problem is only counter-productive for Russia. Following its current line, the Kremlin will never eliminate the terrorist threat to Russia . . .[37]

It appears that the initial usage of suicide terror in Chechnya was just the tip of the iceberg in what has become an increasingly deadly tactic over time and increasingly focused on civilian versus military targets The contagion effect in Chechnya revolves around its link to the mujahideen training camps in Afghanistan, financial support from Arab governments, and possible al Qaeda connections to the Chechen rebels. This link to international terrorism is alleged by government officials. "Russian officials have argued that there is a 'Palestinization' of the conflict—proof of the links they claim exist between Chechnya and international terrorism."[38]

> The leaders of the Chechen separatists use the propaganda experience of other Islamic groups that have their websites on the Internet. A proclamation, which is most likely copied from texts written in the Middle East, [which] became very popular among Chechens. They assert that it is a "sisters' duty" to help Mujahideen—even on the battlefield.[39]

Trenin argues that there is a potential demonstration effect from Chechnya to other parts of the Russian Federation—that repercussions exist for Dagestan, Ingushetia, and states in the Southern Caucasus.[40] Sergei Yastrzhembsky, President Putin's senior advisor on Chechnya, and other officials have provided evidence of links to international terrorism. However, they know little about how the suicide attacks have been planned, organized and carried out.

The Chechen leader, Shamil Besayev, has led open military raids into neighboring Dagestan and taking refuge in Nazran, Ingushetia—presiding over a brazen raid on police and government targets which left more than 90 dead in that republic. Besayev took 1,500 hostages and the Russian authorities blame him for the attack in Beslan in North Ossetia that led to the deaths of 329 hostages. According to the Kremlin, the 32 terrorists at Beslan were a mixed group including Arabs, possibly from Syria or Jordan and several people from Ingushetia and allegedly some Kazakhs in addition to the Chechens. (However, many of the hostages denied that there were any Arabs in the group.) There were 1,181 hostages held in the school including children, their pre-school siblings, mothers and fathers, grandfathers and grandmothers, teachers, the school's administrative staff, and people who lived in the building's immediate vicinity. Besayev was reported to be giving the orders via phone.[41]

Long before events unfolded in Baghdad between U.S. forces and Iraqi insurgents, Besayev had perfected the use of roadside bombings directed against Russian military convoys and rocket propelled grenade attacks in which guerrillas blended back into the civilian population after the initial attack. Besayev is also credited with taking over hospitals, hijacking planes, assassinating a pro-Moscow Chechen leader and training fleets of female snipers and suicide bombers.

There exists an indirect contagion effect, one of a positively reinforced demonstration from one conflict to another. Palestinian women have been inspired to commit their acts of martyrdom by these Chechen women. According to some sources, the inspiration among women flows in the other direction.

> Arab mercenaries are preparing female suicide bombers for terror acts in Chechnya . . . According to [Russian Intelligence sources], no less than 30 women, most of them are wives or relatives of Chechen rebels and even field commanders, are currently being prepared in training camps located, primarily, in the mountainous regions of Chechnya. They are being prepared by Arab instructors from Khattab's gang. Female terrorists, who have completed the course, have already conducted a number of attacks . . .[42]

Thus it is difficult to discern who has influenced whom. Although many analysts have used the term "Palestinization" of Chechnya, it was Chechen women who provided the template for Palestinian women to beseech their leaders to permit female martyrdom operations. In several letters to Hamas, women argued if suicide terror was permitted for Chechen women they too should be permitted to participate.

Significant for feminist theory, there has been a transition in women's roles in conflict from that of the *revolutionary womb* (giving birth to future fighters), to the *exploding womb*—using the IED (Improvised Explosive Device) in such a way as to mimic pregnancy to avoid detection. Women's role in the Chechen resistance appears to be a growing one. In the summer of 2004, women were once again at the forefront of suicide terror. In August: "Amanat Nagayeva and Satsita Dzhbirkhanova checked in for two flights leaving Domodedovo Airport near Moscow and, according to Russian officials, detonated explosives that brought down both airliners, killing 90 people. A week after those bombings, a woman believed to be Ms. Nagayeva's younger sister, Roza, blew herself up outside a Moscow subway, killing at least 10 people."[43]

Significantly, between two and four women were among the attackers in the rebel siege of Middle School No. 1 in Beslan, in North Ossetia, though they were not identified. Since the airplane bombers' roommate, Mariyam Taburova, remained at large there was no way of knowing how many women had been or would be involved in future terror attacks.

Chechens themselves have not embraced a cult of religious martyrdom, as have, for example, many Palestinians in the Occupied Territories, insurgents in Iraq, or groups like al Qaeda. In Grozny, there are neither posters nor graffiti celebrating the martyrs. Chechen Imams do not preach fiery sermons revering them although Shamil Besayev is often compared positively to the legendary Chechen warrior priest, Imam Shamil, who led a twenty year guerrilla war against Imperial Russia in the mid-1800s and made his last stand near the village of Vedeno, Besayev's birthplace. Initially a secular nationalist, Besayev became radicalized by reading militant Saudi and Pakistani religious tracks and incorporating Arab veterans of the Soviet War in Afghanistan into the Chechen ranks. Besayev even talked of taking the fight beyond the borders of Chechnya to establish a pan-Islamic state across the northern Caucasus. That Besayev's *Slakhin Riadus Shahidi* organization would go to the extreme measure of taking children as hostages was foreshadowed by the takeover of the hospital in Buddenovsk in 1995 but only 10 hostages were killed then as compared to 329.[44]

The preliminary reports of the events at Beslan in which more than 300 children and their parents died, indicate that the Chechens might have gone too far. The attacks appear to be alienating the larger public. According to the reports sentiment, even among Chechens, was decidedly unsupportive. The attack "exposed the deep schisms that are tearing apart Chechnya, where few people interviewed here spoke warmly of Russia or the Kremlin, but where all expressed horror at the bombings, the school siege and other attacks carried out for the sake of Chechnya's independence."[45]

The use of suicide terror as a tactic and women operatives spread beyond Russia's border to Uzbekistan and the Islamic Movement of Uzbekistan (IMU). From Chechnya, the intersection between crime and terror has spread into neighboring countries, helped by porous borders and political infighting. The Pankisi Gorge which links Chechnya and Georgia and the Kadori Gorge, a valley situated between Georgia and the irredentist region of Abkhazia, has a thriving smuggling industry.

With the Fergana Valley as a transit point, Afghans have transferred weapons and personnel into Central Asia. They use the valley as a transshipment point for drugs produced in Afghanistan en route for sale in Europe, the proceeds of which go to al Qaeda to finance terrorist operations. Groups in Afghanistan use opium-derived income to arm, train, and support fundamentalist groups including the IMU and the Chechen resistance. Another narcotics route is via Turkey to the Balkans (Bosnia and Kosovo), where the drugs can then be marketed to Western Europe. Colombia has experienced a similar pattern, with both leftist and rightist terrorist groups protecting coca fields and cocaine processing facilities in return for a share of the proceeds. The "brown zones," represented by offshore banking centers, facilitate the interconnection of terrorist groups with the narcotics trade by allowing terrorist groups to deposit funds and use them later on.[46]

A series of violent incidents and suicide terror attacks struck Uzbekistan on March 28–30, 2004, leaving 40 people dead. Among the suicide bombers were several women who wore veils and allegedly spoke some incomprehensible Central Asian language. The first explosion, near a children's store at the market entrance where policeman usually gathered, killed seven policemen and a female suicide bomber whose torso was blown off. A second female suicide bomber reportedly blew herself up at the Chorsu bus stop, killing a small girl and wounding a policeman.[47]

Islam Karimov, the Uzbek President, asserted that extremists received foreign assistance. Uzbekistan has been a strong supporter of the U.S. led campaign in Afghanistan, providing a vital airbase for U.S. troops in military operations there following the September 11, 2001 attacks. Uzbek Foreign Minister Sadyk Safayev said the attacks were aimed at breaking the anti-terror coalition similar to the attacks in Madrid. Safayev added that the attacks "were committed by the forces of international terror," and "showed the hallmark of acts [we have already] witnessed abroad." Rashid Kadyrov, the Uzbek Prosecutor-General, blamed Hizb ut-Tahrir, Wahhabis, and the Islamic Movement of Uzbekistan.[48]

For Aleksei Malashenko of the Carnegie Moscow Center, "In addition to the goals set by al Qaeda and other international Islamist organizations, there was another goal here—to show Karimov and the entire Uzbek establishment that they're not the sole rulers of the country. Uzbek Islamist terrorists are trying to influence the domestic situation and pursuing their own goals."[49]

It appears that one of the motives for the attack was to spark a general uprising. Since the main targets of the violence were the police, those who perpetrated the terror attacks hoped to obtain popular understanding and support—given most people's attitude towards the police. But the vast majority of Uzbeks, however much that they viewed the police force as corrupt and brutal, repudiated the attacks. For journalist Sergei Yezhkov, the plan to incite the population misfired.[50] Thus, it is precisely the role played by domestic politics and the impact of public opinion, which constrains the popularity of violent tactics and underscores the limits of contagion.

A global diffusion of terrorism is evident. New suicide bombers have been reported in locations as far from Palestine and Chechnya as Indonesia, the Philippines, and Malaysia. Young students in Islamic private schools are urged to aspire toward suicide terror throughout Southeast Asia. The impact of early education and the role played by Madrassahs, Pesantrens, and Government schools was documented by the 9/11 Commission report. The question is not only how suicide terror spreads but also where the roots of this terrorism lay and how to remove the continuing sources of inspiration.

However, I have argued earlier in this book that suicide terror is not linked to any particular region, culture, or religion and should not be viewed purely as an Islamic phenomenon even if so many of the groups engaged in suicide terror happen to be Muslim. The effective use of suicide terror in non-Islamic contexts like Latin America and Sri Lanka should disabuse those pundits who view suicide terrorism as the clash of Western versus Muslim cultures or civilizations or as something inherently perverse in the Islamic faith.

DIFFUSION TO LATIN AMERICA?

Suicide terror has even had an impact on Latin America. According to a RAND study, among the most dangerous terrorist groups operating today (along with al Qaeda and the Palestinian Hamas) is the FARC (*Fuerzas Armadas Revolucionarias de Colombia*), a Marxist guerrilla organization that had previously refrained from suicide terror.[51] According to Kalyvas and Sánchez-Cuenca, the FARC attempted to duplicate the September 11 attacks to sabotage the inauguration ceremony for the incoming President Alvaro Uribe. The police foiled the FARC's plan to hire a pilot who would crash a plane into the Presidential Palace. Lacking volunteers, the FARC offered to compensate the family of the pilot with two million dollars and sought pilots from among former members of the Medellin drug cartel.[52] The organization exploded several bombs around the Presidential Palace—killing 17 people and injuring 65 others on the day Uribe took office. And though the FARC did not crash any planes into buildings that day, they have used human bombs since 1998. That year, the FARC concealed two grenades in the body of a dead soldier when a corpse was moved by the army to Bogotá by helicopter and the grenades detonated. Since then, the FARC has employed this technique several times, occasionally using the bodies of children or animals.[53] IRA members are allegedly training the FARC on the use of car bombs and other IEDs (Improvised Explosive Devices) to be used against government forces and state interests. What is particularly interesting is that the Irish police are training the Colombian police while the IRA trains the FARC.[54]

The FARC has used car bombs with great efficacy in Arauca, Colombia. On January 8, 2003, a car exploded as it approached a military base in Arauquita, killing one and wounding four. On January 9, a car drove into a military checkpoint in Fortul killing four and injuring 15. A military checkpoint in Tame was attacked two days later, resulting in four deaths and 14 wounded.[55]

In Peru, the Shining Path (*Sendero Luminoso*) has used children and booby-trapped animals during its urban terror campaign.[56] It is significant to note that while the FARC has been effective in using an array of suicide terror techniques, it has generally focused its attacks on military rather than random civilian targets. In this way, the FARC is able to maximize its use of violence but not alienate the civilian population whose support is crucial for its success.

DOGS THAT DIDN'T BARK: THE LIMITS OF CONTAGION

In examining how suicide terror spreads so rapidly within the context of religious or nationalist struggles, it is useful to explain why it has failed to take root in other cases of conflict. We need to examine the ways in which the surrounding community accepts or rejects it as a stratagem. Thus there is a limit to the degree to which the contagion effect can infect further conflicts.

In the cases of Ireland and Spain, public opinion rejected the use of civilian casualties, including the rejection of suicide terror. This led the IRA to alter tactics that involved civilian deaths resulting from their bombing campaigns. According to Richard English, the IRA switched tactics in the aftermath of events in Derry on January 30, 1972 (Bloody Sunday), and the subsequent whitewashing of British responsibility, which produced greater support for violence, a hardening of views, and decreased possibilities for compromise or reconciliation.[57] Nevertheless even against the backdrop of extreme outrage, support for civilian casualties were not widespread among rank-and-file Irish separatists.

Supporters of the Irish Republican Army tended toward greater moderation than the organizations and rejected the indiscriminate attacks of civilians. IRA leader Sean MacStoifan was oft quoted as saying that "terrorists are actors and their activities are performed as an operational drama with the world as an audience." To that end, symbolic attacks were far more valuable to the IRA and civilian casualties did not resonate positively the way attacking British military targets did. In Spain, the ETA never made civilians indiscriminate targets on the scale of the March 11, 2004, train bombings. Its highest known death toll was 21 persons in June of 1987, when it attacked a Barcelona supermarket in what it later termed a "mistake." Furthermore, the group has often telephoned warnings about imminent strikes.[58]

Were the ETA or the IRA engaged in the indiscriminate bombings, support among important sectors of the nationalist community would wane and the pool of volunteers would likely shrink. In fact, these organizations are well aware of the feelings of revulsion that some particularly bloody, brutal attacks provoke among supporters: this explains why ETA or the IRA have denied responsibility for some of the worst attacks they have carried out.[59]

On March 4, 1972 a provisional IRA bomb exploded in a packed Belfast Abercorn Restaurant. Two young women were killed and 136 others injured; some of the injuries were truly horrific, according to English. The IRA denied responsibility for the attack.[60] Additional examples of denying responsibility include a bomb that exploded without warning in a restaurant on Railway Street in Coleraine on June 12, 1973 killing two women and injuring over a hundred customers; three car bombs that exploded on July 31, 1972 on Main street in Claudy without warning, killing nine; May 17, 1974, UVF bombs exploded in Dublin and Monaghan killing 33, and the IRA alleged that the British Intelligence was ultimately responsible; two pubs in Surrey on October 5, 1974 which killed five; two pubs in Birmingham (the Mulberry Bush and the Tavern in the Town) exploded on November 21, 1974, killing 19 people and injuring 182;[61] and a bomb exploded outside of Harrods department store in London on December 18, 1983, killing six. The IRA issued a statement explaining that, "while the Army Council did not authorize this specific operation at Harrods, we do not believe that the Volunteers involved set out to deliberately kill civilians."[62]

Even Nationalists repudiated such tactics likening the atrocity in Claudy to the events of Bloody Sunday in Derry. Nationalist MP Ivan Cooper said, "This incident can only be equated with what happened on Bloody Sunday. I cannot express words strong enough to condemn the people responsible for this terrible outrage." The horrific nature of the 1974 pub bombings offset intended IRA gains, such was the popular outrage, and it was eleven years before the IRA admitted responsibility for the campaign.[63]

During the reign of terror in Ireland, "terrorists raised the stakes after each new defensive measure was put into place by employing ever more potent weapons and tactics. That in turn led to a hardening of potential targets after each attack."[64] Sean MacStiofain wrote that "No resistance movement in history has ever succeeded in fighting a struggle for national freedom without some accidental casualties, but the Republican interest in retaining popular support clearly lay in causing as few as possible."[65] Eamon Collins argued that the IRA acted with constraint: "the IRA fought with one hand behind its back: in general it did not carry out the indiscriminate campaign of all-out war which it would have been capable of fighting." He added that the IRA "sought to avoid any operations which had obviously sectarian overtones: a policeman could be justified as a legitimate target, his non-combatant Protestant family could not."[66] Attacks against civilians did not resonate positively with the rank-and-file supporters of the IRA. The few spectacular bombings guaranteed greater approbation than appreciation. Kalyvas and Sanchez-Cuenca explain why this was the case:

> IRA Suicide missions were quickly ruled out after the community's indignation became clear.... the vast majority of Catholics in Derry were sickened by the attack and no doubt let the IRA know what they thought. Likewise ... the IRA stopped the practice of targeting civilians due to its counterproductive consequences in terms of public support.... Gerry Adams explained the degree to which the IRA depended on the community support: "In a war zone it is a necessity, if nothing else, to force the republican movement into a complete and utter reliance on the people's support."[67]

The IRA abandoned violence against civilians when they observed public reaction to Derry, the 1974 pub bombings, and Omagh. In the initial phases, the IRA had been fairly disorganized and divided along a number of subgroups. Within a few years, the IRA worked out a system with the British police wherein they would call in bomb threats prior to the bomb exploding in order to minimize civilian deaths. This covert alert system was necessary because random phone tips initially caused anarchy and thus the IRA and the British police worked out this prearranged system. [68]

There were a few instances in which the IRA attempted to use suicide car bombings as a tactic. However, rather than use dedicated supporters, they employed captured Ulster Orangemen to drive cars laden with explosives into military and police targets in a series of bombings in central London and the city of Manchester in 1996. The tactic was rejected by the larger Catholic community and eventually abandoned.[69]

In Spain, the ETA denied responsibility for civilian deaths when a bomb exploded in a restaurant on September 13, 1974 killing 13 people and injuring over 70. The ETA likewise disavowed its bloodiest attack when a bomb exploded a supermarket in Barcelona that killed 21 people and injured 40 on June 19, 1987. This action was rejected not only by the more diffuse community, but also by Basque hard-liners. As a former member of ETA said: "We really fucked it up. I think there is a wide feeling among a lot of people that can be described as 'These guys [the terrorists] don't care at all.' Fuck, we messed up!"[70] Thus, when the Spanish government attempted to lay the blame of the Madrid train bombings on March 11, 2004, in which 191 people were killed and almost 1,500 injured on the ETA, most analysts were skeptical. (See photo 6.)

The IRA and ETA have always been very close in thinking and style—although ETA has always been the junior partner. IRA figures said that the ETA was more likely to pursue an Ulster-style peace process. ETA saw what happened to the Real IRA after the Omagh bombing—it lost its support and became an international pariah. I can't believe ETA would follow that tactic.[71]

The contagion effect of suicide terror and mass killing is inherently limited by how the tactic is received by the community the terrorists represent. In some cases, there is widespread support for violence regardless of whether civilians are involved or not. This has important ramifications for the current war on terror. The reactions in the aftermath of 9/11 certainly represent a spectrum of support and repudiation. What was interesting at the time and remains so is that support or repudiation was not linked to which countries had good relations with the United States and which ones were considered rogue states. There were prayer vigils and candlelight ceremonies in Teheran and yet conspiracy theories of Israeli or American complicitness were rampart in Cairo and Riyadh.

TRENDS AFTER SEPTEMBER 11TH

The events of 9/11 are part of a larger trend toward the increasing lethality in suicide terrorism. We see the increasing violence in Palestine and in Chechnya, the development of more sophisticated technologies in the IED, and the tactical use of women, which always yields more casualties and more publicity. This trend stands in stark contrast to previous acts which wedded suicide and politics such as IRA hunger strikes, the Brahmin self-immolations of the twentieth century, and hundreds of immolations by high-caste students in the 1990s in Ambala and Luknow against the Mandal commission—acts in which the person committed suicide but did not kill anyone else in the process. In the previous trend, the only casualty was the militant himself or herself.[72]

There are fewer symbolic acts, conducted in a measured manner either for bargaining purposes or to extract specific concessions such as the release of prisoners. The current tendency is simply to punish a perceived adversary or cause generalized fear. There is no way to anticipate all of the potential reactions to suicide terror. Nevertheless, certain trends have emerged in the last few years which might actually have unintended negative consequences for the groups that utilize suicide terror to tactical advantage. By failing to discriminate civilians from military casualties, suicide terror can potentially alienate the population the terrorists purport to represent and turn some people against them. For example, Palestinian suicide missions have repeatedly killed Israeli Arabs, Chechen attacks have killed other Chechens, the World Trade Center attack killed Muslims and, the al Qaeda suicide attacks in Riyadh and Casablanca (May 24, 2003) and Istanbul (November 2003) killed many other Muslims or Arabs.[73] The tactic has spread from the Middle East and South Asia to Southeast Asia (the Philippines, Bali), and Western Europe (Spain and preempted attacks in Great Britain—see figure 6.1 in the appendix).

Setbacks have forced al Qaeda to alter its targeting patterns. "Displaced and harried, its operatives must now rely on local groups to carry out their plans and, as a result, have focused on 'softer,' more accessible targets, in places as diverse as Tunisia, Pakistan, Jordan, Indonesia, Kuwait, the Philippines, Yemen, and Kenya. These have included German, Australian, and Israeli tourists; French engineers and a French oil tanker; and such long-standing targets as U.S. diplomats and servicemen."[74]

After the suicide bombings in Istanbul, the Turkish military and intelligence determined to "liquidate"(their term) the perpetrators of the November 2003 attacks. Strong Turkish nationalist sentiments fed popular anger at al Qaeda and "the Wahhabis" for these attacks. The individual bombers were Turkish nationals who were previously affiliated with the extremist Islamic groups in Turkey (Hizb'allah), talent-scouted by al Qaeda when they expressed dissatisfaction with the local agenda, sent to various well known training camps for further indoctrination, and fed back into Turkey. Consistent with this argument regarding public acceptance or revulsion, even the Turkish religious leaders have condemned the perpetrators "in this world and the next one!"[75]

It is impossible to analyze the contagion effect of suicide terror without acknowledging the role played by al Qaeda and the Soviet invasion of Afghanistan. Innumerable terrorists passed through the Mujahideen training camps throughout the 1980s during the war in Afghanistan. The second wave of attacks showed that the smaller organizations, most of whose leaders were trained in al Qaeda camps in Afghanistan, have fanned out, imbued with radical ideology and the means to create or revitalize local terrorist groups. The main link between these small groups is their shared experiences in the training camps. Approximately 20,000 people from 47 countries passed through the camps in the mid-1990s until the U.S. invasion in October 2001. "Osama bin Laden's network, now run largely by midlevel operatives, relies increasingly on these groups to carry out jihad, or holy war, against the United States and its allies. Al Qaeda has turned to inspiring and instigating such attacks."[76]

The 2001 trial of Madji Hasan Idris, an Egyptian member of the Al Wa'd organization, revealed the extent to which terrorism has adopted a global business model.

Al Wa'd would send young Egyptian recruits to camps in Kosovo or Pakistan and then dispatch them to serve in the Philippines, Kashmir, or wherever else they were needed after their training and indoctrination were complete. Cell phones and e-mail kept the network in constant contact, while couriers provided cash advances, airplane tickets, and passports to facilitate operations. The objectives of terrorist organizations such as al Qaeda and the symbiotic organized-crime networks that help sustain these groups are also not confined territorially or ideologically to a particular region. They are instead explicitly global in orientation.[77]

The tactical spread of terror as well as al Qaeda's diffusion of capital and unofficial financing networks (often called Hawala networks) came to light in the aftermath of 9/11. Al Qaeda members have taught individuals from other groups how to use the Internet to send messages and how to encrypt those communications to avoid detection. Bomb and chemical-making techniques have been passed around.[78] One can trace the financial links between the groups as diverse as the IRA and Iraq, the LTTE and the Palestinians, Hizb'allah and Iran, and the Saudis and Abu Sayyaf in the Philippines.

Much of al Qaeda financing derives from charitable organizations subsumed under its structural umbrella. An extensive investigation of the connections between charitable trusts and terrorist financing is being undertaken by the U.S. government and various international intelligence agencies. The links are extensive and overlapping.[79] It is exceedingly difficult to differentiate between the charitable works of groups and their more radical, militant wings who engage in acts of terrorism against civilians. The distinction is an important one in places like Sri Lanka and the Palestinian Territories where the population suffers from extreme poverty and economic stagnation—both breeding grounds for yet more terrorism. The crux of the problem remains that financial contributions to such areas by terrorist groups enhance their organizational profile. Preventing money from going to these areas may also contribute to an atmosphere in which terrorism is deemed the only option. A Catch-22 situation thus emerges.

Moreover the financial structure of al Qaeda shifted because of the war in Afghanistan and financial checks on terrorist funding. Globalized terror has a more local focus.

There is no longer a set pool of money from which the groups can draw. There is no longer a fairly knowable group of large donors or entities. Now groups in Indonesia raise money there. Groups in Malaysia raise money there. There are many more targets, and much harder to find.

Many of the local groups, unable to draw on the web of organizations and donors that have supported al Qaeda, rely on petty crime, drug trafficking, and extortion to pay the bills ... because the groups are hitting softer targets in attacks that require less sophistication to carry out, money is not a major obstacle.[80]

Many of the Islamist groups were historically weak and poorly funded—until Bin Laden and his network of sponsors strengthened them militarily and financially. In Chechnya, the Jordanian Arab leader Khattab (an alias) befriended Besayev in Pakistan and traveled to Chechnya funded by Saudi money to establish training camps there. Bin Laden underwrote the establishment of Jihad in Chechnya by contributing $25 million toward the cause after which Chechens were instructed to become self-sufficient, along the model established by the Afghani Mujahideen by linking up with the local criminal economy, generating profits from counterfeiting, kidnapping, the drug trade, and smuggling contraband, especially guns. A full investigation into how these finances contribute to the contagion effect of suicide terror is necessary, but beyond the scope of this present study and awaiting declassification of materials. Allegations of the direct financial involvement of Bin Laden continue even after the war on terror has allegedly disrupted the financial links between al Qaeda and its franchises. One such example is the allegation that al Qaeda bankrolled the attack in Beslan. "President Putin argues that the tactics used by the terrorists are those of al Qaeda, therefore the funding must come from it too."[81] Yet the economic connections together with the ideological influences and tactical training are all inextricably linked to form a contagion and diffusion of suicide terror.

ASSESSING SUCCESS OR FAILURE?

The international repercussions of suicide terror can be either positive or negative. Spectacular bombings might be a method of raising funds, mobilizing support, recruitment, or attracting international attention to a long-forgotten conflict—forcing the international community to place the conflict on the front burner. Terror may potentially backfire, because it alienates a diaspora community or brings down international condemnation upon the group—especially if civilian casualties are excessive. The publicity effect of suicide attacks may be so beneficial as to offset the potential costs. According to a Rand report,[82] LTTE fundraising was positively correlated to spectacular attacks. For instance, after Rajiv Gandhi was assassinated in 1991 or President Kumaratunga was attacked in December 1999, funding from the Tamil Diaspora increased significantly. This strategy appears to have worked well in the Israeli-Palestinian dispute as well in the Chechen civil war, although it has seemingly failed as part of al Qaeda's strategy.

This globalization of terror and the geographic extension of violence beyond the immediate conflict area has made possible, for example, terrorist attacks by Lebanese Hizb'allah against Jewish and Israeli targets in Argentina. A large number of simultaneous bombings were carried out by anti-Indian terrorists in Bombay in 1993 and by the Kurdistan Workers Party, or PKK, in offensives against Turkish targets in Europe in the early 1990s. On August 7, 1998 al Qaeda perpetrated simultaneous bombings of U.S. Embassies in Nairobi, Kenya (in which 247 were killed and 5,500 injured) and Dar Es Salaam, Tanzania (in which 11 died and 51 were injured—see figure 6.2 in the appendix and photo 4).

The links between the groups outlined in this chapter and sharing of information are clear and undisputed although inherently difficult to prove. The number of smoking guns are few and far between. However, the transfer of information from Lebanon to the Palestinians via the Marj al Zahour expellees proves convincing as a form of contagion. Reports exist that LTTE cadres were trained by Palestinians and the Hizb'allah. Therefore it is no coincidence that within a year of the training, suicide bombing was imported to the island in 1987 and was subsequently perfected over the course of more than 200 suicide attacks. Finally, one cannot ignore the proliferation of this tactic in the last decade and the necessity of devising successful strategies to combat the growing global phenomenon of suicide terror.

CHAPTER SEVEN

FEMINISM, RAPE AND WAR:
ENGENDERING SUICIDE TERROR?

"You've come a long way, baby!" Virginia Slims cigarette ads used to read. After years of struggle, the women's movement in the 1970s brought men and women in the first world to a level of relative parity in most areas of employment, status, and opportunities. However, in the rest of the world, the position of women remains seriously disadvantaged compared to that of men. According to a well cited UNDP report, women in Africa and the Middle East suffer most from inequality.[1] In one area, however, women in the developing world seem to be making their mark in achieving parity with men—in perpetrating suicide terrorism. The common stereotype is exploited by terrorists in order to magnify their cause is that women are gentle, submissive and nonviolent. On the one hand, despite the prejudices describing women as good wives and mothers, they are still capable of murder by engaging in suicide terror.[2]

Historically, women have been involved in conflict in supporting roles. Most often, women's primary contribution has been to perpetuate the conflict by giving birth to many fighters and raising them in a revolutionary environment.

> Society, through its body of rules and its numerous institutions, has conventionally dictated [women's] roles within the boundaries of militancy. Assisting in subordinate roles is welcomed and encouraged . . . fighting in the war is not. Yet women have demanded to be integrated in all aspects of war including frontline fighting.[3]

According to many International Relations theories, women are more likely to choose peaceful mechanisms for conflict resolution than men—suggesting that women are inherently more peaceful in their attitudes toward international conflict and are more disposed toward moderation, compromise, and tolerance.[4] What previously seemed highly unlikely because of the existing notions of women as *victims* of war rather than as perpetrators, women are now taking a leading role in conflicts by becoming suicide bombers—using their bodies as human detonators for the explosive material strapped around their waists. To complicate the notions of femininity and motherhood, the Improvised Explosive Device (IED) is often disguised under the women's clothing to make her appear as if she is pregnant and thus beyond suspicion or reproach. The advent of women suicide bombers has transformed the revolutionary womb into an exploding one. Approximately 17 groups have started using the tactical innovation of suicide bombing, women have been operatives in more than half of them in the Middle East, in Sri Lanka, in Turkey, in Chechnya, and in Colombia.[5]

Why? Motives vary: revenge for a personal loss, the desire to redeem the family name, to escape a life of sheltered monotony and achieve fame, and to level the patriarchal societies in which they live. What is incredibly compelling about delving into how and why women become suicide bombers is that so many of these women have been raped or sexually abused in the previous conflict either by the representatives of the state or by the insurgents themselves. Targeting women through rape in war has many unintended consequences which I explore elsewhere.[6]

Organizational Benefits

The female suicide bomber is not a new phenomenon in the Middle East. The first female suicide bomber, a 17-year-old Lebanese girl named Sana'a Mehaydali, was sent by the Syrian Socialist National Party (SSNP/PPS), a secular, pro-Syrian Lebanese organization, to blow herself up near an Israeli convoy in Lebanon in 1985. Out of 12 suicide attacks conducted by the SSNP, women took part in five of them. From Lebanon female bombers spread to other countries from Sri Lanka to Turkey, Chechnya, and Israel. The upsurge in the number of female bombers has come from both secular and religious organizations.

Israel's restrictive checkpoints and border policy proved fairly effective against Palestinian insurgent organizations inside the Occupied Territories. Since the mid 1990s, it has been almost impossible for unmarried men under the age of 40 to get legitimate permits to cross the border into Israel—for any reason. Terrorist groups have therefore looked further afield for volunteers including women and even children. Women don't arouse suspicion like men and blend in more effectively with Israeli citizens.

Attacks perpetrated by women have tended to be those where the terrorist planners needed the perpetrator to blend in on the Israeli "street."

These female terrorists . . . westernize their appearance, adopting modern hairstyles and short skirts.[7]

The use of the least-likely suspect is the most-likely tactical adaptation for a terrorist group under scrutiny. A growing number of insurgent organizations have adopted suicide bombing not only because of its tactical superiority to traditional guerrilla warfare, but also because suicide bombing, especially when perpetrated by women and young girls, garners significant media attention. There has been a significant public relations boon to sending, for example, 18-year-old Ayat Akras, into the Supersol supermarket to set off a bomb.[8] Young women combating Israel by blowing up their bodies is a powerful image that generates more press. The image of women, defying tradition to sacrifice their lives for the Palestinian cause, has drawn more attention to the despair of the Palestinian people. "Suicide attacks are done for effect, and the more dramatic the effect, the stronger the message; thus a potential interest on the part of some groups in recruiting women."[9] The Al Aqsa Martyrs' Brigades have drawn propaganda mileage from their female bombers. This tactic also makes them appear more threatening since it has erased the barriers between combatants and noncombatants, terrorists, and innocent civilians.

The underlying message conveyed by female bombers is: Terrorism has moved beyond a fringe phenomenon and insurgents are all around you. Akras' death demonstrated that the Palestinian secular militant groups are not all composed of religious fanatics who necessarily believe they will be granted entrance to paradise or because God will reward them with 72 virgins (*houris*). Nor are the organizations' leaders gripped by a burning desire to see all females locked behind black veils. This is a political war, not a religious war; and the suicide bombings are being carefully planned and executed as a part of a precise political strategy.[10]

Until recently, a female bomber was almost certainly sent by a secular organization. The campaign by Chechnya's Al Ansar al Mujahideen provided the first hint of a blurring of a religious inspired militant organization and the use of female operatives.

The growth in the number of Chechen female suicide bombers signaled the beginning of a change in the position of fundamentalist Islamic organizations regarding the involvement of women in suicide attacks—a change that [has since] become devastatingly apparent.[11]

The use of women by insurgent organizations can mobilize greater numbers of operatives and shame men into participating. This has parallels to right-wing Hindu women who goad men into action through speeches saying "don't be a bunch of eunuchs."[12] This point is underscored by the bombers themselves. A propaganda slogan in Chechnya reads: "Women's courage is a disgrace to that of modern men."[13] Before Ayat Akras blew herself up, she taped her martyrdom video and stated, "*I am going to fight* [emphasis added] instead of the sleeping Arab armies who are watching Palestinian girls fighting alone," in an apparent jab at Arab leaders for not being sufficiently proactive or manly.[14]

INDIVIDUAL MOTIVATIONS

When men conduct suicide missions, they are motivated by religious or nationalist fanaticism, whereas women appear more often motivated by very personal reasons. In Chechnya, the female operatives called "Black Widows"—operatives who have lost a loved one—are mobilized by their personal tragedy.

> Zarema Mazhikhoyeva, a widow from Ingushetia, was arrested as she walked along 1st Tverskaya Yamskaya Ulitsa on July 10, 2003, carrying a homemade bomb. In an interview published in *Izvestia*, Mazhikhoyeva agreed to be recruited by Chechen rebels as a suicide bomber, in exchange for $1,000 in compensation to her relatives to repay for jewelry she had stolen from them. . . . When the rebels sent her to Moscow to carry out her mission, she changed her mind and got herself arrested by police.[15]

Mazhikhoyeva was the first bomber to be captured alive. When the court convicted her and gave her the maximum sentence of twenty years regardless of the fact that she had voluntarily opted not to explode her cargo, Zarema shouted, "Now I know why everyone hates the Russians!"—adding that she would return and "blow you all up."[16]

Palestinian women have likewise suffered personal losses and some feel that becoming a martyr is their sole expression of outrage. Palestinian women are also motivated by the desire to recover their family honor. Tamil women allegedly raped by the Sinhalese security services and military at check points join the Tamil Tigers, joining the "birds of paradise" unit of Black Tigresses, while Kurdish women allegedly raped in Turkey by the military joined the PKK. Additionally, the insurgent organizations may provide a potential avenue for advancement beyond what their traditional societies offer.

> There is a difference between men and women suicide attackers: women consider combat as a way to escape the predestined life that is expected of them. When women become human bombs, their intent is to make

a statement not only in the name of a country, a religion, a leader, but also in the name of their gender.[17]

Women are not new to insurgent or terrorist activities. Revolutionary women in radical secular organizations have engaged in anti-colonial and revolutionary struggles in the Third World and elsewhere. Female terrorists have come from all parts of the globe; Italy's Red Brigades, Germany's Baader-Meinhof faction, The Black Panthers, the Weathermen, and the Japanese Red Army—occasionally even as leaders in their own right. Women have played vital support roles in the Algerian Revolution (1958–1962), the Revolution in Iran (1979),[18] in the War in Lebanon (1982), the First Palestinian Intifada (1987–1991) and the current Al Aqsa Intifada (since 2000). Women have supported the revolution, constructed the identities and ideologies of children, and funneled arms and ammunition to the men. In a few instances, women have been on the front lines of combat demonstrating that their revolutionary and military zeal is no less than that of the men. Even Al Qaeda has used women but only for fulfilling tasks in the rear.

Palestinian women have been implicated in terrorism for more than thirty years. Dalal Maghribi was involved in one of the worst terrorist incidents in Israel's history when more than thirty passengers were massacred in a bus hijacking in March 1978. In 1970, Leila Khaled, was caught after attempting to hijack an El Al flight to London. In her book, she explains a woman's rationale. For Khaled, violence was a way of leveling the patriarchal society through revolutionary zeal—the women would demonstrate that their commitment was no less than those of their brothers, sons, or husbands. Strategically, women were able to gain access to areas where men had greater difficulty because the other side assumed that the women were second class citizens in their own society—dumb, illiterate perhaps, and incapable of planning an operation.[19] According to Khaled in an interview with the *Corriere Della Sera*, "We [Palestinians] are under attack . . . [and] women are ready to sacrifice themselves for the national struggle for the respect of just rights."[20] Men gained prestige and status from sustained militancy, "women gain status if they go beyond what is expected and achieve martyrdom or are wounded, carry out incredibly heroic acts, or abide by high moral standards."[21]

According to some authors, women have been radicalized because the Israeli Defense Forces (IDF) and the security apparatus, the Shin Bet, have deliberately targeted them in specific ways as to exploit the patriarchal divisions within their society.[22]

Suha describes a recent incident—one among many, she says—when she was traveling between the West Bank cities of Nablus and Ramallah. She says an Israeli soldier forced her and a man to sit in the dirt at a checkpoint for an hour. He gave them no reason for the delay. "He started by verbally abusing me. The way he was looking at my ID card was humiliating, not to mention the [sexual] passes (that Israeli soldiers) make at us women," she says. "Life is worth nothing when [we] are being humiliated on a daily basis."[23]

In Turkey and Sri Lanka, women's militant activism has a different history—women have participated fully in the early stages of the political resistance at all levels. Women in Sri Lanka fight on the front lines and have their own military units in the LTTE. Palestinian women's participation as suicide bombers or those in Chechnya emerged recently,[24] and against all expectations. In the past, only secular nationalist organizations like the LTTE, Al-Aqsa Martyr's Brigades, or the PKK permitted women to be suicide bombers. Islamic religious organizations, like Hamas, initially refused to permit women to become martyrs and turned at least one woman away (Darine Abu Aisha, who joined one of the secular groups and committed the act on their behalf). Although a patriarchal structure dominates all these societies, the degree to which women participate actively or in support roles varies from place to place and appears to be evolving. Nevertheless, women's roles on the front lines of conflict remained the exception rather than rule.

PALESTINIAN SHAHIDAS

The idea of violence empowering women has spread throughout the West Bank and Gaza. This militant involvement by women has had an extreme effect on the existing cultural norms of Palestinian society. Palestinians have long had a cultural set of rules that describe and limit gender roles. These rules have dictated the separation of the sexes and prescribed that women restrict themselves within the private space of the home. Through violence, women have placed themselves on the frontlines, in public, alongside men to whom they are not related. This results in a double trajectory for militant women—convincing society of their valid contributions while at the same time reconstructing the normative ideals of the society.[25]

Palestinian women have torn the gender classification out of their birth certificates, declaring that sacrifice for the Palestinian homeland would not be for men alone; on the contrary, all Palestinian women will write the history of the liberation with their blood, and will become time bombs in the face of the Israeli enemy. They will not settle for being mothers of martyrs.[26]

The first Palestinian woman to perpetrate an act of suicide terror on January 27, 2002, Wafa Idris, belonged to a secular organization. She was a 27-year-old aid worker for the Palestinian Red Crescent Society from the Al-Am'ari refugee camp near Ramallah. Her death was allegedly accidental. She was carrying a backpack with explosive materials on her way to deliver it to someone else, but it detonated when she got stuck in a revolving door.[27] The public reaction to her death inspired other women to emulate what she did and transformed her into a cult heroine.

> The bomb in her rucksack was made with TNT packed into pipes. Triacetone triperoxide, made by mixing acetone with phosphate, is ground to a powder. In a grotesque parody of the domestic female stereotype, it is usually ground in a food mixer, before being fed into metal tubes.[28]

She killed one Israeli civilian and wounded approximately 140 others. The military wing of Fatah, the Al-Aqsa Martyrs' Brigades, took responsibility for the attack three days later. Bir Zeit students appealed for more women to emulate Wafa Idris. Commenting on Idris' death, women students were quoted as saying, "the struggle is not limited strictly to men. . . . It's unusual [for a Palestinian woman to martyr herself], but I support it. . . . Society does not accept this idea because it is relatively new, but after it happens again, it will become routine."[29]

Idris' death caused a great deal of publicity throughout the Arab World. In an editorial entitled, "It's a Woman!" *Al-Sha'ab* proclaimed:

> It is a woman who teaches you today a lesson in heroism, who teaches you the meaning of Jihad, and the way to die a martyr's death. It is a woman who has shocked the enemy, with her thin, meager, and weak body. . . . It is a woman who blew herself up, and with her exploded all the myths about women's weakness, submissiveness, and enslavement. . . . It is a woman who has now proven that the meaning of [women's] liberation is the liberation of the body from the trials and tribulations of this world . . . and the acceptance of death with a powerful, courageous embrace.[30]

The Al-Aqsa Martyrs Brigade even set up a special unit to train female suicide bombers and named it after Wafa Idris.[31] "We have 200 young women from the Bethlehem area alone ready to sacrifice themselves for the homeland," according to one Al-Aqsa leader.[32] After Idris' death, Palestinian women began begging the Islamic authorities to be more involved in armed conflict; Matti Steinberg describes how Hamas' bi-monthly publication—

dedicated to women—was replete with letters to the editor from Palestinian women to permit their direct participation in the conflict and asserted their right to be martyrs.[33]

The Islamic leadership initially opposed women's activism and banned women from becoming suicide bombers on their behalf; only a handful of clerics endorsed the operations. The Saudi High Islamic Council gave the go ahead for women to be suicide bombers in August 2001 after a 23-year-old Palestinian mother of two was seized by Israeli security as she brought explosives to Tel Aviv's central bus station. Religious leaders in Palestine disagreed regarding the role of women in martyrdom operations. A theological debate rages as to whether women should or could be martyrs and the organizations have been adaptable with regard to permitting women's participation. Several Palestinian leaders gradually accepted women as Shahidas.[34]

Isma'il Abu Shanab, a Hamas leader in Gaza, said, "Jihad against the enemy is an obligation that applies not only to men but also to women. Islam has never differentiated between men and women on the battlefield."[35] Another Hamas leader, Sheikh Hassan Yussef, concurred: "We do not act according to the opinion of the street or of society. We are men of principle. . . . A Muslim woman is permitted to wage Jihad and struggle against the occupation. The Prophet [Muhammad] would draw lots among the women who wanted to go out to wage Jihad with him. The Prophet always emphasized the woman's right to wage Jihad."[36] And according to Jamila Shanti, head of the Women's Activities Division of the Palestine Islamic Movement:

> The issue of martyrdom [operations] has gained much popularity in Palestinian society. There is no difference between the martyrdom of sisters and the martyrdom of brothers, because the enemy [Israel] does not differentiate between firing on men and firing on women. . . . Islam does not prohibit a woman from sacrificing herself to defend her land and her honor. . . . Jihad is a personal imperative for her and no one can prevent her from waging it, provided . . . she avoids fitna [in this case: inappropriate behavior]—Perhaps these activities require the woman to wear a particular garment in order to mislead the enemy, and therefore she may have to relinquish part of her veil when she goes to martyrdom.[37]

Hamas' former spiritual leader, Sheikh Ahmad Yassin, argued that women's appropriate role in the conflict was in supporting the fighters. "In our Palestinian society, there is a flow of women towards Jihad and martyrdom, exactly like the young men. But the woman has uniqueness. Islam sets some restrictions for her, and if she goes out to wage Jihad and fight, she must be accompanied by a male chaperon."[38] Sheikh Yassin further rationalized his reservations—not because of *Shariah* (Islamic religious law), but because women martyrs were unnecessary.

> At the present stage, we do not need women to bear this burden of Jihad and martyrdom. The Islamic Movement cannot accept all the Palestinian males demanding to participate in Jihad and in martyrdom operations, because they are so numerous. Our means are limited, and we cannot absorb all those who desire to confront the enemy.[39]

This situation is alarmingly true. Most of the militant organizations in Palestine cannot fill positions for martyrdom operations fast enough. Nasra Hassan observed this fact years ago.[40]

After January 2002, when Wafa Idris blew up in downtown Jerusalem, Yassin categorically renounced the use of women as suicide bombers or assailants. In March 2002, when another female bomber from Fatah carried out an attack in a Jerusalem supermarket, Yassin said that Hamas was far from enthusiastic about the inclusion of women in warfare, for reasons of modesty. Unlike other organizations, Hamas refrained from using women in front-line roles, but has not hesitated to use them as conduits for money, suicide bombers and ammunition.

Sensing the increasing support for women martyrs and bowing to public pressure and demands, Sheikh Yassin amended his position, saying that a woman waging Jihad must be accompanied by a male chaperon only "if she is to be gone for a day and a night. If her absence is shorter, she does not need a chaperon." In a second statement, Yassin granted a woman's right to launch a suicide attack alone only if it does not take her more than 24 hours to be away from home. This point underscores the irony of Yassin's position, since the female martyr will be away from home for much more than 24 hours if she succeeds in her mission.[41]

Yassin and Sheikh Qardawi found religious justification to allow women's involvement in suicide operations. In the case of Darine Abu Aisheh, she is reported to have gone first to Hamas to volunteer, but was turned down and 'Itaf 'Alayan attempted to carry out a suicide attack in Jerusalem, but was arrested; she was eventually released after the signing of the Oslo Accords.[42] In January 2004, Hamas finally sponsored a female bomber, Reem Riashi, a mother of two. (See photo 10.) Yassin's endorsement of Riashi and encouragement of other Hamas women was part of a campaign to launch Hamas' own line of female suicide bombers. While Yassin pointed out that it was Hamas' armed wing that decided where and when attacks would take place, his comments included quotes from the videotape that Riashi recorded before carrying out her attack, about how she hoped her "organs would be scattered in the air and her soul would reach paradise."[43] Yassin added:

> The fact that a woman took part for the first time in a Hamas operation marks a significant evolution for the Izz Eddin al-Qassam brigades. The male fighters face many obstacles on their way to operations, and this is a new development in our fight against the enemy. The holy war is an imperative for all Muslim men and women; and this operation proves that the armed resistance will continue until the enemy is driven from our land. This is revenge for all the fatalities sustained by the armed resistance.[44]

The Islamic organizations have found justification for shifting their ideological support for women's activism. Sheikh Ali Abu Al-Hassan, chairman of the Religious Ruling Committee at Egypt's Al-Azhar University, stated that suicide attacks by women were permitted, even though the Grand Sheikh of Al-Azhar, Muhammad Sayyid Tantawi, ruled against them. "The martyrdom operation carried out among the Israelis by the young Palestinian woman [Idris] is an act of Jihad permissible according to the Shari'a, and on this there is no disagreement," stated Sheikh Abu Al-Hassan. "If the enemy has conquered and plundered a single inch of Muslim land, Jihad becomes a personal duty of man, woman, slave, and master. [In such a case], the woman wages [Jihad] without her husband's permission, the slave without his master's permission, and the debtor without his creditor's permission."[45] It is interesting to note that each of the relationships mentioned, women are in subordinate, subaltern subject positions.

Sheikh Tantawi then reversed his original opposition and on November 2, 2003 stated that suicide-bombers who are defending their land are seen as martyrs in Islamic Shari'a law. "Anybody blowing himself up in the face of the occupiers of his land is a martyr," said Tantawi. He stressed, however, that Islam did not allow the killing of innocent civilians and children but only invaders and aggressors.[46]

In an interview with Al Jazeera television, Shi'a cleric and the spiritual head of Hizb'allah, Sheikh Muhammad Hussein Fadlallah, stated: "It is true that Islam has not asked women to carry out Jihad, but it *permits them* [emphasis added] to take part if the necessities of defensive war dictate that women should carry out any regular military operations, or suicide operations," he said. "We believe that the women who carry out suicide bombings are martyrs who are creating a new, glorious history for Arab and Muslim women."[47]

The theological refusal of militant Islamic organizations to permit women's participation in suicide bombing evolved. Although Hamas initially rejected the use of female martyrs, Yassin began to shift his ideological opposition slowly, and partly in response to Palestinian women's demands.

> We have entered a new phase of history, in which Palestinian women are willing to fight and to die a martyr's death as the men and youths do. This is from the grace of Allah. But, meanwhile, women have no military organization in the framework of the [Islamic] movement. When such an organization arises, it will be possible to discuss wide-scale recruitment of women.[48]

Hamas lagged behind the Palestinian Islamic Jihad, which in early 2003 launched a campaign to recruit women, and upgraded its operational capabilities by the introduction of a new modus operandi to elude Israeli efforts to thwart and profile suicide attackers. The PIJ focused its recruitment efforts in the northern part of the West Bank, and Jenin in particular, and established a well-trained network of operatives, including some highly skilled women. Two female PIJ operatives carried out suicide bombings in 2003. The PIJ's first success was Heiba Daragmeh, a 19-year-old student from al-Quds Open University from Tubas. On May 19, 2003, she detonated an explosive device strapped to her body in front of a shopping mall in Afula, killing three civilians and injuring 83. On October 5, 2003, Hanadi Jaradat, a law student from Jenin walked into Maxim's, a crowded restaurant in Haifa, and killed 19 civilians while injuring dozens more.[49]

According to reports, Jaradat wore the explosive belt around her waist feigning pregnancy. This tactic unites women suicide bombers in places as diverse as Turkey and Sri Lanka. Police reports in Turkey have emphasized caution with regard to Kurdish women who may appear pregnant because of the fact that several female PKK fighters disguised themselves this way in order to penetrate crowds of people more effectively and avoid detection, assuming—quite rightly—that they would not be frisked or subject to intense scrutiny. The first female PKK bombing in June 1996 killed six soldiers using this tactic. In another incident discussed in chapter 5, while the police fruitlessly searched for a female police officer to conduct the search (out of deference and respect for the women) Otas Gular detonated the device, killing herself and several police officers on October 29, 1996 emulating the same strategy employed four days earlier by Laila Kaplan.[50]

The trend toward women suicide bombers appears to be contagious. In 2002, Indian security forces twice went on high alert, in January and again in August, to guard against possible attacks by female suicide bombers. The suspects sprang from Pakistan-based Islamic organizations Jaish-e-Mohammed and Laskar-e-Tayyaba, both associated with Al Qaeda. Wherever there is a threat of terrorism and suicide terror, women appear to be playing an increasing role. In March 2003, *Asharq Al-Awsat* published an interview with a woman calling herself "Um Osama," the alleged leader of the women Mujahedeen of Al Qaeda. The Al Qaeda network claimed to have set up squads of female suicide bombers under orders from Bin Laden to target the United States. The women bombers purportedly include Afghans, Arabs, Chechens and other nationalities.

> We are preparing for the new strike announced by our leaders and I declare that it will make America forget . . . the September 11 attacks. The idea came from the success of martyr operations carried out by young Palestinian women in the occupied territories. Our organization is open to all Muslim women wanting to serve the (Islamic) nation . . . particularly in this very critical phase.[51]

Even al Qaeda has begun to employ women bombers. An indication of its ideological shift was the capture of two young women in Morocco en route to a suicide attack. Within weeks of the United States' invasion of Iraq, on March 29, two women (one of whom was pregnant) perpetrated suicide attacks against the Coalition forces. Al-Jazeera television reported on April 4, 2003 that two Iraqi women who vowed to commit suicide attacks had videotaped their intentions: "We say to our leader and holy war comrade, the hero commander Saddam Hussein that you have sisters that you and history will boast about." In a separate video, another woman, identified as Wadad Jamil Jassem, assumed a similar position: "I have devoted myself [to] Jihad for the sake of God and against the American, British, and Israeli infidels and to defend the soil of our precious and dear country."[52]

A report in *Pravda* suggested that Chechen rebels, with the assistance of Arab trainers, were training large numbers of women for terrorist attacks.[53] We can observe the role played by women in Chechnya and the Islamic *Fatwas* (religious rulings) that have sanctioned women's martyrdom there. Chechen women have proved to be a model for Palestinian women and so both conflicts have influenced and infected each other. The phenomenon indeed appears to be spreading.

BLACK WIDOWS IN CHECHNYA

Until recently, the Chechen leadership of *Al Ansar Mujahideen* did not require women's participation in military actions. Initially, female insurgents merely supplied medical aid, food and water to the men; they carried weapons and ammunition across enemy territory and played an important role in maintaining the guerrillas' morale during battles. According to reports, at the Dubrovka theatre siege, women and men had different roles: the men took care of the explosives and intimidation, while the women distributed medical supplies, blankets, water, chewing gum and chocolate. Though, at times the women allegedly toyed threateningly with their two-kilo bomb belts. Women's most relevant role, historically, was to raise children, form their character, and make them strong so that they became Mujahideen when they grew up.

Things changed, however, because of military losses and the ideological influence of Islamic volunteers from abroad. Dozens of terrorists from Europe and Northern Africa, willing to help Chechen insurgents, poured into the region and influenced the Chechen ideology regarding women suicide bombers. Shamil Besayev incorporated them into his Salakhin Riadus Shakhidi. The first Russian "Black Widow" (*shahidki*), Hawa Barayev killed 27 Russian Special Forces on June 9, 2000.

> Using women as suicide bombers in crowds is a new method in . . . subversive activities. The "Black Widows" are sisters, mothers or wives of Chechen men that have been killed in battles with federal troops. "Black Widows" choose to die as a bomber in order to show the strength of the resistance. They can wear kamikaze bomb-belts, or drive a truck that is full of explosives. Chechen guerrillas are inspired with the image of Khava Barayeva—the first to walk the way of martyrdom. Chechen rebels portray her as a hero, and they write poems and songs about her.[54]

Suicide terror has become one of the Chechen insurgents' methods of choice, evidenced by the growing number of attacks in recent years. The attacks typically involve women, exclusively or as part of a group. Of the seven suicide attacks by Chechen separatists on Russia in 2003, six were carried out by women.[55] In total the attacks killed 165 people. On October 23, 2002, a band of Chechen militants including 18 women seized the Dubrovka Theater in Moscow—taking the audience of more than 700 people hostage and threatening to blow everyone up—themselves included. The rebels and 129 hostages were killed by the subsequent Russian "rescue" in which they sprayed the arena with Fentanyl gas to overcome the insurgents.

According to one analyst, the key factor that made Chechen women turn to terror was the failed operation at the Dubrovka. In the First Chechen War, hostage-taking operations, for example, Shamil Besayev's 1995 raid on Budennovsk, were pivotal episodes for the outcome of the war. Besayev launched what appeared to be a suicidal operation against a Russian target, yet emerged victorious, with few casualties, and safe passage out. The raid resulted in widespread international media attention for the Chechen cause and outspoken Russian public criticism of the war as Russians blamed their own government for its incompetence and heavy-handed tactics. In 2002, the Chechens who took part in the Dubrovka hostage-taking might have hoped to duplicate the success of Besayev's raid seven years earlier. The operation might have been intended to take hostages rather than kill civilians, to regain some measure of sympathy from the West—the support from which had diminished since the American War on Terror in 2001.[56]

However, the events at the Dubrovka produced little sympathy for the Chechen cause abroad and none whatsoever in Russia. The response of the Russian security apparatus, to gas both hostage-takers and hostages (more than a 120 of whom were killed by the gas) and then slaughter all the hostage-takers probably persuaded many Chechens that the only remaining solution was to engage in suicide bombings of the type that the Arab extremists in Chechnya have long favored. In the aftermath of the failed hostage taking at the Dubrovka, a new wave of suicide attacks plagued Moscow civilians and Russian soldiers.

There appears to be a growing lethality in the Chechen resistance to Moscow, toward more terrorist attacks on traditional Russian territory and an increasing involvement of suicide bombers which is changing the character and dynamic of the conflict. In the short term, these attacks have led to increased Russian domestic support for the war against Chechnya; but over time they may gradually undermine the willingness support the war.

One of the more devastating suicide bomb attacks, in December 2003, destroyed government headquarters in Grozny and killed 80 people. On May 14, 2003, a suicide truck-bombing killed 72 people and a female operative, Shakhidat Baimuradova, blew herself up at an Islamic festival in the village of Ilishkan-Yurt in Gudermes. Pretending to be a journalist, she detonated a bomb hidden in a video camera in a crowd of people close to the head of the Chechen administration, Akhmad Kadyrov. As a result, 26 people were killed and 150 wounded. According to the Russian Interior Ministry, Baimuradova [was] one of 36 suicide bombers that were trained by Besayev.[57]

The trend in Chechnya was to take the fighting from the homeland to the Russian heartland.

On July 5, 2003 there was a double bombing at the Tushino airfield northwest of the capital during the fourth annual "Krylya" rock concert in Moscow that killed 15 and a failed attack in which Zulikhan Yelikhadzhiyeva exploded.[58] On July 9, Zarema Mazhikhoyeva, a 23-year-old Chechen was arrested before detonating the 1.5 kilograms of military issued explosive bomb in her purse at a café on Tverskaya-Yamskaya Street. Mazhikhoyeva claimed that she deliberately botched her mission, but an explosives expert died trying to defuse her bomb[59]

Evidence emerged that these events were just the tip of the iceberg in what was supposed to be a systematic campaign of urban terror. That week the Russian authorities discovered a cache of explosives and suicide belts in a house in the village of Tolstopaltsevo, 30 kilometers (19 miles) southwest of Moscow. According to the General Prosecutor's office: "The design and components of the devices were identical" to those used in the incidents on July 5 and July 9, described above.[60]

During four months in 2003, seven suicide attacks, all but one of which was carried out by women, spread fear across Russia, killing 165 people. Most Chechens, however, have not embraced the cult of martyrdom, as have, for example, Palestinian suicide bombers in the Gaza Strip and the West Bank. In Kurchaloi there are no posters or graffiti celebrating Yelikhadzhiyeva's martyrdom. People in Chechnya have professed shock and horror about female suicide bombers. However, one of the earlier female bombers, Elza (Luisa) Gazuyeva who on November 29, 2001 killed herself and a Russian Commander, Geidar Gadhiyev, the man who had allegedly ordered her husband's death, is revered. Thus it is possible that Chechens discriminate between women who attack military targets and those who target passengers and children.

Amanat Nagayeva brought down Volga-Aviaexpress Tu-134 flight from Moscow to Volgograd, which crashed about 100 miles south of Moscow and Satsita Dzhbirkhanova downed Sibir Airlines Tu-154 flight en route from Moscow to the Black Sea resort of Sochi near the southern city of Rostov-on-Don on August 22, 2004. Preliminary analysis of the Russian Federal Security Service (FSB) indicated that the explosive they used was hexogen, according to Sergei Ignatchenko the FSB spokesman. That was the same explosive substance used in a series of Russian apartment building bombings in 1999, which Russia cited as partial justification for launching the second war against Chechen separatists and helped propel then Russian prime minister Vladimir V. Putin to victory in his first presidential bid in 2000 with 52 percent of the vote because of his get tough policies against terrorism. However, rumors persist that the FSB was involved in the attacks. According to an *LA Times* report, "The bombings, by triggering Russian outrage, brought political benefit to Putin, because of a notorious incident in which FSB agents were caught in September 1999 placing what appeared to be explosives in an apartment building in the city of Ryazan."[61]

Amanat's younger sister Roza killed herself and ten people outside the Moscow subway (the attack was claimed by the Islambouli Brigades) and several more were involved in the takeover of Middle School No. 1 in Beslan.

(Maryam Taburova the fourth woman, who roomed with the three bombers, remains at large). The shock of women's increasing involvement has intensified exponentially since the attack in Beslan. I argued in chapter 6 that this event might be the turning point that turns public opinion against the resistance or minimally forces the Chechen resistance to rethink its casualty strategy.

Most of the Chechen attacks against Russia in 2004 have involved "Black Widows" wishing to avenge the deaths of family members in Russia's conflict in Chechnya. In total, female bombers have taken part in more than 18 major attacks since the outbreak of the second Chechen War, although not all the women were really widows. Reports suggest that the Nagayev sisters were divorced because they were unable to have children, a major stigma in Chechen society. Having said that, the sisters did lose their brother Uvays, who was beaten to death by Russian soldiers.[62]

Female Chechen suicide bombers have recently developed into an increasingly serious threat. Previous acts of violence were primarily aimed at military targets and took place in the Northern Caucasus, and did not aim to kill large numbers of Russian civilians. The attacks by female suicide bombers have reversed these patterns. While this is unlikely to change the course of the war, it will have important implications for Russia's leadership, which is now being forced to provide what its rhetoric has always promised: security for Russia's citizens from terrorist attacks. It is also having a negative effect on the prospects for democracy in the region. Imran Yezhiyev, of the Chechen-Russian Friendship Society in Ingushetia, stated: "Suicide attacks were an inevitable response to the "most crude, the most terrible" crimes Russian forces had committed against Chechen civilians during the war. When Russian soldiers kill children and civilians and demand payment for their return, many in Chechnya are outraged and vow revenge. One woman, Elvira, whose 15-year-old son had been killed by Russian troops who demanded $500 to return his corpse stated: "Oh, yes, I want to kill them. Kill Russians, kill their children. I want them to know what it is like."[63]

Chechens are desperate because they see no prospect of this horrible war ending."[64] Stories about Russian soldiers laughing as they charge Chechen fathers 300 rubles (nearly $15) not to rape their daughters circulate widely throughout Chechnya, adding credibility to the notion that Russian Counter Terror tactics have morphed into a cruel sadistic justification for violence against women. According to Human Rights Watch, more than 80,000 Chechens and 6,000 Russian troops have died. President Vladimir Putin's strong-arm tactics have turned Chechnya into an anarchic wasteland where Russian soldiers roam freely, dispensing summary justice in house-to-house raids and skirmishing with armed rebels.

Sergei V. Yastrzhembsky, Putin's senior advisor on Chechnya, suggested in the newspaper *Sobesednik* that Islamic extremists had coerced the Black Widows against their will to become suicide bombers. "Chechens are turning these young girls into zombies (*Zombirovaniye*) using psychotropic drugs. . . . I have heard that they rape them and record the rapes on video. After that, such Chechen girls have no chance at all of resuming a normal life in Chechnya. They have only one option: to blow themselves up with a bomb full of nails and ball bearings."[65]

The expansion of suicide operations to other parts of the Muslim world is a source of anxiety to regimes in the Middle East and Asia. There is a concern among moderate Islamic scholars about the rise of Islamist activists who have no formal religious education or authority who write self-described *fatwas* that are highly regarded by their followers and have a lot of support among the larger population. Beginning in 2001, we observe the Islamic *fatwas* that have sanctioned women's participation in martyrdom operations.

The Islamic theological debates regarding women suicide bombers might mislead the reader into thinking that martyrdom is an exclusively Islamic phenomenon. The cases presented in this book should prove that there is a spectrum of religious affiliation and degree of religiosity. In some cases, the religion of the bomber was incidental, notably among the secular organizations. Sri Lanka provides an important example of a secular non-Muslim group engaged in suicide bombing and one where the use of women was perfected and very effective.

NON-ISLAMIC FEMALE MARTYRS

The most notorious female insurgents come from the Tamil Tigers of Sri Lanka. In contrast to the Palestinians, they have not been stigmatized because of their gender: they are trained and prepared like men, given arms, and taught how to use them; and they regularly go on suicide missions. Women appear more willing to sacrifice and, as we have noted, they are better able to avoid detection. The critics of the LTTE claim, however, that women are chosen because they are more malleable and easy to control.[66] Since 1999, roughly 35 percent of the 210 attacks have been perpetrated by women.

The "phenomenon" of the LTTE female suicide bomber has raised several important, timely and difficult questions for feminist inquiry, offering, from the particular context of Sri Lanka, a rich analytical site for an understanding of the overlay of violence, militarism, patriarchy and gender. The issues of autonomous choice, agency, feminist politics, cultural role models, and the gendered nature of sacrifice/martyrdom have accrued around the figure of the female suicide bomber.[67]

Tamil society, like that of Chechnya and Palestine, is a traditional one, and some women perceive the LTTE as an entity that allows them equality. "We are given moral support by our leader [Prabhakaran] and we have reached this position only because of him."[68]

Women in combat belong to a totally new world, a world outside a normal woman's life.... They have taken up a life that bears little resemblance at all to the ordinary existence of women. Training and carrying weapons, confronting battle conditions, enduring the constant emotional strain of losing close associates, facing death almost every day, are situations that most women not only wish to avoid, but feel ill at ease with. But not the women fighters of the LTTE. They have literally flourished under such conditions and created for themselves, not only a new women's military structure, but also a legend of fighting capability and bravery.[69]

Women also join the LTTE because they have lost a loved one or because of a degree of community peer pressure.

One woman joined after her boyfriend was arrested, killed and the corpse left in the village market for public to see ... another one told me that one night she was alone at home thinking and listening to LTTE's songs ... the next day she and a few of her friends left their school to join. Once girl in a village joins there is a snow ball effect of others wanting to join the organization.[70]

The most famous among the women was Dhanu, who hid her explosive beneath her sari, giving her the appearance of pregnancy, and went to meet Indian Prime Minister Rajiv Gandhi on May 20, 1991. When he clasped her hand as she respectfully kneeled before him, she detonated the device, killing both of them and several bystanders instantly. Dhanu became a heroine and symbol of the LTTE. The story of Dhanu reached mythic proportions. The perceived heroism of this woman, who committed suicide for her people and her faith, is used as an example to win over new recruits.[71]

When women began to join the LTTE in the mid-1980s many were allegedly rape victims of either the Sinhalese or of the Indian Peacekeeping troops that had entered the country in 1987 and would remain until 1990. Dhanu herself was supposedly the victim of rape although other sources claim that it was her mother who was raped by Indian security services during the Indian Intervention between 1987-1990 and that she was avenging her mother when she killed Prime Minister Gandhi. According to the Hindu faith, once a woman is raped she cannot get married nor have children. Fighting for Tamil freedom might have been the only way for such a woman to redeem herself. The idea of sacrifice is ingrained in Tamil culture. Women are taught from an early age to subordinate themselves to the needs or desires of men. The self-sacrifice of the female bombers is almost an extension of the idea of motherhood in the Tamil culture.

> Tamil mothers make great sacrifices for their sons on a daily basis; feeding them before themselves or the girl children, serving on them and so on. Acting as a human bomb is an understood and accepted offering for a woman who will never be a mother. Family members often encourage rape victims to join the LTTE.[72]

Was Dhanu seeking to avenge her ruined honor, to achieve status within her culture, or to express her personal rage? It is impossible to know for sure. However, the abuse of women is a factor that has changed little during the decades of civil war in Sri Lanka. According to one report, in one typical search at a checkpoint, a woman was ordered to raise her hands:

> One of the officers pointed a gun at her threatening to shoot her. She started crying and shouted in Sinhalese "*Mata Wedithiyanna epa. Mata lamayek innawa*" ("Don't shoot me. I have a child.") She was then ordered to raise the top part of her dress and also ordered to raise the brassiere. Thereafter she was told to take down the lower part of her garment including the knickers up to her knees. She was asked to undress after which she was thoroughly "checked."[73]

The woman was mistaken for a Tamil because of her clothing and proved to be Sinhalese. Nevertheless authorities dismissed her mistreatment when they discovered that she was a sex worker (and not entitled to privacy and dignity).

There have been massive human rights abuses in the north and east in the Tamil areas.[74] According to Darini Rajasingham-Senanyake, Government violence had been organized and routinized through a systematic campaign of disappearances, turning a blind eye toward the use of rape, checkpoint searches aimed at dehumanizing Tamils, widespread torture, and the elimination of whole villages in remote areas.[75] Rajasingham-Senanyake adds that, "check point rape and murder are well documented in Sri Lanka, in this context militant groups who infiltrate camps have little difficulty in recruiting new cadres from deeply frustrated and resentful youth, men and women, girls and boys."[76] The motivations for women to join the LTTE range along a spectrum from their personal experiences to the experiences of the Tamil community as a whole.

> Witnessing rape, witnessing or hearing about rape from other villagers and the Army's killing of Tamil youth (girls and boys arrested by Sri Lankan Army) . . . and the feeling of helplessness in not being able to defend against the Sri Lankan Army, are the main reasons for the girls joining the LTTE.[77]

Such tactics have only emboldened the LTTE and solidified their control of Jaffna.[78] Civilian deaths caused by the government made the LTTE stronger and soured the Tamil population on government assurances of devolution and equal rights. The government forces have not been mindful to differentiate civilian noncombatants from combatants and militants.

Women are better able to avoid detection since they pass through security checks more easily than Tamil men, their dresses and saris allow them to hide the bombing device more easily. "Women are less threatening in public places because of the cultural taboo, it is [more difficult] for male soldiers or police to frisk a woman, therefore women get through security points more easily than men."[79] In an interview with an ex-LTTE cadre, Bernard-Henri Levy reported that women's training includes hiding a hand-grenade in their vaginas.[80]

In Sri Lanka a recent report links the abuse of women to the phenomenon of suicide terrorism but argues that violence has not had an appreciable impact on women in the society. Violence against women has been exacerbated during the long years of armed conflict and rape and sexual harassment by armed forces and use of child soldiers and female suicide bombers are all examples of extreme violence. At the same time women are not represented in the official peace process or in positions of leadership at the local or national levels.

> There are no women in leadership positions in trade unions. Women's multiple roles and time constraints often limit their aspirations but norms of male leadership, and in the case of politics, the present pervasive environment of political violence are also barriers to participation. The fact that Sri Lanka has had the first woman Prime Minister and a woman President for eight years has not made an appreciable difference.[81]

CONCLUSIONS

When analyzing female suicide bombings, specifying the terrorist organization and the larger society from which the women come become important factors in the analysis. Boaz Ganor of the International Institute for Counter-Terrorism says, "if you analyze the motivations of women who commit such attacks, it's the same as the men: they believe they are committed, patriotic, and this is combined with a religious duty. Many were not trained or prepared psychologically for the suicide attack."[82]

However, the reasons for women's participation vary greatly from country to country. Past experience shows that there is generally no single overriding motivation, but rather a number of overlapping motivations working in concert.

> These motivations interact with the potential attacker's emotional predispositions, creating an explosive mixture that needs only some traumatic event to release all its hidden destructive energy. A skillful terrorist operative can easily identify a candidate in this emotional state, and coolly manipulate her into becoming a weapon for his organization.[83]

Similarities exist between the cases. In Sri Lanka or in Turkey, female members of the terrorist organizations were encouraged to participate in suicide bombing and coerced by peer pressure. Both the Tamils and the Kurds share common features such as traditional societies where women's roles are determined and static. The LTTE and the PKK offered women the opportunity that no other arrangement in society could ever offer them, a degree of equality. Both groups were commanded by charismatic, unchallenged leaders, who trained women to kill and die for the cause. Women were also eager to prove their devotion to the group, or were dictated to do so, as has been pointed out earlier concerning Sri Lanka.

According to several of the preliminary studies that have been done on Palestinian female bombers, they represent a new model of suicide attackers. Seven women who, because of their gender, do not—or at least did not—fit the established profile of a Palestinian suicide bomber: one a seamstress, one an ambulance worker, two in college, one in high school, one a law school graduate, and one mother of two who left families stricken and shocked.[84] Some analysts have suggested that these women were misfits or outcasts in their society. An article on the Israeli government website states:

> Any hint of impropriety, no matter how minor, can have serious consequences for the woman involved, even prompting male family mem-

bers to murder her in a so-called "honor" killing. Such personal mo-tives have been well exploited by the terrorist organizations when they approach women in order to recruit them for suicide attacks. Recent intelligence information, gathered by Israeli liaison and coordination officials, have identified a clear effort . . . to recruit as suicide terrorists those young women who find themselves in acute emotional distress due to social stigmatization.[85]

Barbara Victor corroborates this hypothesis when she links the first four female Palestinian suicide bombers as having been placed in positions where the act of martyrdom was their sole chance to reclaim the family honor that had been lost by their own actions or the actions of other family members.[86] Allegations abound that the first female Hamas suicide bomber, Reem Riashi, was coerced by both her husband and lover—as a way of saving face after an extramarital affair. Thus at some level, all the women were motivated by highly charged emotional and personal reasons. The suicide bombers who brought down Russian jets in August 2004 were two women who were unable to have children, a source of stigma in Chechen society. Finally, there is evi-dence that the women who were previously raped and ordinarily killed them-selves (to avoid bringing shame on the family) are now being funneled into the Black Widows. During the first Chechen War there was a significant rise in women who committed suicide—including many who were expecting. The numbers of women who committed suicide dropped during the second Chechen War. According to Valerie Zawilski, the same women who commit-ted suicide before were being funneled into the insurgent organizations.[87]

The selection of women for suicide operations and the methods used to persuade them are similar in some respects to those employed for men, across a range of countries and cultures and by both secular and religious organizations.

Taking advantage of candidates' innocence, enthusiasm, loss of focus and often personal distress and thirst for revenge, "persuaders" subject women as well as men to intense indoctrination and manipulation. They offer the would-be bombers a sense of direction, as well as seem-ingly magical solutions to their problems, overlaid with national or religious symbolism, and promises of concrete [financial] rewards for them and their families, in the next world if necessary.[88]

However, there are allegations that women are subjected to special treat-ment by the recruiters such that women are abused in some fashion deliber-ately to coerce them into becoming bombers. In addition to Israeli allegations that Palestinian women have been deliberately seduced by militants who used their violation of the honor code to convert them to bombers, in Sri Lanka there have been similar allegations that Tamil insurgent groups have used all means at their disposal to induce women to join the organizations.

In the fall of 2002 three young Tamil women presented themselves to an international aid organization claiming that they had been raped by persons who spoke to them in Sinhalese but discovered later on that their attackers were Tamils. Although the women did not report the attacks, they were approached within days by members of the LTTE and coerced into becoming Black Tigresses—to recover the family honor of having had sex with Sinhalese men. Such allegations are shocking since the LTTE traditionally has never abused women nor has advocated or permitted the use of rape against enemy women.[89] Several young women have been kidnapped by the LTTE and eventually escaped back to their villages. The Sri Lankan police established a set of parameters wherein women who were kidnapped had to report to the local police station and fill out a report detailing their experience. To make matters worse, by admitting LTTE membership, the police occasionally used this information as an excuse to rape the women and so they have faced a lose-lose scenario.

The common link between the cases, whether they reflect the facts or construct a fiction, is that women are more vulnerable in such patriarchal settings and occasionally susceptible to mobilization against their will.

GENDER EQUALITY PROGRESSED OR REGRESSED?

In describing his sister Darine Abu Aisha's death her brother stated, "she [was] a real man. . . . the role of women in Palestinian society is not only to cry and keep the household, but to participate in such acts."[90]

Are women suicide bombers portents of gender equality in their societies? Unlikely. Fanaticism and death cults generally do not lead to liberation politics for women. Women may exhibit courage and steely resolve as terrorists but, if they are part of a system that affords them unequal status, then feminism doesn't apply.[91] The Chechen Black Widows, according to Russia's elite Alfa anti-terrorist unit which monitored the Moscow siege, were not permitted to detonate their bombs without the specific command from their male leader. Palestinian female cadres are not welcomed into the paramilitary terrorist factions, which remain dominated by men. Even in the Al 'Aqsa Martyrs Brigades, women are not welcomed by the ranks of the male fighters. In Sri Lanka, while women constitute 30 percent of the suicide attackers and form crucial conventional fighting units, there are few women among the top leadership. In fact, the LTTE has attempted to compel married Tamil women, including former retired female cadres, to adopt more traditional and conservative forms of dress (the sari and head coverings) and not wear trousers in the LTTE controlled areas. "Those who send these women [bombers] do not really care for women's rights; they are exploiting the personal frustrations and grievances of these women for their own political goals, while they continue to limit the role of women in other aspects of life."[92]

There is a difference between the lower-ranking female operatives in terrorist groups and women who are planners and leaders, such as Ulrike Meinhof, who provided the intellectual backbone of the Baader-Meinhof organization. The assassination of Czar Alexander II in 1881 was an operation organized by a woman. Many other nineteenth-century revolutionaries were female. Nevertheless, women's participation as suicide bombers has not equalized their societies.

We can draw similarities to the roles women have played in revolutionary movements in Iran, Palestine, Algeria; and yet women were not included in the leadership of the successor regimes. Palestinian women differ from the female bombers from other countries because they seemingly have options; they could have had a future, yet they chose to die as martyrs for the sake of their communities. The women suicide bombers in Sri Lanka and Turkey have few, if any, career options; many of them are unsophisticated and poorly educated, and simply follow their leadership blindly. The participation of women in Palestine poses a challenge to understanding why educated women react in this fashion.

The problem lies in the fact that women, by operating under such archaic notions of patriarchy—assumptions that they are less warlike or the stereotypes about motherhood— all reinforce the inequalities of their societies, rather than confront them and explode the myths from within. The traditional patriarchy has a well-scripted set of rules in which women sacrifice themselves, the patriarchal ideal of motherhood is one of self-denial and self-effacement. Although the woman is portrayed as supportive this is accomplished when she gives up herself and her sense of self. The motivation to become a martyr is a twisted ultimate fulfillment of patriarchal ideals. These phenomena don't challenge the patriarchy but are clear examples of it: women are more socially vulnerable, especially because widows and rape victims are stigmatized; it is therefore not surprising that these women are recruited. These victims of their society are more easily devalued, while at the same time their deaths are easily exploited. If women want to equalize the society, playing the stereotypical female is decidedly not the way to accomplish this task. Rather placing the women in leadership roles and giving them the opportunity to have a greater say in their futures might be a better way to level the unequal societies in which they live.

CHAPTER EIGHT

CONCLUSIONS AND PROSPECTS FOR THE FUTURE: WILL IRAQ CAUSE SUICIDE TERROR AT HOME?

Prior to September 11, 2001, the United States had a few, albeit violent, encounters with Middle Eastern suicide bombers. The first warning of things to come occurred in Lebanon. On October 23, 1983, a truck filled with 2,250 kg (5,000 lbs.) of explosives detonated when a Hizb'allah driver rammed it into the U.S. Marine barracks in Beirut, killing 241 Marines. In 1993, al Qaeda operatives tried and failed to bring down the World Trade Center by planting a truck bomb..In the past, terrorists seemed more interested in publicity than in killing large numbers of people and thus tended to keep violence within self-imposed bounds. September 11 ushered in a new era of terrorism where the primary goal was to inflict wanton carnage and destruction. This is also unfortunately the clearest expression of how terrorism is an amorphous and constantly evolving phenomenon.

Unfortunately, the U.S. has long had reason to be concerned. In recent years, al Qaeda bombings of the Khobar Towers in Saudi Arabia (June 26, 1996), U.S. Embassies in Nairobi, Kenya and Dar es Salaam, Tanzania (August 8, 1998), and attacks on the destroyer USS *Cole* (October 12, 2000) provided strong warnings of the growing danger of suicide terror against the United States. Several weeks later, President Clinton ordered retaliatory strikes. The criticism was considerable from Republicans. It was not that we should have done much more, but that the attacks were an effort to divert attention from the President's legal troubles [related to Monica Lewinsky] as a sort of "Wag the Dog" scenario. Most worrisome a series of attacks inside the United States that were constantly foiled signaled a new phase, where acts of suicide terrorism on U.S. soil, would become more likely. Some counter-terrorism experts recognized the threat; however, they were either silenced or sidelined by political administrations who prioritized other issues or were distracted by domestic scandals.

"Dick Clarke was sort of a Cassandra, because he was always talking about this issue and was dedicated to, if not obsessed by, destroying al Qaeda. He had reason to be. If you go through 1998, 1999, and 2000, [U.S. authorities] were successful in foiling plots by al Qaeda on American soil."[1] There were legitimate concerns of a terrorist attack to coincide with the millennium. As a result, security and government intelligence organizations were placed on high alert.

On March 1, 1999, the threat of domestic suicide terror came to light when a federal court in Brooklyn sentenced Ghazi Ibrahim Abu Maizar (a Palestinian from Hebron) to life in prison for conspiring to use a weapon of mass destruction. When the police had raided his apartment on July 31, 1997, they found evidence that he was on the verge of setting off a pipe bomb on a New York subway train. Abu Maizar had planned to detonate the bomb on the line that runs from the northern tip of Manhattan to Coney Island "because there are a lot of Jews that ride that train." He spoke openly of killing "as many [Jews] as I could. . . . I always dreamed to be a martyr"; he acknowledged supporting Hamas, and demanded the release of several Islamic fundamentalists imprisoned in the United States.[2]

Abu Maizar's arrest and the whole incident received scant attention except from a handful of conservative pundits who raised their concerns and voices about the dangers of militant Islam in America. Until September 11, these voices were considered on the fringe or limited to academic or counter-terrorism circles. Now, such concerns have moved into mainstream discussions and have dramatically changed our perspective and sensitivity to potential domestic threats.

In the first year of the U.S.-led war on terror, a proliferation of reports and studies analyzed al Qaeda and Osama Bin Laden from every conceivable angle—and with good reason. . . . The attacks in New York, Virginia, and Pennsylvania could never have been carried out without the tremendous logistical assistance of a sophisticated and well-entrenched support network. Indeed, the nineteen al Qaeda hijackers were funded and facilitated by dozens of individuals, cells, front organizations, and affiliated groups that provided a variety of logistical support activities essential to carrying out an operation of this magnitude.[3]

The question always asked of me is why have there been no new attacks since 9/11 against the United States? Experts from the FBI, Porter Goss, former chair of the House Intelligence Committee and now Director of the CIA, and Vice President Dick Cheney have all argued that it is simply a matter of time before there are more suicide attacks on U.S. soil.[4] Ongoing investigations against threats to railways, ports, and other infrastructure on the

East Coast underscore the danger of sustained suicide attacks in the United States. The increased levels of violence by suicide bombers abroad and the terror attacks against American soldiers and contractors in Iraq raise serious questions about national security overall. Finally, the spread of suicide terrorism to South Asia, Africa, and Southeast Asia only serves to demonstrate that the scourge is definitely growing. One of the key errors we make is to assume that just because there has not been an attack, it is because they cannot or because they are weak. Al Qaeda has a very long time horizon as we have seen and Bin Laden tends to prefer spectacular attacks to a series of small acts of violence.

We have few metrics by which to judge this threat and counter-terrorism policies by their nature are largely reactive. One of the few indicators we have to assess the danger is American policy vis-à-vis the Middle East, especially in its occupation of Iraq. Although terrorism might not be organizationally connected with Middle Eastern groups, it may nevertheless be inspired by events there or by the call to action to perpetrate attacks. As al Qaeda has decentralized and increasingly relied on national or regional groups to continue its war against America, understanding events in the Middle East have arguably become more important in assessing radical attitudes toward the United States and understanding the changing tactics of these groups. In this chapter I will explore the growing threat to the United States by examining the trends in suicide terror against American and international targets in Iraq.

During the build-up to the war in Iraq in 2003, Abdel Aziz al Rantisi, the Hamas leader assassinated by Israeli forces, urged Iraqis to copy Hamas' tactics against the Israelis and send thousands of bombers with explosives strapped to their bodies into a battle against the occupiers. He told a rally in Jebalya refugee camp: "We call on the Arabs and Muslims to burn the land under the feet of the American invaders, especially our brothers in Saudi Arabia because this war is not against Iraq, it's against the Islamic nation."[5]

During and after the war, several Iraqi former regime elements and foreign volunteers did just that. There have been scores of suicide attacks against American military forces since March 30, 2003, when Ali Hammadi al Namani carried out Rantisi's edict, killing four Americans at a checkpoint south of Najaf. During combat, Iraqi General Hazem al Rawi claimed that thousands of volunteers from all over the Arab World were prepared to become suicide bombers against the Coalition forces in Iraq.[6] Volunteers poured across poorly defended borders from Saudi Arabia to Syria. For instance, a Lebanese teacher from the Beka'a Valley slipped into Iraq via Syria with the intention of becoming a martyr. "I decided on Jihad because I wanted to stop the occupation, not out of the love of blood." His anger was fueled by almost daily scenes on television of Iraqi women and children dying, not to mention

Palestinians suffering the same fate. According to reports, he found himself in a safe house in Baghdad with dozens of Saudis, Libyans, Egyptians and Kuwaitis all wanting to become suicide bombers too. "Arab governments and Western intelligence officials express growing concern that Iraq is becoming the training ground that Afghanistan was in the 1980s, breeding another generation of fanatical warriors ready to carry their Jihad back home."[7] In the first year after the war, there were forty suicide attacks against American forces. From March 2004 until the U.S. occupation formally ended on June 28, there were thirty more. By the fall of 2004 suicide bombing had become an almost daily occurrence against American forces and Iraqi civilians. See figures 8.1, 8.2, and 8.3 in the appendix.

The militant forces in Iraq consist of residual nationalist elements of the Ba'ath Party as well as a limited numbers of foreigners drawn to the conflict as they were to Afghanistan in the 1980s. For some analysts, the attacks in Iraq can be cleanly divided in two groups: conventional insurgent tactics against the British and U.S. occupying forces most likely perpetrated by former regime loyalists using road mines and snipers and the suicide attacks that have been apparently perpetrated by the foreign elements.[8] The images of the two armies, Israel in Palestine and the Americans in Iraq, are virtually indistinguishable from each other for most Muslims. Many of these foreign volunteers would likely prefer to fight Israelis in Palestine, but the Israeli border is virtually impenetrable. Iraq and killing U.S. soldiers is the next best option. It is conceivable that these volunteers will play a greater role in the future as an underground railroad funneling fighters is cultivated—increasingly making Iraq a beacon for terrorism in the Arab world. According to intelligence sources, this is precisely the point; some members of the Administration mistakenly assume that if the volunteers flock to Iraq, they will not be attempting to penetrate the U.S. This follows from President Bush's theory that we are fighting them there so that they are not here. However, it is a crucial mistake to assume that there is a set and finite number of militants that will either go to one location or another. In fact, the war is less a flame drawing in the current moths, than a chrysalis in which many more are being created.[9]

More important, and unlike native-born Iraqis, such foreigners are not subject to that same public opinion that might potentially constrain their behavior against Iraqi civilians and limit their strategies. Many of the American tactics in Iraq have ignored the influence of domestic public opinion, and there has been a growing trend in favor of supporting the insurgents. The domestic environment is becoming increasingly hostile in part because of the nature of U.S. counter-terrorist strategies.

The suicide attacks in Iraq can be divided into three phases: the first consisted of attacks on U.S. troops by former regime loyalists; in the next phase, during the summer and fall of 2003, there were attacks on the international coalition supporting the occupation (including NGOs); the third phase, which continues, has featured attacks on Iraqi "collaborators" in an attempt to create civil strife—as outlined in a letter intercepted from Abu Musab al Zarqawi (Ahmed al-Khalayleh). This includes the significant increase in attacks in 2004 against Iraqis who work for the coalition provisional authority and for the new independent Iraqi government. (See the Appendix for a partial list of the attacks.)

Zarqawi's letter was released to the *New York Times* with great fanfare in February 2004 as a way to demonstrate that the U.S. led coalition against Iraq was winning (the tone of the letter bordered on despondent) as well as to demonstrate the connections between Iraq and al Qaeda that some in the Bush Administration have long alleged. Zarqawi, according to the Bush Administration was a well-known and close affiliate of Osama Bin Laden, implicated in the "Millennium Plot" in which al Qaeda planned to blow up the Radisson Hotel and religious sites in Amman in 1999. He was also convicted in absentia in the October 2002 slaying of a high-ranking USAID employee, Laurence Foley, in Amman.[10] However, a CIA report found no link between Saddam's regime and Zarqawi prior to the conflict and Zarqawi only formally pledged his allegiance to Osama Bin Laden in October 2004 after the U.S. occupation in Iraq had lasted for over a year. Moreover, the occupation has galvanized Arab public opinion against the U.S. in a way that nothing has done in the past.

The Zarqawi letter was a blueprint for resistance to the American forces and called for the incitement of a sectarian war between Sunni and Shi'a. According to the letter:

> The Shi'a in our opinion, these are the key to change. Targeting and striking their religious, political, and military symbols, will make them show their rage against the Sunnis and bear their inner vengeance. If we succeed in dragging them into a sectarian war, this will awaken the sleepy Sunnis who are fearful of destruction and death at the hands of these Sabeans, i.e., the Shi'a. . . . Most of the Sunnis are aware of the danger of these people and they fear them. . . . The Shi'a have taken on the dress of the army, police, and the Iraqi security forces, and have raised the banner of protecting the nation, and the citizens. Under this banner, they have begun to assassinate the Sunnis under the pretense that they are saboteurs, vestiges of the Ba'ath, or terrorists who spread perversion in the country. This is being done with strong media support directed by the governing council and the Americans, and they have succeeded in splitting the regular Sunni from the Mujahidin. For

example, in what they call the Sunni triangle, the army and police are spreading out in these regions, putting in charge Sunnis from the same region. . . . So I say again, the only solution is to strike the religious, military, and other cadres of the Shi'a so that they revolt against the Sunnis. Some people will say, that this . . . will bring the Islamic nation to a battle for which the Islamic nation is unprepared. Souls will perish and blood will be spilled. This is, however, exactly what we want, as there is nothing to win or lose in our situation.[11]

Zarqawi's letter contributed to the debate as to whether foreign elements played a significant role in the insurgency in Iraq. In the letter Zarqawi alleges:

Despite few supporters, lack of friends, and tough times, God has blessed us with victories against the enemy. We were involved in all the martyrdom operations—in terms of overseeing, preparing, and planning—that took place in this country except for the operations that took place in the north. Praised be to Allah, I have completed 25 of these operations, some of them against the Shi'a and their leaders, the Americans and their military, the police, the military, and the coalition forces. There will be more in the future, God willing.[12]

Since then, suicide attacks against American targets have escalated sharply. The coalition blamed two of the most devastating attacks in Iraq—the bombings of the UN headquarters in Baghdad and the Ali Imam mosque in Najaf—on Zarqawi. The coalition doubled the bounty for his capture to $10 million and he is the most wanted man in Iraq to date. However, law-enforcement sources say that, as far as they know, forensic tests have not tied Zarqawi to either. The U.S. Army commanders downplayed the likelihood that the attacks have been coordinated and planned by outsiders.[13]

For some critics of the Bush Administration, the government's insistence upon highlighting the role of Zarqawi was intended to create a new enemy who was not Iraqi and could link the war in Iraq with the war on terror in Afghanistan—something that the Bush Administration needed to justify the ill conceived war in Iraq.

However, Zarqawi swims in a soup of other groups which include Iraqi nationalists who have nothing to do with the former regime but oppose the occupation. Outsiders (Zarqawi and al Qaeda operatives) play a much smaller role on the ground than we would assume considering his cult-like status in the U.S. media. There are between 500 and 700 foreign elements in Iraq fighting the coalition forces. The vast majority of the Mahdi of Moqtada as Sadr and the Shi'a militants are purely Iraqi—who have a strong sense of national identity and are unabashedly opposed to occupation. People have reacted to the occupation with feelings of deep resistance. Young Iraqi men feel emasculated by the presence of foreign troops, engaging in violence makes them feel manly and proactive that day. Nevertheless, secular Ba'athist groups, who would ordinarily vilify Zarqawi and reject al Qaeda's brand of religious millenarianism because of the occupation, now applaud him. On Haifa Street in Baghdad or in Samarra in the Sunni triangle young men brandish Al Zarqawi flags because it is the ultimate admonishment to the Americans. The longer the United States stays, the more Americans will be hated and attacked. This increases the chances that suicide bombing will be imported here.

Rather than firmly connecting the regime of Saddam Hussein with al Qaeda, the Zarqawi letter implies what Richard A. Clarke testified before the 9/11 commission: that the war in Iraq gave insurgents a greater opportunity and the mobilization capabilities for a global campaign of terrorism. According to Clarke, in the days after 9/11, "Rumsfeld said that we needed to bomb Iraq, and we all said, "al Qaeda is in Afghanistan. We need to bomb Afghanistan." Rumsfeld allegedly grumbled there were not any good targets in Afghanistan. However, Clarke retorted, "There's absolutely no evidence that Iraq was supporting al Qaeda, ever. Clarke later testified, "I think the way [President Bush] has responded to al Qaeda, both before 9/11 by doing nothing, and by what he's done after 9/11 has made us less safe. Absolutely."[14]

This lack of any clear connection was enunciated by Secretary of Defense, Donald Rumsfeld, at a presentation to the Council on Foreign Relations on October 4, 2004. On the record and in front of hundreds of council members and the media, Rumsfeld said that there was *no real* connection between Saddam Hussein and al Qaeda. The White House spent the rest of that week back tracking and trying to spin the secretary's comments because of the Presidential election and the Vice Presidential debates the following evening. However, the majority of the American electorate continues to believe that a connection exists and thus a justification for the war in Iraq is part of the war on terror. What causes concern is that half the American people still wrongly believe that Iraq had links with al Qaeda and a hand in the 9/11 attacks. This misconception is a major misreading of Saddam Hussein's regime and remains an urban legend along with alligators in the New York sewer system. Although Iraq was a brutal genocidal state, it was not a haven for terrorists until the war. This misconception also cushions the outrage Americans should feel about the tens of thousands of dead Iraqi civilians, as well as our own soldiers. It also masks the fact that the war has spilled over into Saudi Arabia, about which we hear very little. The daily shootouts between militant Islamists and government forces in Saudi Arabia should cause alarm according to the CIA chief Bin

Laden specialist Anonymous, Michael Scheuer who emerged from anonymity after quitting the CIA after twenty two years. Scheuer is highly critical of the Bush Administration's handling the war on terror and expresses concern over the war in Iraq. This is especially salient since according to Scheuer, "We found that Bin Laden and al Qaeda were involved in an extraordinarily sophisticated and professional effort to acquire weapons of mass destruction. In this case, nuclear material . . ." To make matters more worrisome, in May 2003 Bin Laden secured an Islamic *fatwa*, a religious ruling by a Saudi cleric by the name of Hamid Bin Fahd that allows for Bin Laden's use of nuclear weapons against the U.S. because of the theory of reciprocity. According to the ruling, because the United States is responsible for millions of Muslim deaths, a nuclear weapon would be a perfectly commensurate response.[15] The war in Iraq provides a justification for such an attack and the increasing number of Iraqi casualties, both military and civilian place Americans at greater risk.

The concern over the long term effects of the war was echoed off the record to this author. According to a high ranking Arab diplomat, prior to the war he prophesized to the secretary of defense that occupying Iraq would be like swallowing a razor. He added, there would likely be six days of fighting, six weeks of honeymoon after liberation, six months of reconstruction, six years of fighting and six decades before the Muslim world would forgive and forget the occupation. To date, many of these prophecies have come true and the extraordinarily well planned and executed war was followed by an extremely poorly planned peace and a worsening quagmire which has the potential to become the next Vietnam.

According to Scheuer, "right or wrong, Muslims are beginning to view the United States as a colonial power with Israel as the surrogate, and with a military presence in three of the holiest places in Islam, the Arabian Peninsula, Iraq (where the Shi'a holy places of Najaf and Karbala are located), and Jerusalem."[16] Furthermore, it appears that American tactics in Iraq have created a situation similar to that created by the Israelis in the occupied territories, especially when they surround villages with barbed wire and bulldoze the homes of suspected operatives. The more the U.S. military employ Israeli-style tactics, the more they appear as occupiers; and the more likely they would be attacked by local and foreign elements alike. Also, similar to the Israelis, the U.S. military has made broad use of checkpoints, transfers of populations, and detained village officials. Men aged 18 to 65 were ordered to get identification cards. In one case, the American military detained the local town council and the police chief for 72 hours and erected a razor wire fence—copying the model used in October 2003 to subdue Auja, Saddam Hussein's home village to the north.[17] American forces also sealed off three towns in western Iraq for several days.

The Americans embarked on their get-tough strategy in early November [2003], goaded by what proved to be the deadly month for American forces in Iraq, in which 81 soldiers were killed by hostile fire. The response they chose . . . echoes Israeli counterinsurgency in the occupied territories. . . . In Abu Hishma, encased in a razor-wire fence after repeated attacks on American troops, Iraqi civilians line up to go in and out, filing through an American-guarded checkpoint, each carrying an identification card printed in English only. In selective cases, American soldiers are demolishing buildings thought to be used by Iraqi attackers. They have begun imprisoning the relatives of suspected guerrillas, in hopes of pressing the insurgents to turn themselves in.[18]

Abu Hishma was locked down for 15 hours a day, so that residents were unable to go to the mosque for morning and evening prayers. The curfew did not allow for sufficient time to stand in the daylong lines for gasoline and get home before the evening curfew. Mostly, the villagers talked about the loss of their dignity as contributing to their antagonism against the Americans.[19]

For decades, Israeli soldiers in the Gaza Strip and the West Bank have used this practice of destroying buildings from which insurgents are suspected of planning or mounting attacks, a practice now emulated in Iraq by U.S. forces. The Israeli Army imprisons the relatives of suspected terrorists, in the hopes of pressuring suspects to surrender. They also cordon off villages and towns thought to be hotbeds of guerrilla activity, to control the flow of people moving in and out. American military personnel threatened to displace 7,000 residents from their village, 75 kilometers north of Baghdad, if mortar attacks did not stop against Base Anaconda, a key coalition supply hub and air strip.[20]

American officials say they are not purposefully mimicking Israeli tactics, but acknowledge that they have studied closely the Israeli experience in urban fighting. [Prior to the Iraqi war,] Israeli defense experts briefed American commanders on their experience in guerrilla and urban warfare.[21]

The American attitude vis-à-vis the Iraqis was equally problematic and betrays some of the fundamental errors made in the Occupied Territories. "You have to understand the Arab mind," according to a company commander with the Fourth Infantry Division, "The only thing they understand is force, pride and saving face."[22]

Earlier in this book I have argued that such counter-terror tactics might be effective in the short term, but tend to inflame public opinion against the occupying forces—a dangerous legacy for Iraq. "An Iraqi man named Tariq muttered in anger. "I see no difference between us and the Palestinians," he said. "We didn't expect anything like this after Saddam fell."[23] Abderrahim Foukara has said that the images in the Arab media of the Israeli Occupation of Palestine and the American Occupation of Iraq are virtually indistinguishable from each other in the minds of most Arabs and the images broadcast on the news are equally transferable. This is exacerbated by the fact that the Israelis are using American made weapons and armor and so the images truly blend one into the other.[24] By April 2004, even former allies of the U.S., the Shi'a, echoed their resentment of the U.S. occupation and declared their admiration for Hamas and Hizb'allah style tactics. (See photo 16.) For example, Shi'a cleric Mustaga al Yacoubi, an aide of the radical cleric Moqtada As Sadr, who was arrested on April 4, 2004, in the Shi'a holy city of Najaf. Another senior cleric urged his followers: "Terrorize your enemy, as we cannot remain silent over its violations."[25]

There has been growing resentment of the U.S. liberators during the course of the American occupation. Anger over the U.S. support for Israel, the occupation, and the abuse of prisoners at Abu Ghraib, is endemic in the Arab World. The insurgency has included the spectrum of Iraqi society including men and women, the old and the young. Iraqi Shiite women, members of Moqtada as Sadr's "Mahdi Army," march to protest the American occupation.[26] Guerrillas regularly target U.S. troops, but increasingly kill local politicians, policemen, Iraqis working for foreign companies and foreign civilians—anyone seen as cooperating too closely with the occupying forces.

As the casualty rates of U.S. soldiers mounted (more than 1,300 by January 2005), attacks have become increasingly brutal including the videotaped beheadings of Nicholas Berg, Paul Johnson, Kenneth Bigley as well as a Turkish contractor, Maher Kemal and an Iraqi Kurdish translator, Lugman Hussein by *Tawhid wal Jihad* (Unity and Holy War) and the *Ansar al Sunnah* Army. Jon Lee Anderson refers to these shocking videos as snuff films intended to mobilize greater support. Insurgents in Iraq have kidnapped over 150 foreigners in their campaign to drive out coalition forces although most have been kidnapped for ransom and have been subsequently released.

The March 31, 2004, attack in Falluja was evocative of the attacks that repelled U.S. forces from Somalia. Four Americans were mutilated and their corpses dragged in the streets. This scene was broadcast on news channels all over the Muslim world and there were threats of further bloodshed if the U.S. forces responded too harshly.

A cheering crowd in Falluja, known for its hard-line resistance to the U.S.-led occupation, burned and kicked the corpses, dragging them through the streets. Images of charred corpses hanging from a bridge were flashed across the world, raising new questions about the occupation. But residents in the hostile town said the military should think carefully about how to react. "If they enter Falluja and use force it will only be met with force and this will happen over and over. . . . This is Falluja. Everyone is angry with the occupation and there are many tribes, which means there will be revenge. The Americans should just keep out."[27]

In all likelihood this was the turning point in the war. The Americans subsequently withdrew and left the militants in Falluja. During the uprising, the American forces used loyal militias (Shi'a and Kurdish) to fight the militants. Whereas the Iraqi defense forces either refused to fight or mutinied or joined the insurgency. This is the same group President Bush expects to take over from U.S. forces and ensure free and fair elections in January 2005. Between 50 and 53 percent of the Iraqi electorate turned out at the polls on January 30. Voter turnout in the Shi'a south and Kurdish north exceeded 90 percent; however, Sunnis did not vote in large numbers. The lack of Sunni involvement in the process will create greater opportunities for militants to spoil any peace and ruin any future prospects for a democratic outcome. Assuming the militants continued their strategy of attacking Iraqi civilians waiting to join the National Guard or the Police, they struck at polling stations, even though polling locations were kept secret until the eleventh hour. Sunnis' rejection of the election may lead to greater sectarian strike and the possibility of an escalating violence which could result in civil war.

From the perspective of Osama Bin Laden: The United States is a hegemonic power, propping up Israel and other morally bankrupt regimes that would not exist save for American backing (for example, Egypt, Saudi Arabia, the Persian Gulf, Pakistan, and Uzbekistan). Although the United States is a hegemonic power, it cannot bear the pain or the losses inflicted by terrorist attacks—as was the case in Lebanon after the 1983 bombing of the U.S. Marine barracks, and when it withdrew from Somalia following the deaths of eighteen U.S. Rangers and Delta Force commandos, in 1993. Thus, in Bin Laden's view, terrorism against the United States—and allied Western countries—works.[28] Thus the U.S. is deterrable.

The Americans have likewise engaged in a limited policy of targeted assassination of insurgent leaders (when arrests were impossible). During the course of the U.S. occupation, several mid-level insurgents were killed or captured. However, a large number of micro-cells remained intact. The concern, echoed by testimonies to the 9/11 Commission is that because of U.S. policies abroad in Iraq or Afghanistan, the American homeland will be targeted. The key question is—could what has happened in Israel against transportation, cafés, supermarkets, or pizzerias in Sri Lanka, against politicians and military personnel, or in Iraq against servicemen religious leaders, and international organizations—spread to the United States?

The greatest fear concerns the possibility of sleeper cells associated with 9/11 that may still be at large, and will perpetrate further suicidal terrorist acts. The fear is exacerbated by concerns that terrorists could make suicide belts potentially more deadly by using nuclear hazardous waste (dirty bombs) to carry out bombings across the country. Unfortunately, this scenario remains a possibility. Increasingly so after the Abu Ghraib prison scandal and thousands of civilian deaths in Iraq.

Many people ask: why there has not been another incident since 9/11? With every major holiday, sporting event, or anniversary, law enforcement agencies are on guard for some impending attack. The fact that, at the time of this writing, there has not been a repeat of 9/11 could be the result of law enforcement vigilance, al Qaeda's own weaknesses, or just plain luck. One should not forget how long it took to plan the events of 2001 and recognize that the terrorists' time horizon is normally quite long. Bin Laden and other extremists view this as a centuries-long struggle. If the attacks against the World Trade Center were the culmination of the failure to bring down the building in 1993, it is conceivable that terrorists will strike years from now. Al Qaeda tends to favor fewer spectacular attacks, even if spaced years apart, over small-scale attacks that require significantly less planning but have less impact. For some, this means nuclear or biological weapons. At the same time, the decentralization of al Qaeda under continuous American pressure means that the United States may face a series of smaller attacks planned by local groups sympathetic with its aims. Al Qaeda's successful attacks in Madrid may well have shifted the outcome of a national election. Osama Bin Laden's tape to the American people, timed four days before the elections appears to have been his attempt to ensure a second Bush presidential term. The coincidence of these events is unsettling.

Anti-terrorist agencies approach the problem in a variety of ways. They recognize that they must upset the terrorists' networks, limit the funds available to carry out operations, and investigate any potential threat on U.S. soil. Thankfully, much of what makes terrorism easy abroad, access to weapons, explosive materials, and an existing infrastructure is largely unavailable here. The most notable contrast with the U.S. is with Israel where the production of suicide belts has unfortunately become a cottage industry and the costs of producing one is $150.00 or less.

In the Middle East or Sri Lanka would-be bombers have readier access to explosives than they would in the United States, where it is not so easy (although far from impossible) to procure these materials. Making sure that the chemical supply houses, construction companies, and demolition firms are visited by police and asked to notify them of sudden purchases of small or medium-sized quantities of explosives by previously unknown customers is one type of precaution. For instance, the Home Depot stores report any sales of fertilizer in excess of 500 pounds to authorities.

The other major difference between the United States and other countries facing terrorist threats regards existing infrastructure. At present there is insufficient terrorist organization and structure to produce the sustained intensity of suicide bombings abroad. Terrorist infrastructures require years to develop and execute, and operatives must insinuate themselves into the local community. The Egyptian Islamic Jihad (EIJ) agents who attempted to assassinate President Hosni Mubarak in Addis Ababa, Ethiopia (January 13, 1999), had immigrated years before the attack, and even married local women to blend in better with the population. To be successful, terrorist groups require a full network of operatives to support the actions of a few bombers.

The Terrorist Organizations that make use of suicide bombing practice a division of labor and comprise several elements: *Quartermasters* who obtain explosives and other materials, *Bomb Makers* who build the bomb, *Minders* who sequester the bomber in a safe house, *Film crews* who make a video of the operative (partly for propaganda and partly to ensure the bomber does not back out), *Reconnaissance Teams* who scout the area or recover information and pass information onto the handlers, and, finally, the *Handlers* who deliver the bomber as close to the target as possible, avoiding detection.[29]

There is a possibility of a single attack, or a series of related attacks, against the United States but a sustained campaign of terrorism would be unlikely without a fairly complicated organizational structure as described above. Despite the horror involved, a one-time suicide attack is fundamentally different from a continuous campaign. Suicide attacks in Israel and Sri Lanka have, on occasion, reached the intensity of one a day. In Israel over the past four years, there has been in excess of 140 suicide bombings and a far greater number that were successfully thwarted by the Israeli authorities.[30] (See appendix fig. 2.4.) The dangers of suicide bombing in the U.S. are not the same as in Israel or Sri Lanka but attacks there provide insight into which counter-terror strategies work or fail.

According to terrorism expert Bruce Hoffman, it is important to adjust American expectations regarding suicide terror:

> The Israelis know that they're not going to stop every attack, but that doesn't mean that they don't do something about it. And that doesn't mean that what they're doing is not effective. The difference is that

with the IDF deployed in the West Bank they are stopping 80 percent of the [attacks]. Now, there's a completely different dynamic in the United States. We don't have a hostile population right across the border that provides a pool of recruits for suicide bombing. So if suicide terrorism were to commence in the United States, it would be different in many ways from what we see in Israel. And also our defenses, by the same token, would have to be different. We're a different country.[31]

Militant Islamic groups present in the country are one of the main foci for U.S. counter-terrorism. Since September 11 government agencies have begun rooting out the sources of militant Islam, shutting off fund-raising, tracking down funding recipients, and encouraging moderate Islamic leaders to emphasize the inclusive (as opposed to the exclusive) writings of the Qur'an and the more pluralistic commentaries of the Hadith.

However, in limiting the spread of militant Islam (often called *Salafism*) Washington has been unwilling to risk a rupture with its two closest Muslim allies, Pakistan and Saudi Arabia. The Bush administration has had to face the fact that Riyadh was—and remains—the main ideological and financial sponsor of Islamic extremism worldwide. Unfortunately, the Saudi government has been seriously constrained in its ability to combat terrorism. As a recent Council on Foreign Relations report noted, Saudi Arabia is the largest source of financing for al Qaeda. The report also blamed the Saudi government for not being resolute enough in the war on terror.[32]

Since its alliance with the United States in the first Persian Gulf War, American relations with Saudi Arabia have been increasingly strained. In 1994, Mohammed al-Khilewi, the first secretary at the Saudi Mission to the United Nations, defected to the United States. In seeking political asylum, he brought with him 14,000 internal government documents depicting the Saudi royal family's corruption, human-rights abuses, and financial support for terrorists. He had evidence that the Saudis had given financial and technical support to Hamas.[33] American administrations have chosen not to confront the Saudi leadership over its financial support of terror organizations and its refusal to help in the investigation of 9/11. In fact, all testimony related to Saudi Arabia to the October 2002 Joint Congressional Commission of Inquiry was redacted by the Bush White House.[34]

Saudi Arabia would not or could not stem terror because of its own internal weakness. For Seymour Hersh:

> The Saudi Arabian royal family, headed by King Fahd is a regime increasingly corrupt, alienated from the country's religious rank and file, and so weakened and frightened that it has brokered its future by chan-

neling hundreds of millions of dollars in what amounts to protection money to fundamentalist groups that wish to overthrow it. By 1996 Saudi money was supporting Osama Bin Laden's al Qaeda and other extremist groups in Afghanistan, Lebanon, Yemen, and Central Asia, and throughout the Persian Gulf region.[35]

The suicide bombing attacks in Riyadh in May 2003 demonstrated the Saudi government's laxity with regard to rooting out al Qaeda operatives even though they had advance warning from U.S. Intelligence that al Qaeda was planning an operation on Saudi soil weeks prior to the attack.

The situation in Pakistan is particularly alarming. Pakistan remains crucially important in al Qaeda operations, serving as a clearinghouse of sorts for operatives and would-be recruits at the individual and group levels. Much of the remaining Taliban infrastructure immigrated to Pakistan during the war in Afghanistan and the Musharraf Government has been unable to keep track of Taliban leaders, even after Afghan President Mohammed Karzai provided President Musharraf with a list of known Taliban operatives.[36] According to his critics, Musharraf is much more interested in his own political survival than American security.

The question is not only how violence spreads but also where the roots of terrorism lie and how to remove these continuing sources of violence. The Pakistani Islamic schools (madrasas) have been identified by Secretary of Defense Donald Rumsfeld and highlighted by the 9/11 Commission Report as breeding grounds for future terrorists. One of the most influential, the Haqqania school outside Peshawar, graduated much of the Taliban's senior leadership—including at least nine Americans. A recent study by the International Crisis Group suggests that students of a religious boarding school in Central Java, Indonesia, may compose the core of Southeast Asia Islamist network.[37] It is said to have graduated a who's who of Southeast Asia's terrorist network, including two of the Bali bombers and several captured bomb makers. The madrasas and pesantrens inculcate anti-Western and especially anti-American sentiment as well as indicate the failure of the existing educational systems in the Middle East and Islamic World. This is partially the result of domestic politics in places like Pakistan, which give preference to military spending and the nuclear arms race with India over educational investment for the future. President Bush has promised millions to reform the Indonesian school system in order to offset the influence of the militant Islamic schools. However, research on state run schools' textbooks in Pakistan reveals that they are just as likely to inculcate anti-American sentiment and contain many anti-Western ideas.[38] Secretary Rumsfeld has argued that radical Islamic militant extremism doesn't depend on al Qaeda alone, and that there is no fixed collection of terrorists for the United States to combat but rather an environment that produces extremism because of closed political systems and economies that prevent people from having a voice in their government or being able to provide for a family. Widespread alienation and extremism are thus unsurprising outcomes. However true, this view still fails to take into account how U.S. policy has an exacerbating effect on this alienation and has led violent anti-Americanism to find resonance within the Islamic world. For many in the Arab world, U.S. policies have exacerbated feelings of anger and the likelihood of terrorism. We must remember that the goal of the guerrilla warfare is not to win, but rather to turn the civilian population against the occupying army. The war in Iraq has been most successful at this. When radical Sunnis and radical Shi'a work together, then the Bush Administration managed to do something even Saddam's state terror was never able to do: get enemies to cooperate against a common enemy.

The Bush Administration must keep in mind, military force is a hammer but not every problem is a nail.

CHALLENGES AHEAD

Although we have fairly good strategic intelligence about the groups that threaten us— their objectives, capabilities, and the methods they might use—we seldom obtain the sort of tactical intelligence—about the date, place, or method of attack—specific enough to foil a plot and prevent it. This underscores a chronic problem for any counter-terrorism strategy. Terrorists will always have the advantage of picking the time, place, and manner of their attack.

Intelligence agencies seldom obtain detailed information in advance because of the inherent difficulty of penetrating or otherwise learning the plans of terrorist groups—that is, the operational cells which actually carry out terrorist attacks. These cells tend to be small, secretive, suspicious toward outsiders, ruthless toward anyone suspected of betraying them, and highly conscious of operational security. "Good strategic intelligence and a lack of tactical intelligence:" was the conclusion of the commission led by General Downing that studied the bombing of Khobar Towers in 1996; it was a conclusion of the panel chaired by Admiral Crowe that looked at the embassy bombings in 1998; and this was also the conclusion of the 9/11 Commission. Moreover the very success in disrupting al Qaeda's command and control has led the organization to decentralize and depend on ideologically sympathetic groups. This makes getting hold of such intelligence that much more difficult.

In one sense, every terrorist attack represents an intelligence failure, since conceivably one could have obtained specific information, and with it, foiled the plot. But by that definition, a world without intelligence failures would be a world without terrorism—something historically unprecedented. Using a sensible definition of intelligence failure—where there was information that reasonably could have been collected but wasn't, or that was collected but was misanalyzed, misused, or ignored—and reflecting on what we know today about the September 11 operation, there were serious errors made. According to Richard A. Clarke:

> The US response to al Qaeda following 9–11 has been partially effective. Unfortunately, the US did not act sufficiently quickly to insert US forces to capture or kill the al Qaeda leadership in Afghanistan. Nor did we employ sufficient US and Allied forces to stabilize that country. . . . There have been more major al Qaeda related attacks globally in the 30 months since 9–11 than there were in the 30 months preceding it. Hostility toward the US in the Islamic world has increased since 9–11, largely as a result of the invasion and occupation of Iraq. Thus, new terrorist cells are likely being created, unknown to US intelligence.[39]

The 9/11 hijackers took the simple yet bare minimum precautions needed to keep their plot under wraps, which meant doing their planning and plotting behind closed doors, and not saying anything to anyone outside of their cell, or through any means that could be intercepted. They did make serious errors (for instance casing planes together in groups of 4 prior to the attacks and arousing suspicion in the process) but the reports filed with the FAA were lost in the bureaucratic shuffle.

The September 11 attacks may have a certain demonstration effect, although as far as major attacks against the U.S. homeland are concerned, the bombing of the World Trade Center in 1993 and the Oklahoma City bombing had already shown the way. The September 11 hijackers demonstrated a major vulnerability in aviation security but the new high awareness of that particular vulnerability, and the countermeasures taken to lessen it, will make it harder for them to use the same technique again. Terrorists are strongly motivated to hit the United States again. In particular, they may stage attacks in direct reprisal for U.S. counter-terrorist actions in response to the original attack—including two major military offensives in Iraq and Afghanistan. These operations along with the prisoners sequestered at Guantanamo and the prison abuse scandal at Abu Ghraib, have stirred opposition and resentment in much of the Muslim world.

The level of risk to domestic security depends heavily on the future course of U.S. military operations. Over the longer term a key question is whether the use of American armed forces in the name of counterterrorism will betray the democratic principles the United States seeks to spread globally. The Bush Administration has made the spread of democracy a key part of both its counter-terrorism strategy and a justification for the war in Iraq. Unfortunately, there is a major tension between this democratization strategy and the short-term needs to fight terrorism and work with Arab allies. There are additional questions as to whether the United States will continue to take an offensive stance against what it designates as "rogue states"—beyond Afghanistan and Iraq and on to Syria and Iran. Expanding Bush's war on terrorism to any additional targets would be a terrible mistake.

The war in Afghanistan was seemingly more successful than the American adventure in Iraq. This was partly the result of a cohesive coalition facing the Taliban and the fact that the United States had the clear support of the rest of the world in the aftermath of the September attacks. Hoffman, however, argues that the loss of Afghanistan may have little effect on the strength of al Qaeda. Several of al Qaeda's most devastating attacks—the 1993 bombing of the World Trade Center, and Ramzi Youssef's failed plot to bomb twelve U.S. commercial aircraft over the Pacific—predate al Qaeda's strong presence in Afghanistan. For al Qaeda, Afghanistan was more important as a base from which to carry out a conventional civil war against the Northern Alliance.[40] Arguably, Afghanistan drained resources while simultaneously providing a logistical and training base of operations.

The war in Afghanistan in 2002 stands in stark contrast to the U.S. war against Iraq the following year. The U.S. led war against Iraq sustained and fed the worst misperceptions of the Arab world regarding American intentions in the Middle East and allegations of neocolonialism. According to Clarke:

> Osama Bin Laden had been saying for years, "America wants to invade an Arab country and occupy it, an oil-rich Arab country." . . . This is part of his propaganda. So what did we do after 9/11? We invade an oil-rich and occupy an oil-rich Arab country which was doing nothing to threaten us. In other words, we stepped right into Bin Laden's propaganda. And the result of that is that al Qaeda and organizations like it, offshoots of it, second-generation al Qaeda have been greatly strengthened.[41]

Part of the problem with the U.S. policy in Iraq is that it yields a potential lose-lose scenario. If the U.S. stays in Iraq, as an occupying power, the violence will increase as this book predicts. However, if the U.S. pulls out of Iraq prematurely, before the stated task of regime change is successfully completed, it would lose credibility in the Middle East, appear as a "paper tiger," and allow the supporters of al Qaeda to argue that they have once again vanquished a superpower. Continued instability might also turn parts of Iraq into a terrorist haven drawing in Jihadis from near and far. This is particularly dangerous given Iraq's strategic geographic location bordering on Iran, Turkey, Syria, Kuwait and Saudi Arabia. [42]

There was a great deal of discussion about the role that terrorism plays in the domestic politics of democratic countries. Much has been written about how the bombing of a train in Madrid affected Spain's electoral process. A week after the Madrid attack, the Abu Hafs al-Masri Brigades claimed responsibility for the bombing on behalf of al Qaeda and promised a truce in Spain if the new government withdrew its troops from Iraq. The declaration also turned its attention to President Bush, saying: "A word for the foolish Bush. We are very keen that you do not lose in the forthcoming elections as we know very well that any big attack can bring down your government and this is what we do not want. We cannot get anyone who is more foolish than you, who deals with matters with force instead of wisdom and diplomacy. Your stupidity and religious extremism is what we want as our people will not awaken from their deep sleep except when there is an enemy. Kerry will kill our nation while it sleeps because he and the Democrats have the cunning to embellish blasphemy and present it to the Arab and Muslim nation as civilization. Because of this we desire you [Bush] to be elected."[43]

Nevertheless, on September 7, 2004, less than a month before the U.S presidential election, Vice President Dick Cheney, announced that the U.S. would risk another terrorist attack if voters make the wrong choice in November. "It's absolutely essential we make the right choice on 2 November because if we make the wrong choice, then the danger is that we'll get hit again and we'll be hit in a way that will be devastating from the standpoint of the United States." However partisan this comment was, it fails to take into account the "incumbent phenomenon."[44]

Across the cases discussed in this book, terrorist violence against civilian targets increased significantly when the incumbent leader of the target state is given a second term in office. This has been evident in Russia during the second Putin term, in Israel after Sharon was reelected, in Sri Lanka when Kumaratunge was reinstalled as president and likely now against America.

Bush's particular global unpopularity exacerbates this existing incumbent dynamic and the dangers to the United States. The logic, from the perspective of the terrorists, is that if the larger public reelects a leader they perceive as their enemy, then that civilian public is also to blame for his (or her) policies. Osama Bin Laden released an eighteen minute video on October 29, 2004, four days before the U.S. presidential election, asserting that

Bush had dragged his country into a quagmire in Iraq and warned of future retaliation. In a section of his videotaped speech in which he harshly criticized George Bush, Osama Bin Laden stated: "Any U.S. state that does not toy with our security automatically guarantees its own security." The media mistranslated the words "ay wilaya" (which means any state or each state) as "country" or "nation" whereas the word for country would be *dawla* or *balad*. The threat was seemingly directed at each individual U.S. state.

The Islamist website Al-Qal'a explained what this sentence meant: "This message was a warning to every U.S. state individually. When he [Osama Bin Laden] said, 'Every state will be determining its own security, and will be responsible for its choice,' it means that any U.S. state that will choose to vote for Bush as president has chosen to fight us, and we will consider it our enemy, and any state that will vote against Bush has chosen to make peace with us, and we will not characterize it as an enemy. By this characterization, Sheikh Osama wants to drive a wedge in the American body, to weaken it, and he wants to divide the American people itself between enemies of Islam and the Muslims, and those who fight for us, so that he doesn't treat all American people as if they're the same."[45]

What is significant about the role that terrorist threats played in the U.S. 2004 election campaign is that the two places that suffered most from the terrorist attacks of 9/11, New York City and Washington, DC overwhelmingly voted against the President's reelection (between 89-91% in favor of John Kerry) whereas the rural areas of America where terrorism is more theoretical than a reality voted overwhelmingly in favor of George Bush. Thus the election has implications for the potential of terror on U.S. soil in the heartland of America and in the southern states. This also follows the tactical shifts we observe in Sri Lanka, Russia, and Palestine where terrorists shift from attacks within the homeland (their areas of dominance to shake off the foreign occupation) to the heartland of the country that is occupying them to inflict maximum damage and casualties.

In the video, Bin Laden reiterates his perspective that links the Iraqi war to the pursuit of oil. "The black gold (oil) blinded him [President Bush] and he put his personal interests above the general interests of America so the war took place, many died, American money was squandered and Bush was dragged into a quagmire in Iraq which threatens his future." He went on to say: "more than 15,000 of our people were killed and more than 1,000 of your people were killed and tens of thousands were wounded. Bush's hands are sullied with blood of those on both sides just for oil and to employ his private companies." To underscore his point he said: "Remember for every action, there is a reaction."[46]

Finally, the continued occupation of Iraq will place American soldiers and civilians increasingly as risk. The demographic makeup of Iraq complicates the future for our safety even in the event of a January 2005 election. The majority of Iraqis are Shi'ite Muslims. After 1979, it is unlikely that the U.S. Government would be comfortable with another Shi'a dominated government in the Middle East. If a Shi'a government is installed, it would potentially increase radical Sunni Wahhabi antagonism against the United States—which would appear to be siding with the Shi'a against the Sunni. The worst possible scenario would pit radical Shi's together with radical Sunni elements in the common cause against Americans. There seems to be no way to exit from this policy without incurring high levels of antagonism that trigger terrorist motivations. As John Mearsheimer has said: "The United States took a decade to accept defeat and exit Vietnam. The Soviet Union took a decade to reach the same end in Afghanistan, while the Israelis took eighteen years to finally leave Lebanon. How long will it take the U.S. to leave Iraq?" According to the CIA's chief specialist on Bin Laden, "I'm not talking about appeasement. There is no way out of this war at the moment . . . it's not a choice between war and peace. It's a choice between war and endless war . . . it's [about] American self interest."[47]

DOMESTIC COUNTER TERROR STRATEGIES

What precautions can the U.S. government take against the possibility of domestic suicide terror attacks? Layers of Government agencies are busily training law enforcement personnel to identify and infiltrate potential terrorist organizations. Some of the best strategies have involved community outreach programs by the "cop on the beat" in order to alter the perceptions of the communities from which the terrorists spring or take refuge.

The government has managed to disrupt the terrorists' financial networks, freeze their assets, and detain their money handlers. With a few more successes, it is feasible that the government will be able to collapse the al Qaeda network altogether. But unfortunately, even on the verge of collapse, al Qaeda can do a lot of damage and kill lots of people.

Terrorist expert Bruce Hoffman has made the case that the United States has had considerable success against al Qaeda:

Al Qaeda is clearly weaker than it was at the formal commencement of the war on terrorism, on October 7, 2001. It has been deprived of operational bases and training camps in Afghanistan. Its command-and-control capabilities have been disrupted. Its headquarters have been destroyed. Its leaders and fighters have been forcibly dispersed, and they are now consumed as much by providing for their own security as by planning and executing attacks. Communication and coordination among the disparate parts of al Qaeda's global network are more inconvenient—if not necessarily less effective—than ever before.[48]

Other signs indicate that the United States has a great deal more work ahead. Al Qaeda's core leadership is still alive and at large—perhaps only a third of its leaders are dead or captured. Moreover, the two most important figures, Osama Bin Laden and Ayman al-Zawahiri, are still very much alive. Its activities are therefore still somewhat centralized, and controlled by top leaders. The process may be less organized and more fractured than when it was based in Afghanistan, but the looseness of control is not necessarily a liability. Al Qaeda can still fill its mid-level operational command positions—because of the reservoir of fighters and operatives (some estimates place the number as high as 70,000) that the group trained during the 1990s, in the Sudan, Yemen, and Afghanistan. But what makes al Qaeda strong is its continuing ability to recruit and mobilize fighters, supporters, and sympathizers worldwide.[49]

The assumption driving the American war on terrorism is that the United States can win by targeting rogue states and the tyrants who rule them. The war in Afghanistan was about ousting the Taliban and denying al Qaeda a sanctuary; the war in Iraq was about ousting Saddam. This view of the terrorist threat is deeply flawed, quite apart from the dubious claims about the ties between al Qaeda and Saddam. Al Qaeda operates globally and independently of states. They take state support when they can get it but they are not manipulated directly by states, and that makes them particularly dangerous.

Al Qaeda is a less like a state and more like an NGO with multiple independent franchises. Its terrorists can strike-whether in Bali, Casablanca, Riyadh, Istanbul, Madrid, or New York and Washington-without the direct support of states. These franchises are likely to survive the death of its "corporate parent." Al Qaeda is no longer a regular terrorist organization that can be defeated by killing or capturing its leader, it is a global insurgency that spreads revolutionary fervor throughout the Muslim world. We can target its operatives, but its ideas and inspiration are ultimately far more dangerous.

Bruce Hoffman has identified four different types of al Qaeda operatives.[50]

1. *Professional cadres.* The most dedicated element of al Qaeda. Teams are carefully selected, provided with specific instructions, and generously funded.

2. *Trained amateurs.* For example, Ahmed Ressam, arrested in December 1999 at Port Angeles, Washington, after entering the United States from Canada with explosive materials in the trunk of his car. Ressam had some background

in terrorism and belonged to Algeria's Armed Islamic Group. After being recruited by al Qaeda he was given some basic training in Afghanistan. Unlike the professional cadres, however, Ressam was given only open-ended instructions. The team he had been assigned in Afghanistan had decided to attack an airport or foreign consulate in the United States. He received $12,000 in seed money and was expected to raise the rest of his operational funds through petty thievery—by swiping money, credit cards, passports, traveler's checks, and computers from tourists. He was told to recruit members for his terrorist cell from among the Muslim expatriate communities in Canada. Nevertheless, as ill-prepared and as inept as the trained amateurs may be (Richard Reid, the "Shoe Bomber," is another example), their ability to succeed once, and thereby to inflict pain and destruction, should not be dismissed.

3. *Local walk-ins.* Independent Islamic radicals who come up with terrorist-attack ideas on their own and then attempt to obtain funding from al Qaeda. An example is the group of Islamic radicals—not formally a part of al Qaeda—who plotted to attack the American and Israeli embassies and the British and Australian high commissions in Singapore. The Singapore plotters, who were arrested before they could carry out their intentions, spent four years planning their attacks, conducting the kind of detailed and meticulous reconnaissance—including extensive videotaping, with detailed voice-over discussions of potential targets—that is emblematic of al Qaeda operations.

4. *Like-minded guerrillas and terrorists.* This group embraces existing insurgent or terrorist groups that have benefited over the years from either Bin Laden's largesse or his spiritual guidance; that have received al Qaeda training in Afghanistan or elsewhere; or that the organization has provided with arms, materiel, and other assistance in order to further the cause of global *jihad.* Among the recipients of "revolutionary philanthropy" are insurgents in Uzbekistan, Indonesia, Chechnya, the Philippines, Bosnia, and Kashmir. This is designed to harness the energy of geographically scattered, disparate movements and to ensure that al Qaeda operatives can call on these local groups for logistical services and manpower.

With the disruption of the al Qaeda network (and assuming that the United States manages to eliminate Bin Laden), many of the associated terrorist organizations might gravitate toward regional organizations—resulting in a decentralization of terror.[51]

The primary benefit would be the demise of al Qaeda and the elimination of its ability to perpetrate another large 9/11-style attack. It would be difficult for Bin Laden or anyone else to exert command and control over such a decentralized network. Communication within the network, let alone control of the subordinates, would be virtually impossible. Many of the attacks since the war in Afghanistan have often been the work of the local organizations rather than directed from above by Bin Laden although they were most likely funded by him.[52] However, this decentralization has positive and negative implications.

A decentralized terrorist network would be difficult for counter-terrorism agencies to disrupt since it would be more diffuse organizationally, difficult to follow, and harder to monitor. The smaller organizations might ramp up violence in order to distinguish themselves from the crowd and to take a lead in anti-Western activities. Although they would not be able to perpetrate conspicuous or dramatic attacks like 9/11, they might carry out smaller episodes that would result in fewer casualties and less (but perhaps more generalized) popular fears. 9/11 has raised the bar for terrorist activities. Since the smaller groups would not be able to conduct an operation of that caliber or scale, they might have increased incentives to use dirty bombs or weapons of mass destruction to distinguish themselves from the crowd to mobilize support.

Although it is difficult to get military or commercial explosives in the United States, that might only increase the likelihood of a car bomb packed with larger quantities of less efficient explosives (for example ammonium nitrate which was used in Oklahoma City by Timothy McVeigh). Less sophisticated suicide bombs are often made using an acetone-based explosive rather than a military explosive like C-4 or Semtex (which, for example, was used in Richard Reid's shoe bomb).

Given that domestic suicide bombers may use less sophisticated explosives, the U.S. can use additional precautions to protect against attacks like hardening targets, reinforcing park benches, erecting concrete "Jersey" barriers around vulnerable buildings, ensuring that bus and subway windows are shatterproof and that seats are not easily dislodged. Bruce Hoffman recommended a list of precautions to deter domestic terrorist attacks. It is necessary to understand the Terrorists' operational environment: know their modus operandi and targeting patterns. Suicide bombers are rarely lone outlaws and are preceded by long logistical trails. Homeland security can focus on the bombers' infrastructure and develop strong confidence by building ties with communities most likely to be the sources of terror; law enforcement should encourage and cultivate cooperation in a nonthreatening way. They should encourage businesses from which terrorists can obtain bomb-making components to alert authorities—especially if they notice large purchases of ammonium nitrate fertilizer, pipes, batteries, acetone, or other flammable chemicals; First responders on the scene should learn from the experiences abroad and be wary of a second, follow-up attack in the same location. Finally, they need to make informed decisions about sending in emergency crews until an area is secured.[53]

However, evidence from other cases where suicide terror has become a daily fact of life demonstrates that terrorist organizations versus individuals might play a less crucial role than they did in the past. Moreover, the time lag between signing on and committing the act of violence decreases if the population is already convinced that terrorism is a good idea. Therefore, the environment in which would be bombers develops matters. There is little need to indoctrinate Palestinians to convince them to attack Israelis. This trend poses additional challenges for counter-terrorism since we have worked under the assumption that suicide terrorists require a fairly complicated infrastructure in order to conduct suicide bombing campaigns. Among Argo's interviews of bombers:

> Eight of the 15 interviewees volunteered; five of 15 executed their mission within 10 days of committing to it, and almost 90% undertook their mission within one month of being assigned. An individual's psychological preparation for bombing seems to take place often without ties to a cell or institutional training.[54]

Furthermore, the types of counter-terrorist policies have a direct impact on whether violence is well received or repudiated. Allegations in Russia that the security service was behind several attacks to drum up public support for Putin's war on terror have never been fully put to rest. Before the first Chechen War, the Federal Security Service FSB allegedly blew up of the bridge over the Yauza and bus No 33 in Moscow in 1994; the explosions on the metro in June 1996, prior to the presidential elections; and the blowing up of the blocks of apartments in Moscow and Volgodonsk and the attempted explosion in Ryazan in September 1999, occurred right before the State Duma, and the presidential elections, were all organized and carried out by the FSB.[55]

Israel has responded to every ceasefire of Palestinian suicide attacks with a targeted assassination thus unleashing a new round of reprisals and counter attacks. Sharon's refusal to consider burying Arafat in Jerusalem (his last wish) by saying, "not over my dead body" does not hint that such states and their leaders will negotiate or compromise to maintain law and order and restore a semblance of peace.

Why is what Israel does important for U.S policy? Bin Ladin admits that he thought of the idea of attacking the Twin Towers when he saw Israeli aircraft bombing towers in Lebanon in 1982, an invasion which he accused the U.S. of supporting.

"As I watched the destroyed towers in Lebanon, it occurred to me to punish the unjust the same way . . . to destroy towers in America so that it can taste some of what we are tasting and to stop killing our children and women. God knows that it had not occurred to our mind to attack the towers, but after our patience ran out and we saw the injustice and inflexibility of the American-Israeli alliance toward our people in Palestine and Lebanon, this came to my mind."[56]

If suicide bombing has two main purposes—directed against the enemy and used for mobilizational purposes—then we can disaggregate the motivations and the goals according to theories of political science. Suicide terror as "Coercive bargaining" is directed at the enemy to coerce them to leave the homeland territory; there is a phenomenon of outbidding directed toward the domestic population who sponsor, join, support, or "vote" for these organizations. The objectives of suicide bombing are thus multiple and may reinforce or undercut each other depending on specific conditions of each case. The goals are directed against the international opponent (get out of the "homeland"), against the domestic rivals (to achieve dominance), against local collaborators who might also be a source of political rivalry) and/or against a negotiated settlement to which they might not be party (spoil the peace).

There are indicators that popularity which results from suicide terror violence is not ingrained and the domestic population can distinguish between killing civilians and military personnel. In some cases, military targets are acceptable whereas civilian casualties are not. Organizations recognize this and adapt their strategies accordingly. The LTTE has adapted to such limitations because of constraints on its behavior while other groups, like the Chechens and the Palestinians, have not.

Recognizing the impact of public opinion opens up different avenues of response for counter-terrorism. Public opinion not only determines the range of activity, but also affects the types of steps taken against terror, the timing of their activation, as well as their scope and frequency; both on the level of defense such as the reinforcement of the security system, the establishment of designated security units, etc.

Drawing from the lessons learned in other cases of suicide terror, counter-terrorist measures, and the possible rebound effects, a good policy recommendation is to *outbid the outbidders*, in other words, create irresistible rewards that lead to arrests of recruiting agents; information that helps to disrupt an attack in the planning and preparation phases; prophylactic measures to improve standards of living by providing better education, employment, community relations; and meeting the legitimate aspirations and grievances of people who have been deliberately or unknowingly wronged in the past.

Terrorist groups use suicide bombing under two conditions: when other terrorist or military tactics fail and when they are in competition with other terrorist groups for popular/financial support. Suicide bombing is generally found in the second stage of conflicts and becomes particularly acute against civilians during an incumbent's second term in office—and suicide terror spreads in countries where the population is receptive to terrorists targeting civilians. There is a demonstration effect from one conflict to the next and so we should not underestimate the importance of observing other states' policies to observe patterns and glean insights for U.S policy, the future of terrorism in the United States, and the prospect of attacks against American targets abroad. This book may be a cautionary tale of what has worked, what did not and what might make matters worse. There is much to learn from the mistakes of some of the heavy handed counter terror policies in Russia and Israel and the successes of yet other countries facing those—dying to kill.

APPENDIX

The material in this appendix is keyed to the discussions in the texts. For example, figure 2.1 is the first figure referenced in chapter 2.

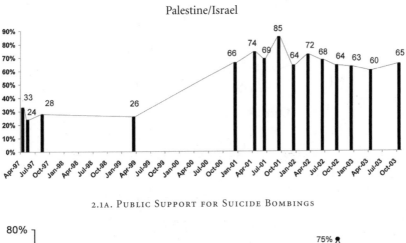

2.1A. PUBLIC SUPPORT FOR SUICIDE BOMBINGS

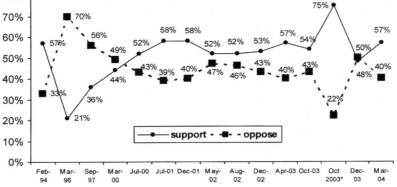

2.1B. PUBLIC SUPPORT/OPPOSITION TO SUICIDE TERROR *Source: Nicole Argo*

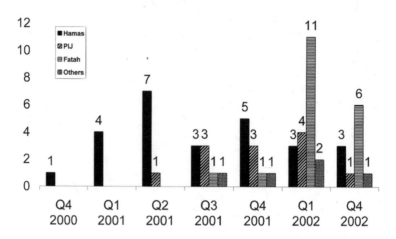

2.2. Proliferation of Terror Groups and Increasing Number of Attacks
Source: Assaf Moghadam

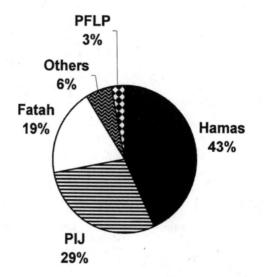

2.3. Percentage of Attacks by Organization 2000-2002

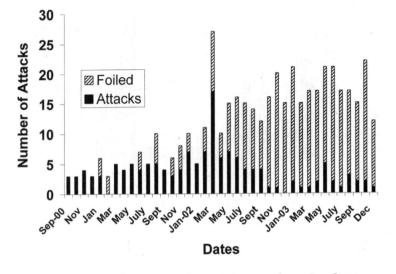

2.4. SUCCESS OF PALESTINIAN SUICIDE ATTACKS *Source: Boaz Ganor*

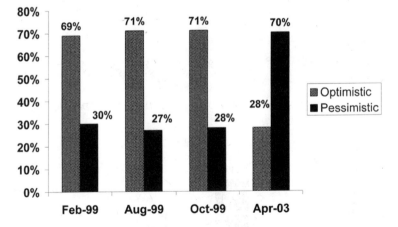

2.5. OPTIMISM FOR THE FUTURE *Source: JMCC polls between 1999 and 2003*

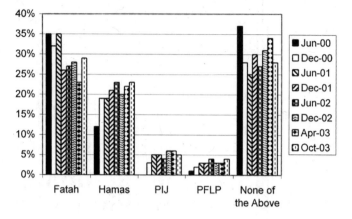

2.6. Trust in Palestinian Political Factions Over Time

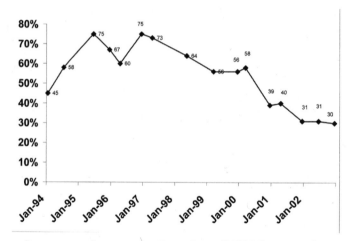

2.7. Palestinian Support for Oslo *Source: JMCC Poll #47 December 2002*

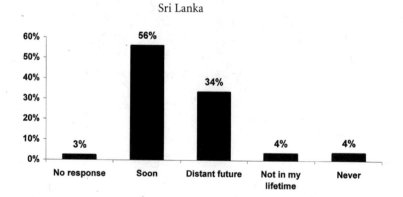

3.1. How Soon Do You Think There Will Be Peace?

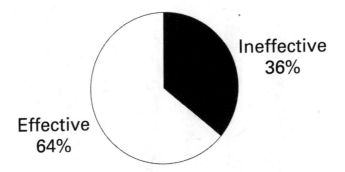

Ineffective
36%

Effective
64%

3.2A. EFFECTIVENESS OF ARMED CONFRONTATION

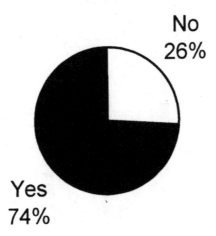

No
26%

Yes
74%

3.2B. HAS THE LTTE GAINED MORE NOW BY USING NEGOTIATIONS
VERSUS VIOLENCE?

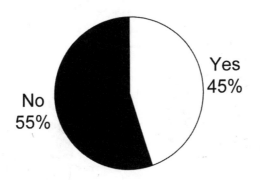

Yes
45%

No
55%

3.2C. HAS THE LTTE GAINED MORE IN THE PAST BY USING
NEGOTIATIONS VERSUS VIOLENCE?

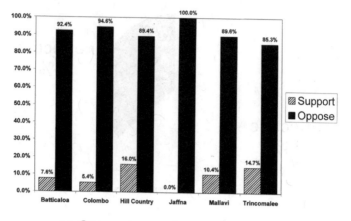

3.3. Civilian Attacks Supported By Region

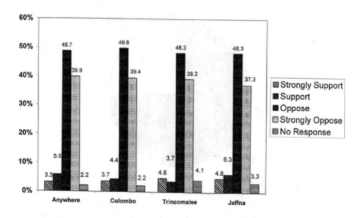

3.4A. Attacks Against Sinhalese Civilians

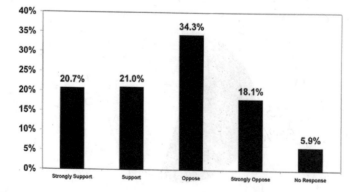

3.4B. Attacks Against Sinhalese Soldiers in Jaffna

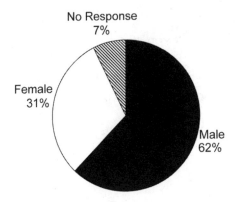

3.5A . GENDER RATIO OF THOSE WHO SUPPORTED THE USE OF VIOLENCE

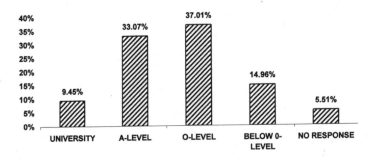

3.5B. LEVEL OF EDUCATION OF THOSE WHO SUPPORTED THE USE OF VIOLENCE

4.1. GARY VARVEL—*The Indianapolis Star-News,* APRIL 15. 2002

Country	Suicide attacks per year per country				Total Attacks	No. of Religious Attacks	Total Dead
	2000	2001	2002	2003			
Afghanistan**				2	2	2	11
Chechnya/Russia**	8	1	1	10	20	20	382
China			2		2	0	5
Indonesia**			1	1	2	2	215
Iraq**				33	33	15	244
Kashmir/Jammu**	17	29	18	11	75	75	409
Kenya*			1		1	1	18
Morocco**				5	5	5	44
Pakistan**			2	2	4	4	84
Palestine/Israel	3	40	64	22	129	78	555
Philippines**			1	1	2	2	24
Saudi Arabia*		1		5	6	6	57
Sri Lanka	14	4		1	19	0	205
Tunisia**			1		1	1	16
Turkey**		1		5	6	4	64
USA*		4			4	4	3002
Yemen*	1				1	1	19
SUM	43	80	91	98	312	220	5354

*al-Qaeda attacks
** Involving al-Qaeda associates

6.1. Contagion Effect of Suicide Terrorism 2000-2003
Source: Scott Atran

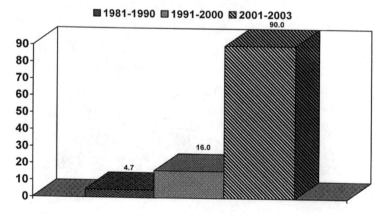

6.2. Increasing Number of Suicide Attacks by Decade
Source: Scott Atran

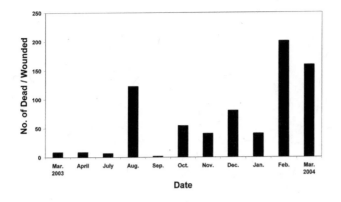

8.1. VICTIMS OF TERRORISM IN IRAQ MARCH 2003-MARCH 2004
Source: Patrick Hynes

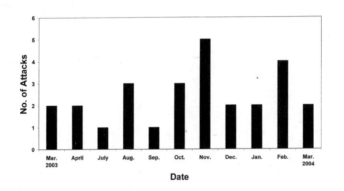

8.2. MAJOR TERRORIST ATTACKS IN IRAQ MARCH 2003-MARCH 2004
Source: Patrick Hynes

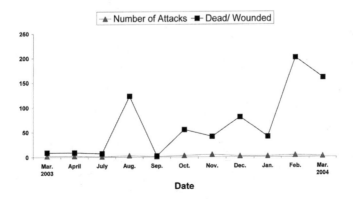

8.3. NUMBER OF ATTACKS VS. NUMBER OF VICTIMS MARCH 2003-MARCH 2004
Source: Patrick Hynes

NOTES

1. THE HISTORICAL ANTECEDENTS OF TERROR

1. Scott Atran, "Who Wants to be a Martyr?" *New York Times*, May 5, 2003, Amira Haas, "Confessions of a Dangerous Mind." *Ha'aretz* April 3, 2003 and Dr. Rita Giacaman, Institute of Community and Public Health at Bir Zeit University, BBC Interview, April 27, 2002 http//news.bbc.co.uk/hi/English/world/middle_east/new-sid_1951000/1951569.stm accessed 20 March 2003. Mark Juergensmeyer, *Terror in the Mind of God: The Global Rise of Religious Violence* (Berkeley: University of California Press, 2000), "Suicide Bombings: The Ultimate Weapon?" Yoram Schweitzer, Israel's Institute for Counter Terrorism (ICT) website (www.ict.org.il) August 7, 2001.

2. Among the groups listed, the majority happen to also be Muslim. This has troubling ramifications for theorizing suicide terror in other contexts. For groups like the PKK or the PFLP, religion is incidental.

3. *Al-Sharq Al-Awsat* London, September 4, 2004 cited by John Kifner, "School Siege in Russia Sparks Self Criticism in Arab World" September 8, 2004.

4. See Alan B. Krueger and Jitka Malekova, "Education, Poverty, Political Violence and Terrorism: Is There a Causal Connection?" NBER Working paper, July 2002, 4.

5. Juergensmeyer, *Terror in the Mind of God*, 214 however, he neglects to mention Sri Lanka—to which I have extended this logic.

6. *The Daily Star* (Beirut), Feb. 8, 2002.

7. Foreign Policy Association, *Great Decisions '86* (New York: Foreign Policy Association), 36.

8. Max Hastings, Comment and Analysis, "These Terrible Tactics May Actually be Working," The Guardian (UK), September 6, 2004, 16.

9. David Rapoport, "Fear and Trembling: Terrorism in Three Religious Traditions," *American Political Science Review* 78 (1984): 653.

10. Herodotus, *The Histories*, trans. Aubrey de Selincourt (London: Penguin 1954, rev. ed. 1996), VII, 85.

11. Rapoport, "Fear and Trembling," p.p 659 ff. Rapoport cites Major General William Henry Sleeman, "Bhowanee is happy and most so in proportion to the blood that

is shed . . . blood is her food . . . she thirsts for blood. WH Sleeman, *Rambles and Recollections of an Indian Official* London: J. Hatchard and Son, (1836), 36.

12. Rapoport, "Fear and Trembling," 663–664.

13. Philip K. Hitti "The Assassins," in George Andrews and Simon Vinkenoog (eds.), *The Book of Grass: An Anthology on Indian Hemp* (London: Peter Owen, 1967)."

14. Bernard Lewis, *The Assassins: A Radical Sect in Islam* (New York: Oxford University Press 1987), 127.

15. James Scott, *Weapons of the Weak: Everyday Forms of Peasant Resistance* (New Haven: Yale University Press, 1990).

16. Their first target was the Grand Vizier, Nizar al-Mulk, chief administrator for Sultan Malikshah, the Seljuk ruler of Persia. Smithsonian Museum, http://www.silent-arrows.com/assassins.html accessed June 20, 2003. Even during the centuries of the Crusades, when fierce European knights and nobles were carving out Christian kingdoms on the eastern shore of the Mediterranean and inland toward the Holy City of Jerusalem, local Assassins still chose to concentrate on the killing of Orthodox Sunni soldiers and spiritual leaders. Twice they tried to kill Saladin, the Sultan and ruler of Egypt who—though he had overthrown the Fatimid Ismaili Caliphate—strove from 1174 to 1192 to unite nearby Islamic peoples against the Crusaders.

17. Eventually, in 1171, Salah ad-Din, in the process of trying to unite Syria and Egypt, toppled the Fatimid Caliphate and took power in Cairo. By that time, Ismailis were divided over the question of which son, Nizar or al-Mustali, should succeed the Fatimid caliph, who died in 1094. In time, the followers of al-Mustali seemingly disappeared but the militant followers of Nizar flourished, proclaiming a doctrine known as the New Preaching which emphasized the role of the living Imam, even at the expense of the original intent of the Qur'an. For all Nizar Shi'ites thereafter, their Imam was the true Imam and all others imposters. Ibid.

18. The most important of which is the *Fada'ih al-batiniyyah wa fada'il al-mustazhiri-yyah* or *al-Mustazhiri* ("The Infamies of the Batinites and the Excellences of the Mustazhirites"), composed in 1094 AD (487–488 AH), which he dedicated to the Caliph al-Mustazhir. http://www.muslimphilosophy.com/gz/articles/gz2.htm accessed June 20, 2003.

19. Rapoport, "Fear and Trembling," 666; Marshall GS Hodgson, *The Order of the Assassins* (The Hague: Mouton Press, 1955), 115.

20. Interview with the author, October 5, 2004, see also Giles Kepel, *The War for Muslim Minds*, Cambridge: Harvard University Press, 2004).

21 http://homepage.ntlworld.com/anthony.campbell1/assassins/decline.html accessed June 20, 2003.

22. The Zealots hoped to inspire the Greeks to rebel against Roman oppression as well as inspiring Jews; however their campaign proved disastrous and led to the Temple's destruction in 70 AD, the desolation of the Holy land, the Jewish Galut (exile) from the Holy Land (renamed Palestine), and the mass suicide at Masada in 72 AD. Their continued inspiration of revolts led to the decimation of the Jewish communities in Cyprus, Egypt, and Cyrene, (now Shahat Libya, North Africa) in 100 AD. In this uprising Jews fought the Romans and were defeated. Cecil Roth (ed.), *Encyclopedia Judaica* (Jerusalem: Keter, 1971), 16: 956.

23. Rex A. Hudson, "The Sociology and Psychology of Terrorism: Who Becomes a Terrorist and Why?" *Report Prepared under an Interagency Agreement* by the Federal Research Division, Washington DC: Government Printing Office, Library of Congress September 1999, 14.

24. Rapoport, "Fear and Trembling," 659.

25. Ibid, 669.

26. David H. Stern (Translator), *Complete Jewish Bible: An English Version of the TANAKH (Old Testament) and B'rit Hadashah (New Testament)* (Clarksville, MD: Jewish New Testament Publications, 1999) (Numbers 25:11).

27. Rapoport, "Fear and Trembling," 670.

28. Flavius Josephus, *The Jewish War*, Trans. H. St Thackery (Cambridge: Harvard University Press, 1999 [1926]), 2: 254–257.

29. Roth, *Encyclopedia Judaica*, 16: 956.

30. Rapoport, "Fear and Trembling," 670.

31. Ibid., 672.

32. Ibid.

33. Josephus, *The Jewish War*, volume 7, 252–404; Paul Johnson, *A History of the Jews* (New York: Harper and Row, 1987), 139–140; David Rapoport, personal correspondence with the author, April 8, 2004.

34. http://homepage.ntlworld.com/anthony.campbell1/assassins/decline.html accessed June 10, 2003. As a minority faction within a minority sect, the Ismailis were compelled to devise ingenious tactics to survive and contend for power. One precautionary device was to maintain that their Imam might choose to remain in hiding, only to reveal himself at a later date. This notion was in turn supported by the principle of *taqiya* (for "precautionary dissimulation'), which allows Muslims, if under threat, to deny their specific faith. Thus an Ismaili, when embattled, could protect himself by pretending to be a Sunni.

35. Stephen Frederick Dale, "Religious Suicide in Islamic Asia, Anti-colonialism in India and the Philippines," *Journal of Conflict Resolution* 32, no. 1, 39, 49.

36. Ibid, 51.

37. In the mid-nineteenth century an Achinese poet named Chik Pantee Kulu wrote a hugely popular 2000-line epic entitled *Hikayat Prang Sabi*, which inspired the Achinese struggle against Dutch colonial rule. Parts of it were read to Achinese fighters prior to battle. Forty years later, the poem's appeal inspired the Achinese in their next struggle—against the Japanese invaders. Ko Kooman, "Can Poetry Be Political?" *Poetry International Web*. http://www.poetryinternational.org/cwolk/view/17579 accessed June 22, 2003.

38. Dale, "Religious Suicide in Islamic Asia, 53.

39. Ibid, 54.

40. Ibid, 57.

41. The Term *Kamikaze* formally refers exclusively to the *Shimpū* (Divine Wind) Special Attack Corps formed at the instigation of Admiral Ōnishi in October 1944.

42. Peter Hill, "Kamikaze; Pacific War, 1943–45," Department of Sociology, University of Oxford Unpublished manuscript, 2.

43. Richard O'Neill, *Suicide Squads: Axis and Allied Special Attack Squads of World War*

Two, Their Development and Missions (London: Salamander Books 1999), 196–197). Cited by Hill.

44. Hill, 55 citing Antony Beevor, *Berlin: the Downfall 1945* (London: Viking Press 2002), 238.

45. Mako Sasaki, "Who Became Kamikaze Pilots, and How Did They Feel Towards Their Suicide Mission?" Quoted by Roman Kupchinsky, in "Smart Bombs with Souls," in *Organized Crime and Terrorism Watch* 3, no. 13 (April 17, 2003): 1

46. According to Hill, Special attack, *tokubetsu kōgeki* or, in its abbreviated form *tokkō*, was the standard military euphemism for missions in which the death of the protagonist was a prerequisite for the mission's success.

47. Ibid, 3–4.

48. Kupchinsky, "Smart Bombs with Souls."

49. T. Yokoi. "*Kamikaze* in the Okinawa Campaign" in David Evans (ed.), *The Japanese Navy in World War II* (Annapolis: Naval Institute Press, 1986), 455; cited by Hill, 9.

50. Hatsushō Naitō, *Thunder Gods: the Kamikaze Pilots Tell Their Story*, (Tokyo: Kodansha International 1989), 22; cited by Hill.

51. Maurice Pinguet, *Voluntary Death in Japan*, (Cambridge: Polity Press, 1993), 228–229 asserts that less than one eighth of planes successfully hit their targets. Raymond Lamont-Brown, *Kamikaze: Japan's Suicide Samurai*, (London: Cassell, 1997), 174 gives a figure of 20 percent at the Battle for Okinawa. Hill states that "only a minority" of the kamikazes hit their targets. The Allied fleets deployed radar ships to spot the enemy planes, after which they bombarded the planes with antiaircraft fire. The Allies also enjoyed air superiority.

52. O'Neill, *Suicide Squads*, 158 cited by Hill.

53. Rikihei Inoguchi, Tadashi Nakajima, and Roger Pineau, *The Divine Wind*, (London: Hutchinson, 1959), 7.

54. Ben-Ami Shillony, "Universities and Students in Wartime Japan," in *Journal of Asian Studies* 45, no. 4 (1986): 783.

55. Jean Larteguy, *The Sun Goes Down: Last Letters from Japanese Suicide-Pilots and Soldiers* (London: W. Kimber, 1956), 130.

56. Hill, "Kamikaze; Pacific War, 1943–45," 28, 37.

57. Ibid., 37.

58. Rohan Gunaratna, "Suicide Terrorism: A Global Threat." *Jane's Intelligence Review*, 20 October 2000 at http://www.janes.com/security/international_security/news/usscole/jir001020_1_n.shtml accessed June 20, 2003.

2. Palestinian Suicide Bombing

1. An earlier version of this chapter appeared in *Political Science Quarterly*, Volume 119, no. 1 Spring 2004, 61–88.

2. Among these are the widely publicized and televised killing of Mohammed al-Durra on September 30, 2000 and 70 other Palestinians killed in the first two months alone, the failing economic situation, Palestinian disillusion with the deadlocked peace process, and Ariel Sharon's visit to the Temple Mount that corroborated Hamas rhetoric that Israel would never fulfill its Oslo obligations. As much as Durra is a symbol,

there are questions as to who is really responsible for his death. See James Fallows, "Who Shot Mohammed al Durra?" *Atlantic Monthly*, June 2003, 49–56.

3. See JMCC Poll #47, December 2002 as well as Interviews with Khalil Shiqaqi with the author, October 17, 2002.

4. "Suicide Bombings: The Ultimate Weapon?" Yoram Schweitzer, (ICT) website (www.ict.org.il) August 7, 2001. Accessed May 20, 2002.

5. Arnon Regular, "PA Document: Hamas and Islamic Jihad Timed Bombings to Derail Peace Processes," *Ha'aretz*, January 8, 2004.

6. Rui De Figueiredo and Barry Weingast, "Vicious Cycles: Endogenous Political Extremism and Political Violence," Paper presented at the annual meeting of the American Political Science Association, September 1998.

7. "Hamas Operations Against Israel Said to Continue," *Al Dustur* (in Arabic) April 14, 1994.

8. "Terrorism: Questions and Answers, Hamas, Islamic Jihad" www.terrorismanswers. com. Accessed May 10, 2002; Ehud Sprinzak interview with the author, April 1, 2002. This is borne out by Palestinian public opinion surveys that cite the targeted assassinations as the factor most harmful to the Palestinians, see *JMCC Poll* 2, no. 6 (October 2001) http://www.jmcc.org/publicpoll/pop/01/oct/pop6.htm. Accessed May 10, 2002.

9. Tony Karan, "Chronicle of a Massacre Foretold," *Time*, January 18, 2002 and Robert Fisk, "Suicide Bombing on Passover Feast Wrecks US Peace Plan," *The Independent*, March 28, 2002.

10. Andrew Kydd and Barbara F. Walter, "Sabotaging the Peace: the Politics of Extremist Violence," *International Organizations* 56, no. 2 (Spring 2002): 263–296.

11. "Peace, Terror and Dissent in Israel: Hamas Goal of Blocking Negotiations," *New York Times*, August 23, 1995.

12. Hillel Halkin, "Bye, Bye Bibi," *The New Republic* June 7, 1999.

13. Interview with Ziad Abu Amr cited in Joyce M. Davis, *Martyrs: Innocence, Vengeance, and Despair in the Middle East* (New York: Palgrave, 2003), 171.

14. Avishai Margalit, "The Suicide Bombers," *The New York Review of Books* 50 no. 1 (January 16, 2003).

15. Ibid.

16. Zeev Ma'oz, "The Unlimited Use of the Limited Use of Force: Israel and Low Intensity Warfare, 1949–2004," Paper prepared for the International Studies Association Meeting, Montreal, March 17–20, 2004, 16.

17. A senior Israeli security official said the attacks (in May 2003) were aimed both at Israel and at Mahmoud Abbas (Abu Mazen), the first Palestinian prime minister, who has promised to disarm militant groups. "Everyone in the terror chain is very worried about this development," he said of the appointment of Mr. Abbas, "They are determined to escalate and make every effort to carry out attacks in this period," James Bennet, "3 Israelis Killed and 50 Wounded in Blast at Mall," *New York Times*, May 20, 2003.

18. There were a series of failed or aborted peace missions. According to public opinion polls, fewer than 18 percent of those Palestinians polled had any confidence in the success of the Zinni or Powell Missions. After the election of Mahmoud Abbas

as prime minister in the spring of 2003, Hamas justified its attacks to ensure that the "Road map for peace" would fail. Ibid.

19. Mouin Rabbani, "Suicide Attacks in the Middle East are Fueled by Alienation and Futility." Palestinian Media Watch, *Middle East News Online*, posted April 4, 2001 http://www.merip.org/mero/mero101700.html. Accessed May 20, 2002.

20. Imad A. Faluji, *Darb al Ashwak: Hamas, al-Intifada ,wa al Sultah* (The Path of Suffering: Hamas, the Intifada, and the Authority) (Arabic), Dar al Shuruq: Amman, Jordan, 2002; interviews of Palestinians with the author, April 12, 2003 names withheld, see also Emile Sahliyeh and Zixian Deng, "The Determinants of Palestinians' Attitudes Toward Peace with Israel." *International Studies Quarterly* 47, no. 4 (December 2003): 706.

21. Raviv Drucker, 'Harakiri' *Yediot Ahronot* (Hebrew), Tel-Aviv 2002, 329.

22. Richard Falk, Interview with the author February 1, 2002.

23. Richard Ned Lebow, *Between Peace and War: The Nature of International Crisis.* Baltimore: Johns Hopkins University Press, 1981.

24. Zeev Ma'oz, "The Unlimited Use of the Limited Use of Force," 14, 16.

25. Ma'mun Basisu, Niqash Sarih li Muntaqidi al-'amaliyyat al-istishadiyya (Frank discussions with the critics of martyrdom operations) (Arabic) *Al-Liwa'* July 6, 2002. See also a Hamas statement which claimed that one purpose of the Netanya Park Hotel Passover Seder attack (March 27, 2002) was to derail diplomatic initiatives at an Arab League summit in Beirut. "The summit resolutions are below the aspirations and the sacrifices of the Palestinian people," said 'Usama Hamdan, a Hamas spokesman in Beirut. The Palestinian Authority agreed that "this operation against Israeli civilians is in essence an attack against the Arab summit and against [U.S. Special Representative Anthony] Zinni's mission." WAFA (official PA news agency), March 27, 2002. Translated from Arabic by Human Rights Watch. HRW Report, *Erased in a Moment: Suicide Bombing Attacks Against Israeli Civilians* (New York: October 2002), 33.

26. Andrew Bilski and Eric Silver, "Dashed Hopes: Rabin and Arafat have become Prisoners of the Peace Process." *Maclean's* 108 (1995): 30–31.

27. Ziad Abu Amr, Palestinian Cabinet Member (Independent) and Minister of Culture, Interview Cited by Joyce M. Davis, *Martyrs*, 168–169.

28. When Palestinians were asked in 1999 about their level of optimism or pessimism about the future, 70.7 percent of the respondents expressed optimism. There were no major differences in the level of optimism about the future between those surveyed in the West Bank and those in the Gaza Strip. By January 2001, when respondents were asked about their level of optimism or pessimism, 48.8 percent stated that they were optimistic, and 50.2 percent were pessimistic about their futures, a significant change from 1999. *JMCC Poll* 2, no.2 (January 2001). By 2003 more than 80 percent were now pessimistic see figures below. Support for suicide operations varied by respondent characteristics. Those living in refugee camps were more supportive of military operations against Israeli targets than respondents residing in cities and villages (79 percent, 75 percent, and 69 percent respectively). Refugees and Gaza strip residents were also more supportive of military operations than non-refugees or East Jerusalem residents and there was 68 percent support

among Palestinians with less than high school education versus 76 per cent support among those with a high school education or higher; and 67 percent of Palestinians 40 years or older versus 76 percent of respondents under 40 supported suicide bombings. As the figures below show, there is a dramatic increase in the level of public support for military and suicide operations against Israeli targets. The level of support for suicide operations against Israeli targets is more than double the level of support during the past five years (26.1 percent in March 1999, 28.2 percent in August 1997, 23.6 percent in May 1997, 32.7 percent in April 1997, and 32.8 percent in June 1995).

29. Yossi Belin, Chief Oslo Negotiator, Interview with the Author, April 16, 2003.

30. "Hamas Divides Against Itself," *Middle East Intelligence Bulletin* June 1999.

31. Yossi Beilin Interview with the author.

32. Ambassador Itamar Rabinovitch (senior Israeli negotiator) Interview with the author, April 19, 2001; Center for Palestinian Research Polls, CPRS Polls Survey Research Unit available at http://www.pcpsr.org/survey/cprspolls/index.html. Accessed May 20, 2002.

33. Assaf Moghadam, "Palestinian Suicide Bombing in the Second Intifada: Motivations and Organizational Aspects," *Studies in Conflict and Terrorism* 26 (2003): 75.

34. Khalil Shiqaqi, "Palestinians Divided," *Foreign Affairs* (January–February 2002): 89.

35. Arieh O'Sullivan, "IDF warns PA losing control of Gaza Strip," *The Jerusalem Post*, Nov. 19, 2001.

36. *The Economist* December 1, 2001.

37. Shiqaqi Interview with the author, October 17, 2002. The April 2003 *JMCC Poll*, no. 48 at http://www.jmcc.org/publicpoll/results/2003/n048.htm. Accessed April 30, 2003.

38. Joyce Davis, *Martyrs*, 167.

39. Ibid, 150.

40. Serge Schnemann, "Israelis and Palestinians Wait for Explosions, and Despair," *New York Times*, March 8, 2002.

41. Abu Amr interview cited in Joyce Davis, *Martyrs*, 168.

42. John Kifner, "As Arafat Critics Close in, Deputies Vie in the Wings," *New York Times*, May 21, 2002.

43. Shaul Mishal and Avram Sela, *The Palestinian Hamas: Vision, Violence, and Coexistence* (New York: Columbia University Press, 2000).

44. Megan Goldin, "Hamas Feeds Struggle Against Israel With Charity," Reuters, January 4, 2001.

45. The interview in Hamas' *Filastin al-Muslimah* (no date cited) is translated and excerpted in "Summary of Information Provided by the FBI to the Department of Treasury in Support of the Designation of the Holy Land Foundation for Relief and Development," no date, provided to Human Rights Watch by the U.S. Department of the Treasury, August 2002.

46. Felicity Barringer, "Israel is Criticized for Restricting UN access in Gaza," *New York Times*, May 20, 2003.

47. Boaz Ganor, "The Islamic Jihad: The Imperative of Holy War," http://www.ict.org.il/articles/articledet.cfm?articleid = 405 and http://www.ict.org.il/inter_ter/orgdet.cfm?orgid = 28. Accessed May 20, 2002.

48. George Habash Interview, June 20, 2002 on PFLP website http://www.pflp-pal.org/opinion/habash29–6-02.html. Accessed May 20, 2003; JMCC public opinion polls "Palestinian Opinion Pulse," 2, no. 4 (June 2001); 2, no. 6 (October 2001); 3, no. 7 (January 2002); 3, no. 8 (April 2002); www.jmcc.org/publicpoll.opinion.html. Accessed May 20 2002; Ben Lynfield, "As Hope Dwindles, Hamas thrives," *The Christian Science Monitor,* December 10, 2001.

49. Roni Shaked, *Yedioth Ahronoth* (Hebrew) 4/25/2003; *JMCC Poll* 3, no. 7 (January 2002) http://www.jmcc.org/publicpoll/pop/02/jan/pop7.htm. Accessed May 20, 2002.

50. The August 2002 JMCC poll and *Ha'aretz*, November 28, 2002 "Poll: Majority of Palestinians support PA crackdown on attacks,"

51. PFLP leader, George Habash denounced suicide bombings in interviews up until 2001.

52. Joel Greenberg, "7 Killed, 17 Hurt in Ambush of Bus by Palestinians" *New York Times*, July 17, 2002.

53. "7 die in terror attack on Immanuel bus," Staff *Ha'aretz*, July 17, 2002.

54. Nichole Argo, "The Banality of Evil, Understanding Today's Human Bombs," Policy Paper, Preventive Defense Project, Stanford University Unpublished ms., 2003, 13.

55. Interview with Abdul Aziz al Rantisi cited in Mark Juergensmeyer, *Terror in the Mind of God: The Global Rise of Religious Violence* (Berkeley: University of California Press, 2000), 187–188.

56. Lori Allen, "There Are Many Reasons Why: Suicide Bombers and Martyrs in Palestine," *Middle East Report* 223 Barriers to Peace (Summer 2002).

57. Palestinian People's Resistance Forces, Martyr Abu Ali Mustafa Brigades, The Military Wing of the Popular Front for the Liberation of Palestine, Press Statement March 15, 2002.

58. Mouin Rabbani, "A Tale of Two Assassinations: Mustafa Zibri and Rehavam Ze'evi," *Washington Report on Middle East Affairs*, August 2002, 13–14.

59. Press statement issued by Nasser Oweis, leader of Al-Aqsa Martyrs' Brigades in Palestine March 22, 2002 (Arabic).

60. Mishal and Sela, *Hamas,* 36.

61. *Ash-Sharq al-Awsat*, April 1, 1996, in FBIS, Apr. 2, 1996.

62. www.ict.org.il and Khaled Hroub, *Hamas: Political Thought and Practice* (Washington, DC: Institute for Palestine Studies, August 2000).

63. CNN World January 16, 2002.

64. Reuven Paz, "Sleeping with the Enemy, a Reconciliation Process as Part of Counter-Terrorism. Is Hamas Capable of *Hudnah*?" June 25, 1998. Institute for Counter Terrorism, Israel http://www.ict.org.il/articles/articledet.cfm?articleid = 37. Accessed May 2, 2002.

65. Khalid Mish'al Interview with Abdullah al-Qaq in Amman, quoted in *Amman al Dustur* (Arabic) February 28, 1998, 10.

66. Human Rights Watch Report, *Erased in a Moment: Suicide Bombing Attacks Against Israeli Civilians* (New York: Human Rights Watch Report October 2002).

67. Ganor, "The Islamic Jihad," 197.

68. Ahmad Rashad, *Hamas: Palestinian Politics with an Islamic Hue* (Annandale: VA, United Association for Studies and Research, 1993), 4.

69. Interviews/Statements issued on Al Manar Television (Arabic), Interview with Avi Jorisch, February 13, 2003.

70. Graham Usher, "Arafat's Shrinking Dominion," *Al-Ahram Weekly* January 24–30 2002.

71. Jonathon Lis and Amira Haas "Israel presents document linking the PA to terror attacks," *Ha'aretz* April 2, 2002.

72. BBC News, February 2, 2002; April 28 2002 PFLP Abu Ali Mustafa Brigades letter to Sheikh Nasrallah of the Lebanese Hizbullah at http://www.tao.ca/~solidarity/texts/palestine/PFLPcommuniques.html. Accessed April 30, 2003. PFLP communiqués begin with "to the masses of the Arab nation" this letter begins with "in the name of Allah, the Mercy giving etc."

73. Joel Greenberg, "Shock at Charges Palestinians Were Sold Israeli Munitions," *New York Times,* July 19, 2002.

74. John Daly, "Suicide Bombing: No warning and No Total Solution," *Jane's Defence Weekly,* September 17, 2001.

75. See UN Security Council Resolution no. 1405 April 19, 2002 and the Human Rights Watch Report, "Israel/Occupied Territories: Jenin War Crimes Investigation Needed," http://www.hrw.org/press/2002/05/jenin0503.htm posted May 3, 2002. Accessed May 20, 2003.

76. Lori Allen, *Middle East Report* 223 (Summer 2002).

77. Mouin Rabbani, "Palestinian Authority, Israeli Rule: from Transitional Arrangement to permanent Authority," *Middle East Report* (Fall 1996); David Plotz, "The Logic of Assassination: Why Israeli Murders and Palestinian Suicide Bombings make Sense," *Slate Magazine,* http://slate.msn.com/?id = 113987, posted Friday August 17, 2001. Accessed April 10, 2002. Although Krueger and Malekova's research proves otherwise, "Education, Poverty, Political Violence and Terrorism: Is There a Causal Connection?" Princeton University Working paper, July 2002, 9, 4, 28; Bruce Bueno de Mesquita, Interview with the author March 18, 2002.

78. Nasra Hassan, "Letter from Gaza: An Arsenal of Believers," *The New Yorker,* November 19, 2001.

79. Khalil Shiqaqi, Interview with the author, October 17, 2002.

80. Lori Allen, *Middle East Report* 223 (Summer 2002).

81. Alan J. Kuperman identifies a "moral hazard problem" in which minority groups deliberately incite the majority to act in a repressive fashion in order to force the hand of the international community to intervene. Palestinian calls for an International Intervention after the Jenin massacre, the deliberate exaggeration of casualties and fake bodies exhumed as evidence would appear to support Kuperman's hypothesis, "The Moral Hazard of Humanitarian Intervention," Paper Prepared for the 2002 Annual Meeting of the International Studies Association, New Orleans, LA, March 25–28, 2002 and discussions with the author March 27, 2002.

82. Amira Haas, "Confessions of a Dangerous Mind," *Ha'aretz* April 3, 2003.

83. Patrick Seale interview, *Al Hayat* (London) September 13, 2001.

84. The killing of Raed Karmi, the head of Fatah's military wing in Tulkarm resulted

in the suicide bombings in early March 2002. In an aerial bombardment of Gaza, the Israeli Army killed Salah Shehada, head of Hamas' Izz Eddin al Qassam Brigades July 22, 2002. Hamas vowed retaliation. "There is nothing in our hands but to respond with whatever power we have," said Dr. Mahmoud al-Zahar, a political leader of Hamas. "Every Israeli is a target now. No one will stop us from defending ourselves." Abdel Aziz Rantisi, vowed revenge against Israelis: "We will hit them hard, they will be targeted, their houses and their families," James Bennet, "Israeli Strike in Gaza Kills a Hamas Leader and 14 Others," *New York Times*, July 23, 2002. On April 28, 2003, Israel killed Nidal Salameh of the PFLP.

85. Danny Rubinstein, "Assassination as a Boomerang," *Ha'aretz*, March 6, 2002.

86. Boaz Ganor, *The Counter-Terrorism Puzzle—A guide for Decision Makers*, (Hebrew), Mifalot IDC Publications, 2003, 125.

87. Simon Reeve, *One Day in September* (New York: Arcade Books, 2000), 70–93, 160–175.

88. Joel Greenberg, "Coat, Backpack, Sweat: Close Call in Israeli Café," *New York Times*, March 8, 2002, sec. A8

89. David Plotz, "The Logic of Assassination; Abd al-'Aziz Rantisi on "Al-Jazeera This Morning," *Al-Jazeera* (Doha), May 20, 2002; Haim Malka, "Must Innocents Die? The Islamic Debate over Suicide Attacks," *Middle East Quarterly* (Spring 2003).

90. George Habash Interview, June 20, 2002 on PFLP website http://www.pflp-pal.org/opinion/habash29–6-02.html. Accessed June 4, 2003.

91. Nichole Argo, "Understanding and Defusing Human Bombs: The Palestinian Case and the Pursuit of a Martyrdom Complex—A Working Paper," Paper Prepared for presentation to the International Studies Association Meeting, Montreal, March 17–20, 2004, 2

92. Richard Falk, Interview with the author May 10, 2002.

93. Avishai Margalit, "The Suicide Bombers," *The New York Review of Books* 50 no. 1 (January 16, 2003).

94. www.cfr.org/background/mideast_postarafat.php accessed November 4, 2004.

95. Interview with the author, NYC December 13, 2003.

96. JMCC April 20, 2003 http://www.jmcc.org/banner/banner1/listmartyr.htm. Accessed May 20, 2003. B'tselem and Palestinian Red Crescent websites, www.btselem. org, and http://www.idf.il/daily_statistics/english/1.gif. Accessed January 11, 2004, http://www.palestinercs.org/crisistables/table_of_figures.htm. Accessed January 11, 2004 and http://news.bbc.co.uk/1/hi/world/middle_east/3256858.stm. Accessed January 12, 2004.

97. Margalit, "The Suicide Bombers."

98. "Fifteen Months: Intifada, Closures, and Palestinian Economic Crisis—An Assessment," *World Bank Report*, March 18, 2002. The UNSCO data is included in the World Bank report at http://lnweb18.worldbank.org/mna/mena.nsf/Attachments/complete/$File/complete.pdf. Accessed 20 April 2003.

99. See Sara Roy, "The Gaza Strip: Critical Effects of the Occupation," *Arab Studies Quarterly* 10, no.1 (Winter 1998).

100. Argo, "Understanding and Defusing Human Bombs," 8

101. Sunhi Asila, "Hal hana waqtu waqf al 'amaliyyat al-istishadiyya?" (Arabic) Has the time come to end martyrdom operations? *Al Ahram*, September 10, 2002, 7.

102. The number of arrests has increased exponentially. On the eve of the first In-tifada's outbreak (December 1987) 200 Palestinians were under administrative detention in Judea, Samaria, and the Gaza Strip. However, during three years of the Intifada 14,000 residents were placed under administrative detention, see Amnon Straschnov, "Justice Under Fire," *Yediot Ahronot* (Hebrew) Tel-Aviv, 1994, 72, 76.

103. Boaz Ganor, "Israel" in Robert J. Art and Louise Richardson, *Democracy and Counter Terrorism: Lessons from the Past.* (Washington: DC, USIP Press,) forth-coming, 41.

104. Israel Ministry of Foreign Affairs, "PM Rabin's Speech to the Opening Session of the Knesset 18 April 1994," www.mfagov.il. See also Robert A. Pape, "Rabin: Kill-ing Civilians Won't Kill the Negotiations," *Jerusalem Post* April 13, 1994; "Strategic Logic of Suicide Terrorism," *The American Political Science Review* 97, no. 3 (August 2003): 343–361.

105. *Ha'aretz* (Hebrew), November 3, 1994. However, Boaz Ganor adds his objec-tion arguing that separating the peace process from the fight against terrorism might have produced a situation wherein the Palestinian Authority had little motivation to strike at Hamas' infrastructure, or pressure them to abstain from attacks. In the absence of such motivation, and the infrastructure of the move-ment was not affected, Hamas had a free hand to carry out attacks as it saw fit, and to convey its objections to the peace process without putting the process and Palestinian national interests in danger. Ganor in *Democracy and Counter Terrorism*, 19.

3. Ethnic Conflict, State Terror, and Suicide Bombing in Sri Lanka

1. An earlier version of this chapter appeared in *Civil Wars* 6 no. 1 (Spring 2003): 54–84.

2. Since the time of this writing, the LTTE has suspended peace talks although con-tinues to pledge its commitment to peace.

3. Andrew Kydd and Barbara F. Walter, "Sabotaging the Peace: the Politics of Extrem-ist Violence." *International Organizations* vol. 56 no. 2 (Spring 2002).

4. Thomas Friedman, *New York Times*, August 8, 2002.

5. According to Sri Lankan sources, the LTTE makes 20 million rupees per month from the A9 highway taxes/tolls alone. Amy Waldman writes that the LTTE is the only terrorist group who issues speeding tickets. Sources indicate that the LTTE Diaspora collects 1 million dollars/day but is unable to transfer this money to Sri Lanka because of the financial and legal limitations regarding support for terror-ist organizations. See http://www.rand.org/publications/MR/MR1405/MR1405.ch3.pdf accessed April 29, 2003.

6. Charles Tilly, *Coercion Capital and European States AD 990–1992* (New York: Black-well, 1992). See also Tilly's article "War-making and State-making as Organized Crime" in Peter Evans, Dietrich Rueschemeyer, and Theda Skocpol (eds.), *Bringing the State Back In* (New York: Cambridge University Press, 1995), 169–191.

7. HRW Report, *Erased in a Moment: Suicide Bombing Attacks Against Israeli Civilians* (New York, October 2002).

8. SJ Tambiah, *Sri Lanka, Ethnic fratricide and the Dismantling of Democracy* (Delhi: Oxford University Press, 1986), 9.

9. The demographics of the Eastern province are significantly different from the rest of the country with 42 percent Tamil, 24 percent Sinhalese, and 35 percent Muslim.

10. The Portuguese and later the Dutch initiated a land registration (*tombo*) to maintain a precise record of land ownership, labor service, dues, and taxation.

11. David Little, "Religion and Ethnicity," in Robert I. Rotberg (ed.), *Creating Peace in Sri Lanka: Civil War and Reconciliation* (Washington, DC: Brookings Institution Press, 1999), 45.

12. Tambiah, *Sri Lanka: Ethnic* Fratricide, 101–105 H.P. Chattopadhyaya *Ethnic Unrest in Modern Sri Lanka: An Account of Tamil-Sinhalese Race Relations* (New Delhi: MC Publications, 1994), 51.

13. Elizabeth Nissan and RL Stirrat, "The generation of Communal identities," in Jonathan Spencer (ed.), *Sri Lanka: History and Roots of the Conflict* (London: Routledge, 1990), 31.

14. Different castes were based on different professions. The Karava, or fishing caste versus the Salagama, or cinnamon peeler caste who were Sinhalese and the Goyigama, Mukkuvar, Vellala, Paravar Shanar, Nalavar and Karaiyar Tamil castes. Chelvadurai Manogaran and Bryan Pfaffenberger, *The Sri Lankan Tamils: Ethnicity and Identity* (Boulder: Westview, 1994), 30.

15. Tambiah, *Sri Lanka: Ethnic Fratricide*, 5–7.

16. Tamil nationalists tried to bring in Muslims into its movement by demonstrating Sinhalese Buddhist chauvinism.

17. MA Nuhuman, "Ethnic Identity, Religious Fundamentalism and Muslims in Sri Lanka." In *Dossier 21* (September 1998): 90–96. This has not always been the case and there have been instances of Muslims joining the LTTE. See Ameer Ali, "The Muslim Factor in Sri Lankan Ethnic Crisis," *Journal of Muslim Minority Affairs* 17, no. 2 (1997): 258.

18. Tambiah, *Sri Lanka: Ethnic Fratricide*, 7.

19. Ibid., 66–68.

20. Ibid., 78.

21. Kumari Jayawardena, *Ethnic and Class Conflicts in Sri Lanka* (Madras: Kaanthalakam, 1987), chs 3 and 5.

22. Nuhuman, "Ethnic Identity, Religious Fundamentalism and Muslims in Sri Lanka," 94 citing Kumari Jayawardena, *Ethnic and Class Conflict*, 24.

23. http://www.lacnet.org/srilanka/issues/kumari.html#a accessed October 24, 2002.

24. Jayawardena. *Ethnic and Class Conflicts in Sri Lanka*, 14.

25. The legislation passed in 1956 by a margin of 56 to 29. Bandaranaike was assassinated three years later by a Nationalist dressed as a Buddhist Monk and succeeded by his wife Sirimavo.

26. Radhika Coomaraswamy, "Myths with Conscience: Tamil and Sinhalese Nationalist Writings in the 1980s," in *Facets of Ethnicity in Sri Lanka* (Colombo: ICES, 1987), 79.

27. Chola was a Southern Indian dynasty from the second to the eleventh centuries

AD that invaded and occupied Sri Lanka only to be expelled by the Pandyan kings. Mudaliyar C. Rasanayagam, *Ancient Jaffna* (New Delhi: Asian Educational services, 1926), 26–29 and K. K. Pillay, *South India and Sri Lanka* (Sir William Meyer Lecture Series, University of Madras, India), 1963, 62.

28. Little in Rotberg, *Creating Peace in Sri Lanka*, 48.

29. Although the Tamil population and language were fully acknowledged by the UNP, they felt slighted by the addition of the word "and" (as in Sinhala *and* Tamil). Secondly, the 1977 constitution moved significant power to the Executive President, and away from the parliament. This had significance for the future, for instance the creation of a provincial system that reported to the president, and not to parliament.

30. Kingsley M. De Silva, *Managing Ethnic Tensions in Multi Ethnic Societies*. (Washington, DC, University Press of America, 1986), 228.

31. Neelan Tiruchelvam in Yash Ghai, (ed.) *Autonomy and Ethnicity: Negotiating Competing Claims in Multi Ethnic States* (London: Cambridge University Press, 2000), 200 It should be noted that Neelan Tiruchelvam, Member of Parliament (TULF) and director of the International Centre for Ethnic Studies (ICES) was killed on July 29, 1999 by LTTE extremists for his views.

32. Different sources place the formation date of the LTTE between 1972 and 1978. Edgar O'Ballance, *The Cyanide War: Tamil Insurrection in Sri Lanka 1973–88* (London: Brassey's, 1989), 12–17.

33. The assassination of the SFLP mayor of Jaffna, Alfred Durayappah by future LTTE leader Velupillai Prabhakaran occurred on July 27, 1973). "This act gave him terrorist standing and prestige, making him the unquestionable leader of his group, and enabled him to formalize the TNT into the broader LTTE." O'Ballance. *The Cyanide War*, 13 The Tamil Tigers also claimed responsibility for at least 11 assassinations in 1978 including a member of the TULF that had defected to the UNP as well as a number of policemen.

34. KM de Silva (ed.), *Conflict and Violence in South Asia: Bangladesh, India, Pakistan, and Sri Lanka* (Kandy: ICES, 2000), 381–382.

35. Tambiah, *Sri Lanka: Ethnic Fratricide*, 42.

36. Ibid., 43. Tambiah notes that the PTA shares several common features with the 1967 Terrorism Act in South Africa and this author would contend with the practices of the Occupation in the West Bank and Gaza.

37. Ibid., 18.

38. Ibid., 78.

39. Ibid., 13. The other example of the 'deadly ethnic riot" was the Sinhalese-Muslim riots of 1915. The riots tended to abate within a few weeks. The other major mob attacks were against the Hindu Nationalist Party in April 1971, the Janata Vimukti Peramuna (JVP). See Rohan Gunaratna, *Sri Lanka: A Lost Revolution, The Inside Story of the JVP* (Sri Lanka: Institute of Fundamental Studies, 1990), 92–105.

40. Little in Rotberg, *Creating Peace in Sri Lanka.*, 51.

41. Tiruchelvam in Yash Ghai, *Autonomy and Ethnicity*, 200.

42. The army was composed of 95 percent Sinhalese and the Tamil minority is virtually excluded from serving in the Armed Forces. In 1956, 40 percent of the armed forces were Tamil and by 1970 only one percent was. There has been no recruitment of

Tamils into the military or the police force for more than 40 years. Smith in Rotberg, *Creating Peace in Sri Lanka*, 35.

43. Anita Pratap, *Island of Blood: Frontline Reports from Sri Lanka, Afghanistan and Other South Asian Flashpoints* (New York: Penguin, 2001), 76–77.

44. Tamil estimates were closer to 2,000 with between 80,000–100,000 refugees who abandoned their homes and were placed in "care and welfare" centers. O'Ballance writes that the Government admitted to 402 deaths *The cyanide War*. 25.

45. Tambiah, *Sri Lanka: Ethnic Fratricide*, 21 and Chattopadhyaya, *Ethnic Unrest in Modern Sri Lanka*. 68.

46. Naxalism draws its name from Naxalbari, a Bengali village in Eastern India inspired by Maoism which was a form of Indian peasant militancy. De Silva (ed) *Conflict and Violence in South Asia*, esp. 235. .

47. Tambiah, *Sri Lanka: Ethnic Fratricide*. 27.

48. O'Ballance, *The Cyanide War*. 25.

49. Tiruchelvam in Ghai, *Autonomy and Ethnicity*, 199–200.

50. Elizabeth Nissan, "Some thoughts on Sinhalese Justifications for the (1983) Violence," in James Manor (ed.), *Sri Lanka: in Change and In Crisis* (New York: St. Martin's, 1984), 176–177; cited in Little in Rotberg *Creating Peace in Sri Lanka*, 51.

51. The dead included a number of Tamil political leaders of the PLOTE, The Secretary general of the Gandhian Society, and TELO in O'Ballance, *The Cyanide War*, 25.

52. Tambiah, *Sri Lanka: Ethnic Fratricide*, 15–16.

53. Interview with the author, Colombo, October 28, 2002.

54. The LTTE's main source of income became taxation imposed on Sri Lankan Tamils while they held the reins of administration in Jaffna. Another source of income was the LTTE small industries that they set up, Chattopadhyaya, *Ethnic Unrest in Sri Lanka*, 48.

55. Chris Smith, "South Asia's Enduring War," in Rotberg, *Creating Peace in Sri Lanka*, 17.

56. HP Chattopadhyaya, *Ethnic Unrest in Modern Sri Lanka: An Account of Tamil-Sinhalese Race Relations* (New Delhi: MD Publications, 1994), esp. 36 and 40. Chris Smith alleges the connection was between People's Liberation Organization of Tamil Eelam (PLOTE) and al-Fatah. Rotberg, *Creating Peace in Sri Lanka*, 32.

57. O'Ballance, *The Cyanide War*, 15. It was their connection to the Hizb'allah in the 1980s that taught them the tactic of suicide bombing. Further O'Ballance adds that the Sri Lankan Government was aided by Israel to combat LTTE terrorism during this same period, 37.

58. Other sources place the figures higher at 100,000 from the Colombo area and another 175,000 countrywide for internally displaced persons (IDPs). Rotberg, *Creating Peace in Sri Lanka*, 7.

59. http://www.lacnet.org/srilanka/issues/kumari.html#a accessed October 24, 2002.

60. Shelton Kodikara, "Internationalization of Sri Lanka's Ethnic Conflict," Paper presented at a Social Science Association Seminar, Colombo, Sri Lanka, 1983.

61. http://www.lacnet.org/srilanka/issues/kumari.html#a accessed October 24, 2002.

Several MDMK leaders were removed from government office and jailed for openly supporting the LTTE in 2002. .

62. Rotberg, *Creating Peace in Sri Lanka*, 8.

63. The accord was opposed by Sinhalese Fundamentalists. The theme of JVP propaganda was the alleged "betrayal of the motherland" which the occupation of part of
the country by an alien army was seen to represent. Eventually the Tamil separatists
likewise opposed the IPKF and led to its departure in 1990.

64. Tiruchelvam in Ghai, *Autonomy and Ethnicity*, 199–200.

65. Smith in Rotberg, *Creating Peace in Sri Lanka*, 20.

66. O'Ballance, *The Cyanide War*, 91–92 The Indian Foreign Minister had voiced his
concern over reports of Pakistani, South Korean and Israeli military advisers "mercenaries" fighting with the Sri Lankan military forces against the Tamils. Interestingly enough, Peiris reports that the LTTE received arms and funding from the
Israelis in a strange geopolitical move to arms and aid both sides in the conflict.

67. GH Peiris, "Secessionist War and Terrorism in Sri Lanka: Transnational Impulses."
Unpublished manuscript, ICES Kandy, 15.

68. Rohan Gunaratna, *Sri Lanka: A Lost Revolution*.

69. Prabhakaran Interview with Pratap, cited in *Island of Blood*, 78–86 Pratap writes,
however, that the IPFK was initially greeted with great enthusiasm by the local
Tamil population who assumed that the Indian Peacekeepers would protect them
from further depredations by the Sri Lankan state like the carpet bombing of towns
in the Jaffna Peninsula of Velvettithurai, Point Pedro, Vasivilan, and Uripiddy, 44.

70. KM de Silva, *Sri Lanka*, 203 citing Dayan Jayatilleka, *Sri Lanka: The Travails of a
Democracy, Unfinished War, Protracted Crisis*, New Delhi: ICES, 1995, 1.

71. Rotberg, *Creating Peace in Sri Lanka*, 25 and http://news.bbc.co.uk/1/hi/world/
south_asia/340717.stm and http://members.tripod.com/~sosl/gandhi.html.

72. De Silva, *Sri Lanka*, 418.

73. Ann Adele, *Women Fighters of the Liberation Tigers* (Jaffna: Thasan Publication
Department of the LTTE, 1993), 45.

74. PLOTE was founded by Uma Maheswaran, an LTTE co-founder.

75. Darini Rajasingham-Senanyake in Rotberg, *Creating Peace in Sri Lanka*, 60.

76. O'Ballance, *The Cyanide War*, 65.

77. According to S. Pulleedevan, of the LTTE Peace Secretariat, Maheswaram was
kicked out of the LTTE for illicit sexual misconduct with Urmila, a well-known
female cadre. Interview with the author, November 2002.

78. O'Ballance, *The Cyanide War*, 49.

79. De Silva, *Sri Lanka*, 407–408. From that point on the LTTE began to systematically
eliminate their rivals including Amirthalingam in 1989 and the whole leadership
of the Eelam people's Revolutionary Liberation Front (EPRLF).

80. Citing an article on April 25, 1986 K. Padmanabha, Secretary General of the EPRLF
alleged he had documentary proof of EROS' responsibility. Much later EROS admitted this to be the case. O'Ballance *The Cyanide War*, 76.

81. There are Women Units for each of the Services operating separately since the creation of an independent fighting force on September 26, 1989. Ann Adele, *Women*

Fighters of the Liberation Tigers (Jaffna: Thasan Publication department of the LTTE, 1993), 24–43.

82. One of the LTTE martyrs was Father F. Bastian, a Tamil Roman Catholic priest who on January 18, 1985 together with eight other Tamils was shot and killed in his church at Vankalai, near Mannar, by security forces who claimed that he was hiding arms and ammunition in his church. Father Bastian's body disappeared. Father Bastian had helped to collect and bury 110 victims of the security services after the December 4 1984 Massacre. O'Ballance *The Cyanide War*, 45.

83. Ibid., 77 .

84. She had also led the campaign against the atrocities committed during the government anti-JVP campaign and attacked the policies of the UNP as a result.

85. The LTTE managed to attack Government naval patrols, conducted three major bombings, and controlled the coastline from Jaffna to Trincomalee.

86. Tiruchelvam in Ghai, *Autonomy and Ethnicity*, 209–210.

87. KM De Silva, *Sri Lanka*, 410–411.

88. Ibid., 412.

89. Vijitha Silva, "Sri Lankan security forces continue witch-hunt against Tamils." February 15, 2000 World Socialist Website, www.wsws.org accessed November 20, 2002.

90. The death toll for the government operations against the JVP exceeded 17,000, these figures are disputed and range from official Government tally of 4,250 to allegations of more than 40,000 dead. KM de Silva, *Sri Lanka*, 205.

91. In July 1997 three national human rights commissions established in 1994 found that there had been 16,742 disappearances since July 1988.

92. Interview with the author, Colombo, Sri Lanka October 25, 2002. .

93. Rajasingham-Senanyake in Rotberg, *Creating Peace in Sri Lanka*, 62.

94. Ibid., 9.

95. Charu Lata Joshi, "Sri Lanka Suicide Bombers." *Far Eastern Economic Review*, June 1, 2000 http://www.feer.com/_0006_01/p64currents.html accessed November 26, 2003.

96. Charu Lata Joshi, "Sri Lanka Suicide Bombers." *Far Eastern Economic Review*, June 1, 2000 http://www.feer.com/_0006_01/p64currents.html accessed November 26, 2003.

97. Ibid.

98. Ibid.

99. Neloufer De Mel, The Body Politics, (Re)presenting the Female Suicide Bomber in Sri Lanka. http://www.aucegypt.edu/igws/deMel.pdf, 7 citing Narayan Swami 2003b: 250 accessed November 20, 2003.

100. Rajasingham-Senanyake Interview. International human rights and international humanitarian law have long prohibited the recruitment and use of children less than fifteen years of age in hostilities. Article 77(2) of Protocol I requires parties to the conflict to "take all feasible measures in order that children who have not attained the age of fifteen years do not take a direct part in hostilities and, in particular, they shall refrain from recruiting them into their armed forces. In recruiting among those persons who have attained the age of fifteen years but who have

not attained the age of eighteen years, the Parties to the conflict shall endeavor to give priority to those who are oldest." Article 38 of Convention on the Rights of the Child, adopted November 20, 1989, requires states parties to "take all feasible measures to ensure that persons who have not attained the age of fifteen years do not take a direct part in hostilities," and to "refrain from recruiting any person who has not attained the age of fifteen years into their armed forces."

Similar provisions exist in international criminal law and international labor law. For example, article 8 of the Rome Statute of the ICC gives the court jurisdiction over the war crime of conscription or enlisting children less than fifteen years into national armed forces or armed groups, or using them to participate actively in hostilities. Convention concerning the Prohibition and Immediate Action for the Elimination of the Worst Forms of Child Labor, adopted June 17, 1999 (entered into force November 19, 2000).

101. Smith in Rotberg, *Creating Peace in Sri Lanka,* 36.

102. Interview with a top ranking International Aid worker, name withheld, December 1, 2003.

103. Ibid.

104. Joshi, "Sri Lanka Suicide Bombers"

105. Interviews with the author, October-December 2002, names withheld.

106. Interview with LTTE leaders, Kilinochi, November 2002.

107. Interview with the author, name withheld, Batticaloa, November 2002.

108. Interview with the author, Kilinochi, November 2002.

109. KM de Silva, *Reaping the Whirlwind,* 268.

110. KM de Silva, *Sri Lanka,* 412.

111. Ibid 269.

112. Unpublished seminar paper, "The Ethnic crisis and Internal Displacement: The Muslim Minority of the Northern Province of Sri Lanka," ICES-Kandy, presented May 1995, 29–33.

113. KM de Silva, *Reaping the Whirlwind,* 413 and author interviews with *Bikkhu* priests at the Dalada Maligawa, Kandy October–November 2002.

114. Kumar Rupesinghe, Interview with the author, Colombo, Sri Lanka, October 28, 2002.

115. There have been allegations that this rioting, between Sinhalese and Muslims rather than Muslims and Tamils is less an ethnic conflict and much more of fighting between rival gangs of organized crime. *Sunday Leader,* November 3, 2002.

116. A memo of understanding between the LTTE and the Sri Lanka Muslim Congress which pledged to recognize Muslim identity in the east.

117. Kumar Rupesinghe, Interview with the author, Colombo, Sri Lanka October 28, 2002.

118. Although I discussed Tamil anti-Muslim agitation earlier in this paper, the Sinhalese had also turned a blind eye to a group of soldiers from the Trincomelee Naval Base who had gone on a rampage against Muslims.

119. Shockingly enough, there is a Sinhalese trend toward extreme anti-Semitism.

120. Interview with a top ranking International Aid worker, name withheld, December 1, 2003.

121. Interviews with UN agencies in Colombo and Batticaloa November 2002.

122. *New York Times* May 29, 1995 cited in KM de Silva, *Sri Lanka*, 414.

123. This is particularly true in the Vanni area under LTTE control. Interview with ICRC Representative, Malavi subdivision, Colombo, Sri Lanka October 26–27, 2002. .

124. "Tamil Threat to Break Away Tiger," BBC News, World Edition March 26, 2004, http://news.bbc.co.uk/2/hi/south_asia/3570427.stm accessed March 30, 2004.

125. BBC World, http://news.bbc.co.uk/go/pr/fr/-/2/hi/south_asia/3872481.stm accessed July 9, 2004.

126. Rohan Gunaratna, *Sri Lanka's Ethnic Crisis and National Security* (Colombo: Unie Arts, 1998).

127. *Sunday Leader*, November 3, 2002 Colombo, Sri Lanka. .

128. BBC World, http://news.bbc.co.uk/go/pr/fr/-/2/hi/south_asia/3872481.stm accessed July 9, 2004.

129. BBC World, http://news.bbc.co.uk/go/pr/fr/-/2/hi/south_asia/3872481.stm accessed July 9, 2004.

130. US Department of State, *Pattern of Global Terrorism* Washington, DC Government Printing Office, 1995, 48–49 cited by de Silva 2000:419.

131. Interview, December 1, 2003.

4. DEVISING A THEORY OF SUICIDE TERROR

1. "Suicide Bombings: The Ultimate Weapon?" Yoram Schweitzer, Institute for Counter Terrorism (ICT) website (www.ict.org.il) August 7, 2001.

2. I am grateful for Martha Crenshaw's observations regarding the need to create a typology of suicide terror. Discussions with the author, November 6, 2003.

3. Scott Atran, "Genesis of Suicide Terrorism," *Science* 299 (March 7, 2003): 1534

4. Avishai Margalit, "The Suicide Bombers," *The New York review of Books* 50 no. 1 (January 16, 2003).

5. Atran, "Genesis of Suicide Terrorism," 1534.

6. Ashutosh Varshney, "Nationalism, Ethnic Conflict and Rationality." *Perspectives on Politics*, Vol. 1 no. 1, March 2003, pp.86.

7. R. E. Bell suggests four ideal models of terrorist funding: 1) popular support model (donations),2) criminal proceeds (drug dealing, bank robbery), 3) state sponsor model,4) entrepreneurial model (where businesses generate funding), to which my argument would add 5) the domestic taxation model, R. E. Bell, "The Confiscation, Forfeiture and Disruption of Terrorist Finances" in the *Journal of Money Laundering* (2003).

8. *Resonance* can result from desperation (after other strategies have failed) or because of intense outrage (hatred of "the other" because of their actions—real or perceived.)

9. Roger Dale Petersen, *Resistance and Rebellion: Lessons from Eastern Europe.* (Cambridge: Cambridge University Press, 2001).

10. Scott Atran, "The Strategic Threat from Suicide Terror," AEI-Brookings, Joint Center for Regulatory Studies, December 2003, 13.

11. Chaim Kaufmann, "Intervention in Ethnic and Ideological Civil Wars: Why One

Can Be Done and the Other Can't," *Security Studies* 6, no. 1 (Autumn 1996): 62–100; Chaim Kaufmann, "Possible and Impossible Solutions to Ethnic Civil Wars," *International Security* 20, no. 4 (Spring 1996): 136–175; and Chaim Kaufmann, "When All Else Fails: Ethnic Population Transfers and Partitions in the Twentieth Century," *International Security* 23, no. 2 (Fall 1998): 120–156.

12. It should be noted that hyper segregation is caused by a variety of state practices which include discrimination in residence, land tenure, economic opportunities or access to education. The hyper segregation is a necessary though insufficient precondition of ethno-nationalist violence.

13. I am grateful to Jeff Goodwin for this observation.

14. For example both the LTTE and Palestinian militants have targeted moderates for assassination.

15. Richard W. Builliet, correspondence with the author June 19, 2004.

16. Paul Pillar Interview, NYC, November 2003.

17. Fareed Zakaria cogently identified how in Turkey, PKK suicide terror was repudiated by the population and then abandoned as a tactic. "Suicide Bombings Can Be Stopped." Fareed Zakaria. MSN op ed, http://www.msnbc.com/news/953555.asp August 2003 www.fareedzakaria.com.

18. Nichole Argo, interview with a 26 year old Palestinian suicide bomber, July 2003, in "Understanding and Defusing Human Bombs: The Palestinian Case and the Pursuit of a Martyrdom Complex—A Working Paper," Paper Prepared for presentation to the International Studies Association Meeting, Montreal, March 17–20, 2004, 6–7.

19. *Yediot Ahronot* (Hebrew), March 11, 1994, 13.

20. Some analysts consider them provocations like Zeev Ma'oz. Stephen David considers the issue of Israeli provocations in "Fatal Choices," Policy Paper, The Begin-Sadat Center for Strategic Studies, 2002.

21. Martha Crenshaw, Ted Robert Gurr, and Robert A. Pape have all integrated terrorism and/or suicide bombing into larger theories of International Relations, combining theory with an attention to detail that stays true to the empirical realities of their cases. Martha Crenshaw, "The Logic of Terrorism: Terrorist Behavior as a Product of Strategic Choice." In Walter Reich (ed.), *Origins of Terrorism: Psychologies, Ideologies, Theologies, States of Mind* (New York: Cambridge University Press, 1990), 7–24; Ted Robert Gurr, "Terrorism in Democracies: Its Social and Political Bases," in ibid., 86–102 and Robert A. Pape, "Strategic Logic of Suicide Terrorism," *APSR* 97, no. 3 (August 2003): 343–361. Andrew Kydd and Barbara F. Walter have also published a theoretical article on suicide bombing, see "Sabotaging the Peace: the Politics of Extremist Violence." *International Organizations* 56 no. 2 (Spring 2002).

22. Crenshaw, "The Logic of Terrorism," 8.

23. Ibid.

24. Syrian President, Hafez al Assad destroyed Hama on February 2, 1982. See Scott Peterson, "How Syria's Brutal Past Colors its Future" *Christian Science Monitor*, June 20, 2000 and Thomas Friedman, *From Beirut to Jerusalem* (New York: Anchor Books, 1990), ch. 4 "Hama Rules," 76–105.

25. Jerrold Post, "The Mind of the Terrorist: Individual and Group Psychology of Ter-

rorist Behavior," testimony prepared for the Subcommittee on Emerging Threats and Capabilities, Senate Armed Service Committee, November 15, 2001, Ehud Sprinzak, "Rational Fanatics," *Foreign Policy* (September/October 2000): 66–73 and Crenshaw, "The Logic of Terrorism, 10.

26. Ashutosh Varshney, "Nationalism, Ethnic Conflict and Rationality." *Perspectives on Politics* 1 no. 1 (March 2003): 85–86.

27. The terrorist organizations are able to effectively manage the individuals' value rationality by providing a means to increasing self-esteem and life-meaning (though at the cost of a short life).

28. Rationality, however, is not a guarantee of success.

29. Argo, interview, 2003.

30. Scott Atran, "Genesis of Suicide Terrorism," 1535

31. This is the main argument of Jessica Stern's, *Terror in the Name of God: Why Religious Militants Kill*. NY: Harper Collins, 2003.

32. Tim Golden, "Young Egyptians Hearing Calls of 'Martyrdom' For Palestinian Cause," *The New York Times International*, April 26, 2002.

33. Nichole Argo, "The Banality of Evil, Understanding Today's Human Bombs," Policy Paper, Preventive Defense Project, Stanford University, 2003.

34. Amira Hass, "Confessions of a Dangerous Mind," *Ha'aretz* Magazine, March 2003, 14.

35. I am grateful to Elisabeth Wood for this observation.

36. Eli Berman and David Laitin, *Rational Martyrs: Evidence from Data on Suicide Attacks*. ISERP Paper, Contentious Politics Seminar, http://www.iserp.columbia.edu/news/calendars/contentious_politics.html

37. Argo, "Banality of Evil."

38. Crenshaw, "The Logic of Terrorism," 26 see also Barbara Victor, *Army of Roses: Inside the World of Palestinian Women Suicide Bombers* (New York: Rodale Press, 2003).

39. Stern, *Terror in the Name of God*, 5.

40. Alan B. Krueger and Jitka Malekova, "Education, Poverty, Political Violence and Terrorism: Is There a Causal Connection?" Princeton University Working paper, July 2002 and David Plotz, "The Logic of Assassination: Why Israeli Murders and Palestinian Suicide Bombings makes Sense." *Slate Magazine*, Friday August 21, 2001.

41. Simon Haddad and Hilal Khashan, "Accounting for Palestinian Perspectives on Suicide Bombings: Religious Militancy, Poverty, and Personal Attributions." Unpublished manuscript no date.

42. David Brooks, "The Culture of Martyrdom," *Atlantic Monthly* 289, no. 6 (June 2002): 18–20.

43. Barbara Victor, Interview with the author, October 24, 2003 see also her *An Army of Roses*.

44. Khaled Hroub, *Hamas: Political Thought and Practice* (Washington, DC: Institute for Palestine Studies), 2000, 245–249.

45. Paul Pillar, Interview with the author.

46. *New York Times*, March 31, 2002.

47. Crenshaw, "The Logic of Terrorism," 10.

48. Ehud Sprinzak, "Rational Fanatics" quoting "Dr. Ramadan Shalah, secretary-general of the Palestinian Islamic Jihad..

49. Ibid.

50. I am indebted to Richard Harknett for the theorization of the model. For a discussion of non-contingent violence see his article, "Barbarians At and Behind the Gates: The Loss of Contingency and the Search for Homeland Security," *The Forum: A Journal of Applied Research in Contemporary Politics*, 1, no.2 (Fall 2002): 1–12. www.bepress.com/forum/vol1/iss2/art1

51. Audrey Cronin, "Studies in Counter Terrorism: Russia and Chechnya." In Robert J. Art, Louise Richardson, and Paul Stares (eds.), *Democracy and Counter Terrorism: Lessons from the Past* (Washington DC: USIP Press, forthcoming), 4

52. Quoted in Hala Jaber, "Inside the World of a Palestinian Suicide Bomber," *The Jordan Times* cited by Argo "Banality of Evil," 10.

53. The IRA briefly attempted to use suicide car bombs, employing coerced Protestant Ulster Orangemen as drivers, but this tactic was renounced by the general population and was quickly abandoned.

54. Argo, "Banality of Evil.

55. Although beyond the scope of this present study, a project regarding the effects of counter terror strategies could be undertaken in the future to test which military tactics are most efficient.

56. Raviv Drucker, 'Harakiri' (Hebrew), *Yediot Ahronot*, Tel-Aviv2002, 310.

57. Boaz Ganor in Art, Richardson, and Stares (eds.), *Democracy and Counter Terrorism: Lessons from the Past*, 24.

58. Ilya Milstein, "A Female Suicide Bomber is more Dangerous than a Nuclear Power." *Gazeta*, October 2003.

59. Kavkaz-Tsentr news agency web site in Russian February 8, 2004.

60. Zeev Ma'oz, "The Unlimited Use of the Limited Use of Force: Israel and Low Intensity Warfare, 1949–2004. paper prepared for presentation to the International Studies Association Meeting Montreal, March 17- 20, 2004, 16.

61. Ma'oz, discusses four such occasions when a Palestinian *Hudna* ended because of a targeted assassination, ibid., 16.

62. Argo, "Understanding and Defusing Human Bombs."

63. Bruce Hoffman, "The leadership Secrets of Osama Bin Laden: the Terrorist as CEO." *The Atlantic Monthly*, April 2003.

64. Meda Ryan, *Tom Barry; Column Commander and IRA Freedom Fighter*, Cork: Mercier Press, 2003.)

65. United States Institute of Peace, cited by Argo, "Understanding and defusing Human Bombs," 21.

66. Nichole Argo, "Expressive Purpose and the Palestinian Martyrdom Complex," Jaffe Center Report, April 2004, 8.

67. Suicide terror became the dominant strategy in Sri Lanka under conditions of outbidding. Once the LTTE eliminated most of its domestic opposition, it became more amenable to negotiations and moderated its demands.

68. LTTE Representative Interview with the author, March 6, 2004, name withheld.

69. Boaz Ganor, interview with Shabtai Shavit, the former head of the Israeli Mossad, 4.11.99.

70. Ganor in Art, Richardson, and Stares, *Democracy and Counter Terrorism*, 42.

71. Mr. Abdallah Baali, Representative, Permanent Mission of Algeria to the U.N, Interview with the author, November 13, 2003.

72. The adjournment of democracy in Sri Lanka by President Chandrika Kumaratunga in November 2003, suspension of Parliament, and military reoccupation of the capital is a step in the wrong direction and may prove disastrous for the negotiations between the LTTE and the Sri Lankan Government. This work posits that only solution to end suicide bombing is to appeal to the rank and file, offer an alternative solution, and negotiate to avoid an endless spiral of violence.

73. If the instance of 9/11 is excluded then both types of groups have fairly equal degrees of lethality. Hoffman and Rand identify the religious based groups as dominant and increasing while nationalist groups appear to be receding.

74. Several formerly secular individuals joined religious groups to volunteer for martyrdom operations. Nichole Argo, Interview with the author, November 23, 2003.

75. Arnon Regular, "Mother of Two Becomes First Female Suicide Bombers for Hamas." *Ha'aretz*, January 15, 2004.

76. Atran, "Genesis of Suicide Terrorism," 1538.

77. Charles Tilly, *Coercion Capital and European States AD 990 – 1992* (New York: Blackwell, 1992). See also "War-making and State-making as Organized Crime" in Peter Evans, Dietrich Rueschemeyer, and Theda Skocpol (eds.), *Bringing the State Back In* (New York: Cambridge University Press, 198)5, 169–191.

78. Kavkaz-Tsentr news agency web site in Russian February 8, 2004.

79. Allistair Lawson, "The Enigma of Prabhakaran" BBC News, November 25, 2003.

80. James Fearon and David Laitin, "Ethnicity, Insurgency, and Civil War." *American Political Science Review*, 97, 1 (February 2003), 75-90.

81. Atran, "Genesis of Suicide Terrorism," 1538.

5. HALTING SUICIDE TERROR FROM WITHIN: THE PKK IN TURKEY.

1. "U.S. State Department Nicholas Burns denounced PKK attacks and said Syria was directly supporting these terrorist groups, and pledged that the United States would provide Turkey with all kinds of support in its fight against these terrorist groups." US Says Syria Responsible, *Turkish Daily News*, October 31, 1996. Furthermore, PKK leader Abdullah Öcalan (aka Apo) was headquartered in Lebanon after having lived in Damascus for many years. Finally, the PKK held its very first congress on the Lebanese- Syrian border.

2. Henri J. Barkey, "Turkey and the PKK," In Robert J. Art and Louise Richardson (eds.), *Democracy and Counter Terrorism: Lessons from the Past* (Washington DC: USIP Press, forthcoming, 2005), 4.

3. Ibid, 5.

4. *Hürriyet*, March 18, 1999 cited by Barkey, Ibid.

5. Henri J. Barkey and Graham E. Fuller, *Turkey's Kurdish Question* (Lanham, MD: Rowman and Littlefield, 1998), xi.

6. Reported by Alan Cowell, in the *New York Times* February 1990 cited in "Destroying Ethnic Identity: the Kurds of Turkey, An Update," *A Helsinki Watch Report*, September 1990, 2.
7. Helsinki Report, 2 .
8. Barkey, "Turkey and the PKK," 2.
9. *The Spectator,* November 28–December 5, 1998.
10. Barkey, "Turkey and the PKK," 15, 6.
11. Michael M. Gunter, *The Kurds in Turkey: A Political Dilemma* (Boulder: Westview, 1990), 58 .
12. Martin Van Bruinessen, "Between Guerrilla War and Political Murder: The Worker's Party of Kurdistan," *Middle East Report*, no. 153 (July–August 1988): 41–42.
13. McDowall, The Kurds, 420.
14. Barkey and Fuller, *Turkey's Kurdish Question*, 24.
15. "Destroying Ethnic Identity: the Kurds of Turkey, An Update." *A Helsinki Watch Report*, September 1990, 37.
16. Ibid, 7.
17. Barkey, "Turkey and the PKK," 2.
18. "Destroying Ethnic Identity: the Kurds of Turkey, An Update." *A Helsinki Watch Report*, September 1990, 1.
19. John B. Grant, "Turkey's Counterinsurgency Campaign Against the PKK: Lessons Learned from a Dirty War," unpublished thesis, Faculty of the Joint Military Intelligence College, June 2002, 39.
20. Barkey, "Turkey and the PKK," 12.
21. Gunter, *The Kurds in Turkey,* 72.
22. For a complete history see, Gerard Chaliand (ed.), *People Without a Country: the Kurds and Kurdistan* (New York: Interlink Publishing Group, 1993); James Ciment, *The Kurds: State and Minority in Turkey, Iraq, and Iran* (New York: Facts on File, 1996); Chris Kutschera, *Le défi kurde, ou le rêve fou de l'indépendance* (Paris: Fayard 1997); David McDowell, *A Modern History of the Kurds* (London: I. B. Tauris, 1999); and Martin Van Bruinessen, *Agha, Shaikh, and State* (London: Zed Books, 1992).
23. "PKK's fine tuned game playing," October 31, 1996, *Turkish Daily News.*
24. Ibid.
25. Barkey and Fuller, *Turkey's Kurdish Question*, 29.
26. "The Price for Respecting Women: Six Deaths" October 31, 1996, *Turkish Daily News.*
27. Ibid .
28. PKK violence continues http://www.turkishdailynews.com/old_editions/03_01_99/feature.htm.
29. Barkey, "Turkey and the PKK," 2.
30. Grant, "Turkey's Insurgency Campaign," 47 cited by Barkey, Ibid.; Hakan Yavuz, "Five Stages of the Construction of Kurdish Nationalism in Turkey," *Nationalism and Ethnic Conflict* 7, no. 1 (Autumn 2001): 14.
31. *Hurriyet* quoting Chief of Staff Ismail Hakki Karadayi. "We could finish off terrorism in 3 months but . . ." *Turkish Daily News*, November 1, 1996.

32. Mehmet Ali Kislali, *Güneydogu: Düsük Yogunluklu Çatisma* (Ankara: Ümit Yayin-cilik, 1996), 224 cited by Barkey, "Turkey and the PKK," 13.

33. Kurdish Rebels Say They Shot Down Turkish Helicopter March 7, 1999 (CNN).

34. Derya Sazak, "Bu Kaçinci Paket?" *Milliyet* March 3, 1999 and *Reuters* March 2, 1999 cited by Barkey, "Turkey and the PKK," 20.

35. Barkey and Fuller, *Turkey's Kurdish Question*, 40 *passim* are the only authors who assert that Öcalan was moderating his position in this time.

36. Barkey, "Turkey and the PKK," 6.

37. Ibid 12–13.

38. U.S. Department of State, *Turkey Country Report on Human Rights Practices for 1998* Released by the Bureau of Democracy, Human Rights, and Labor, February 26, 1999, 3.

39. "Italy Urged to Prosecute PKK Leader Öcalan," *Human Rights Watch Report*, November 21, 1998.

40. Speech delivered by Lt. Gen. Cetin Saner, chief of intelligence of the General Staff, in the briefing organized in June 1997 by the Office of the Chief of the General Staff [OCGS] entitled "Reactionary Activities." *Sabah*, June 12, 1997. [FBIS-WEU-97–114] excerpted in Eli Karmon, "The Demise of Radical Islam in Turkey," *Middle East Review of International Affairs* (MERIA) 1, no. 4 (December 1997), 13.

41. Ibid.

42. *Hurriyet*, February 10, 1993.

43. Ertugrul KURKCU, BIA News Center, November 22, 2003, PKK Website, http://69.57.132.41/~kadek/kurdistan/modules.php?name = News&file = article&sid = 378.

44. Eli Karmon, "The Showdown Between the PKK and Turkey: Syria's Setback," November 20, 1998, http://www.ict.org.il/ and "The Arrest of Abdullah Öcalan: The last stage in the Turkey-PKK showdown?" February 17, 1999, [http://www.ict.org.il/articles/articledet.cfm?articleid = 72].

45. Ertugrul KURKCU, BIA News Center, November 22, 2003, PKK Website, http://69.57.132.41/~kadek/kurdistan/modules.php?name = News&file = article&sid = 378.

46. See "The Islamic Movement in Turkey" by Ismet G. Imset, *Turkish Daily News* (*TDN*) February 8, and May 14, 1993 and *Cumhuriyet* February 4, 1993 Cited by Karmon, "The Demise of Radical Islam in Turkey."

47. Eli Karmon, "The Showdown Between the PKK and Turkey: Syria's Setback," 20 November 1998, http://www.ict.org.il/ and "The Arrest of Abdullah Öcalan: The last stage in the Turkey-PKK showdown?" February 17, 1999, http://www.ict.org.il/articles/articledet.cfm?articleid = 72.

48. See *Anatolia Radio* in English, January 24, 1993.

49. "Italy Urged to Prosecute PKK Leader Öcalan," *Human Rights Watch Report*, November 21, 1998.

50. Karmon, "The Demise of Radical Islam in Turkey," 18.

51. "Kurdish rebels say they shot down Turkish helicopter," March 7, 1999 (CNN) .

52. March 11, 1999, Itar-Tass Cited by Ely Karmon, "Terrorism in Turkey: An Analysis of the Principal Players." *ICT Report*, March 16, 1999 www.ict.org.il/articles/article-det.cfm?articleid = 74.

53. Ibid.

54. PKK violence continues http://www.turkishdailynews.com/old_editions/03_01_99/feature.htm.

55. Barkey, "Turkey and the PKK," 2–3.

56. *Patterns of Global Terrorism 2002*, U.S. Government, Department of State. Washington: DC, 2003.

57. Ibid.

58. Barkey, "Turkey and the PKK," 1.

59. Reuters November 12, 2003.

60. Barkey, "Turkey and the PKK," 3.

61. Sebnem Arsu and Dexter Filkins, "20 in Istanbul Die in Bombings at Synagogues," *New York Times*, November 16, 2003.

62. Military Intelligence sources in Istanbul (name withheld), personal correspondence with the author, November 25, 2003.

63. Selcan Hacaoglu, "Police ID Explosives Used in Turkey Bombs." *The Guardian*, November 27, 2003.

64. Military Intelligence source, Interview with the author.

65. PKK website, http://69.57.132.41/~kadek/kurdistan/modules.php?name=News&file = article&sid = 378 accessed December 1, 2003.

66. Craig S. Smith, "Terror Attacks and Politics Put Turkey's Military on Edge" *New York Times*, November 30, 2003.

67. Louis Mexler, "Suicide Bombs kill 27 injure 450 in Turkey" Associated Press report, November 30, 2003.

6. TERROR 101: THE TRANSNATIONAL CONTAGION EFFECTS OF SUICIDE BOMBING

1. Claire Sterling, *The Terror Network* (New York: Holt, Reinhart, and Winston, 1981), 10, 26; Richard English, *Armed Struggle: the History of the IRA* (New York: Oxford University Press), 2003, 167.

2. Leila Khaled Interview in *Hurriyet* May 26, 1971 cited in Sterling, *Terror Network*, 124.

3. Bruce Hoffman, *Inside Terrorism (New York:* Columbia University Press, 1998, 84).

4. See also Ray S. Cline and Yonah Alexander, *Terrorism: The Soviet Connection* (New York: Crane Russak, 1984).

5. Sterling, *Terror Network*, 135–137; Hoffman, *Inside Terrorism*, 67–68.

6. Hoffman, ibid, 68; For a full description see, Simon Reeve, *One Day in September* (New York: Arcade Publishing, 2000. At the time of the 9/11 attacks, there was considerable discussion about the continued symbolic value of the month of September for terrorist operations. For example see http://nyc.indymedia.org/front.php3?article_id = 9865&group = webcast accessed October 25, 2003.

7. Cited by Hoffman, *Inside Terrorism*, 76.

8. "Arguments concerning demonstration effects assume that followers will learn only one kind of lesson—one that encourages further action, leading to repeated occurrences of the first event . . ." See Stephen M. Saideman, "Is Pandora's Box Half

Empty of Half Full?" ch. 6 in David Lake and Donald Rothchild (eds.) *The International Spread of Ethnic Conflict.* Princeton University Press, 1998. Donald Rothchild suggested a fine tuning of this model during my presentation at the September 2004 meeting of The American Political Science Association (APSA) in Chicago.

9. Edgar O'Ballance, *the Cyanide Wars* alleges that the LTTE (Tamil Tigers) were being trained in Lebanon in the late 1980s and thus learned the tactic of suicide terror directly from the Hizb'allah's successes in 1983, and imported it back to Sri Lanka in 1987. According to Rohan Gunaratna, "Tamil militant organizations (the LTTE and PLOTE) received training with PLO and PFLP in the 1970s and early 1980s. As Indian intelligence started to provide them training from 1983, Palestinian training stopped. Certainly, the Hezbollah attacks, especially the 1983 Beirut attack inspired the group to do their first vehicle bomb suicide attack in 1987." Interview with the author, August 2003.

10. Joyce Davis, *Martyrs* (New York: Palgrave Press, 2003. Martin Kramer enumerates the overall number of suicide operations in Lebanon and credits Hizb'allah with only one-fourth of those operations between the years 1983 and 1986. Martin Kramer, "Hizbullah: the Calculus of Jihad." *Bulletin of the American Academy of Arts and Sciences.* vol. 47 no. 8 (May 1994): 35.

11. Matthew Levitt, Interview with the Author, June 2003.

12. There is at least one civil case against Iran which successfully made this connection. In the case of Weinstein v. Iran, Iran was ordered to pay $183 million (US) in damages to the family of Ira Weinstein, who died in a 1996 bus bombing in Israel. Hamas, which is supported by Iran, claimed responsibility for the attack, which killed 25 people. While court decisions have been rendered against terrorists and state sponsors, few claimants have actually received the money they were awarded. According to the law, the President may block the release of funds from the Treasury for reasons of national security. Citing diplomatic reasons, the Bush administration has thus far blocked efforts by victims to collect compensation from the frozen assets, even after courts have ruled in the victims' favor. See Susan Weinstein v. The Islamic Republic of Iran Civil Action No. 00–2601 *Memorandum & Order* issued July 22, 2003 by Judge Royce C. Lamberth.

13. *Ha'aretz* (Hebrew), March 31, 1993.

14. Anat Kurz, Islamic Terrorism and Israel—Hizb'allah, Palestinian Islamic Jihad and Hamas, (Hebrew), Papirus Publications, 175 cited by Ganor, in Robert J. Art and Louise Richardson (eds.), *Democracy and Counter Terrorism: Lessons from the Past* (Washington DC: USIP Press, forthcoming, 2005), 34.

15. Marilyn Raschka, "Expellees in Lebanon Halved as First Contingent Returns Home." Washington Institute Report, November/December 1993, 53.

16. Giles Kepel, *Jihad, the Trail of Political Islam.* Cambridge: Harvard University Press, 2002, 327.

17. *Yediot Ahronot* (Hebrew), December 1, 1994, 7; Senior FBI analysts, Confidential Interviews with the author, August 2003.

18. http://www.jmcc.org/media/report/97/Oct/1.htm accessed August 11, 2003.

19. Al-Ghoul sold hand grenades for $50 and belts packed with TNT for use in suicide

bombs for $1,000. *Time* Magazine, "How Hamas-Hezbollah Rivalry is Terrorizing Israel." April 23, 2001.

20. *Time* Magazine, Ibid.

21. Boaz Ganor, "Israel" in Art, Richardson and Stares, *Democracy and Counter Terrorism*, 23.

22. David Regev, *Yediot Ahronot*, 19 May 1996.

23. Russ Kick, "9/11: Once Again, the Ignorance Excuse is a Lie." *The Konformist*, June 2002 and corroborated by His Excellency Abdallah Baali, Representative, Permanent Mission of Algeria to the U.N, Interview with the author November 13, 2003.

24. http://newsvote.bbc.co.uk/mpapps/pagetools/print/news.bbc.co.uk/1/hi/world/middle_east/country_profile/811140.stm accessed July 2003.

25. Jeremy Shapiro, "France and the Algerian Islamists," in Art, Richardson and Stares, *Democracy and Counter Terrorism*; Stathis N. Kalyvas and Ignacio Sánchez-Cuenca, "Accounting for the Absence of Suicide Missions," Manuscript 2003. In Diego Gambetta (ed.) *Suicide Missions* (Oxford: Oxford University Press, forthcoming).

26. Robert A. Pape, "Dying to Kill Us." *New York Times*, September 22, 2003.

27. Olga Oliker, *Russia's Chechen Wars 1994–2000: Lessons from Urban Combat*. RAND report, Washington: DC, 2001. In August 1994, Boris Yeltsin stated that "armed intervention is impermissible and must not be done" cited in Matthew Evangelista, *The Chechen Wars*, Washington: DC, Brookings Press, 2002, 31.

28. Oliker, *Russia's Chechen Wars*.

29. Stasys Knezys and Romans Sedickas, *The War in Chechnya* (College Station: Texas A&M University Press, 1999), 50, 65. The fighters were known as "Gazavat" (Holy War) fighters. Yeltsin used to refer to them as "criminals in black headbands." Evangelista, *Chechen Wars*, 31. The attacks also included the destruction by two trucks of Chechnya's main regional government offices in Grozny, killing about 80 people and wounding more than 150 (December 27, 2002); the truck bombing of a government compound in the town of Znamenskoye which killed 59 and injured more than 200 (May 12, 2003). Cited by Kalyvas and Sánchez-Cuenca in Gambetta, *Suicide Missions*.

30. Evangelista, *Chechen Wars*, 40–41.

31. Michael Fredholm, "The New Face of Chechen Terrorism," *Central Asia—Caucasus Analyst*, September 24, 2003.

32. "Inside a Chechen Bomber's Mind." BBC News September 4, 2003.

33. Dimitri Trenin, *Chechnya: Effects of the War and Prospects for Peace*. Carnegie Endowment for International Peace Policy Brief, 1.

34. Evangelista, *Chechen Wars*, 43–44, 80–84. This echoes the traditional Palestinian explanation for why terrorism was an appropriate tactic. According to Abu Iyad the Black September Operation against the Israeli Athletes at the Munich Olympics did not manage to "bring about the liberation of their comrades imprisoned in Israel . . . but did attain two other objectives: World Opinion was forced to take note of the Palestinian drama, and the Palestinian people imposed their presence on an international gathering that had sought to exclude them." Cited in Hoffman, *Inside Terrorism*, 73.

35. Steven Myers, "Putin Offers an Amnesty Plan Covering Most Chechen Rebels." *The New York Times*, May 16, 2003, A5.

36. Michael Wines, "19 Die as Suicide Bomber Destroys Bus Near Chechnya." *The New York Times*, June 6, 2003, A3.

37. Nabi Abdullaev, "Chechnya's Man in Moscow Talks Peace." Global Vision News, http://www.gvnews.net/html/DailyNews/alert4916.html.

38. Steven Eke, "Chechnya's Female Bombers." BBC News, July 7, 2003.

39. Dimitri Sudakov, "Shamil Besayev Trains Female Suicide Bombers" *Pravda*, 5/15/2003.

40. Trenin, *Chechnya: Effects of War*, 4 see also Dexter Filkins, *NYT*, June 12, 2003 and Olga Oliker, Thomas Szayna, eds. *Faultlines of Conflict in Central Asia and the South Caucasus: Implications for the U.S. Army*. Washington DC: Rand, 2003.

41. Andrew Osborne, "The Beslan Massacre, One Siege, Two Stories, How the Truth is Gradually Emerging," *The Independent* (UK), September 8, 2004, 24–25.

42. "Arab Mercenaries Prepare Female Kamikazes In Chechnya," *Pravda* 15: 26 2001–12–11.

43. Steven Lee Meyers, "From Dismal Chechnya, Women Turn to Bombs," *New York Times*, September 10, 2004.

44. Kim Murphy, "Chechen Warlord Always Brazen – but Never Caught." *Los Angeles Times*, September 10, 2004 A1.

45. Ibid.

46. Ray Takeyh and Nikolas Gvosdev "Do terrorist networks need a home?" *Washington Quarterly*, 25, no 3 [Summer 2002]: 100.

47. "Terror in Uzbekistan: A Special Report." Radio Liberty, March 31, 2004 http://www.uzland.uz/2004/april/01/33.htm.

48. "23 dead in Uzbek "terrorist" clash" March 30, 2004 CNN.com, http://edition.cnn.com/2004/WORLD/asiapcf/03/30/uzbek.blast/ and Terror Blasts Rock Uzbekistan, BBC World, http://news.bbc.co.uk/2/hi/asia-pacific/3577803.stm.

49. "Terror in Uzbekistan: A Special Report." Radio Liberty, March 31, 2004 http://www.uzland.uz/2004/april/01/33.htm.

50. Ibid.

51. Kim Cragin and Sara A. Daly (RAND Corporation), *Terrorist Groups: Requirements, Vulnerabilities, and Response*. Paper presented to the International Studies Association. February 25, 2003, B19.

52. Kalyvas and Sánchez-Cuenca, in Gambetta, *Suicide Missions*, 3.

53. Author correspondences with Cynthia McClintock.

54. ENR, "The Economics of Terror Recognizes No Boundaries" *NY* 250 no. 9 (March 10, 2003): 72.

55. Kalyvas and Sánchez-Cuenca, in Gambetta, *Suicide Missions*, 9.

56. According to David Scott Palmer, this was only used in a limited fashion and not as part of a systematic campaign.

57. Richard English, *Armed Struggle: the History of the IRA* (New York: Oxford University Press, 2003), 151.

58. Tom Regan, "Was it ETA or al Qaeda?" csmonitor.com, http://www.csmonitor.com/2004/0312/dailyUpdate.html?s = mits accessed March 22, 2004.

59. Kalyvas and Sánchez-Cuenca, in Gambetta, *Suicide Missions*, 9.

60. English, *Armed Struggle*, 156. Denials included the killing of Jean McConville in 1972 but the IRA finally took responsibility in March 1999.

61. Sean MacStiofain, *Memoirs of Revolutionary* (Edinburgh: Gordon Cremonesi, 1975), 237–238, a former IRA Chief of Staff, denied IRA responsibility. However, David McKrittick, S. Kelters, B. Feeney, and C. Thornton, *Lost Lives: The Stories of the Men, Women and Children Who Died as a Result of the Northern Ireland Troubles* (Edinburgh: Mainstream, 1999), 161 do blame the IRA. The victims were Dinah Campbell and Elizabeth Craigmille both in their 70s, http://www.upmj.co.uk/Martin%20McGuinness.htm accessed August 4, 2003; English, *Armed Struggle*, 159, 167, see also Peter Taylor, *Provos: the IRA and Sein Fein* (London: Bloomsbury, 1997), 173.

62. Liam Clarke and Katherine Johnston, *Martin McGuiness: From Guns to Government* (Edinburgh: Mainstream, 2001), 143–44; cited by Kalyvas and Sánchez-Cuenca, in Gambetta, *Suicide Missions*, 9–10.

63. English, *Armed Struggle*, 159, 170.

64. ENR, "The Economics of Terror Recognizes No Boundaries." 72.

65. MacStiofain, *Memoirs of a Revolutionary*, 214.

66. Eamon Collins, *Killing Rage* (London: Granta, 1999), 8, 295; cited by Kalyvas and Sánchez-Cuenca, in Gambetta, *Suicide Missions*, 9–10.

67. David Sharrock and Mark Davenport, *Man of War, Man of Peace: The Unauthorized Biography of Gerry Adams* (London: Pan, 1997), 159. The conflict in Northern Ireland is characterized by reciprocal restraint. See Kevin Toolis, *Rebel Hearts: Journeys Within the IRA's Soul* (London: Picador, 1997), 21. The British authorities have committed human rights abuses, they "have not ruthlessly and brutally suppressed the population which explicitly or tacitly supports insurrection in the manner experienced by Algerian Muslims, Afghan peasants, Iraqi Kurds, Kashmiri Muslims, Palestinian Muslims and Christians, South African blacks, Sri Lankan Tamils, and Vietnamese peasants" (Brendan O'Leary and John McGary, *The Politics of Antagonism: Understanding Northern Ireland* [London: Athlone, 1993]). As an IRA man was told after his arrest by the security forces: "If this was Beirut we would just take you out into that yard and shoot you" (Collins, *Killing Rage*, 188) Excerpted from Kalyvas and Sánchez-Cuenca in Gambetta, *Suicide Missions*.

68. Louise Richardson, "Ireland" in Art, Richardson, and Stares, *Democracy and Counter Terrorism*.

69. Sean Anderson and Stephen Sloan, *Historical Dictionary of Terrorism* (Scarecrow Press, 1995), 294.

70. Cited in Kalyvas and Sánchez-Cuenca, in Gambetta, *Suicide Missions*, 17.

71. Neil McKay, "Was it ETA or al Qaeda?" *Sunday Herald*, March 14, 2004.

72. Nicholas B. Dirks, *Castes of the Mind: Colonialism and the Making of Modern India*. (Princeton: Princeton University Press, 2001), 275–277.

73. At least 60 Muslims were killed in the WTC attack (see http://islam.about.com/blvictims.htm, assessed June 31, 2003); Neil MacFarquar, "Saudis Arrest 8 in Deadly Riyadh Bombing" *New York Times*, May 29, 2003, "Morocco Arrests Three Tied to Suicide Bombing," *New York Times*, May 25, 2003 and Sebnem Arsu and Dexter Filkins, "20 in Istanbul Die in Bombings at Synagogues," *New York Times*, November 16, 2003.

74. Bruce Hoffman, "The Leadership Secrets of Osama Bin Laden" *The Atlantic Monthly*, April 2003.

75. Military Intelligence sources in Istanbul (name withheld), personal correspondence with the author, November 25, 2003.

76. Douglas Farah and Peter Finn, "al Qaeda's Terror Style Spreading" *Washington Post*, November 21, 2003.

77. Ray Takeyh and Nikolas Gvosdev, "Do Terrorist Networks Need a Home?" *Washington Quarterly*, 25, no 3 (Summer 2002): 97.

78. Ibid.

79. Interviews with senior FBI analysts, as well as with members of the Office of Counter Terrorism.

80. Farah and Finn, "al Qaeda's Terror Style Spreading."

81. Loretta Napoleoni, "Chechnya's Terror Economy is Booming and its bloody trade is being exported," *The Times* [London], September 9, 2004, 20.

81. Rand Report. T/K.

7. FEMINISM, RAPE, AND WAR: ENGENDERING SUICIDE TERROR?

1. UNDP Arab Human Development Report 2002: Creating Opportunities for Future Generations, http://www.undp.org/rbas/ahdr/. Accessed June 6, 2003.

2. Clara Beyer, "Messengers of Death: Female Suicide Bombers". ICT report. February 12, 2003, http://www.ict.org.il/articles/articledet.cfm?articleid = 470. Accessed February 20, 2003.

3. Lucy Frazier, "Abandon Weeping for Weapons: Palestinian Women Suicide Bombers." http://www.nyu.edu/classes/keefer/joe/frazier.html. Accessed November 21, 2003.

4. Emile Sahliyeh and Zixian Deng, "The Determinants of Palestinians' Attitude Toward Peace with Israel," *International Studies Quarterly* 47, no. 4 (December 2003): 701.

5. "From Jerusalem to Jakarta and from Bali to Baghdad, the suicide bomber is clearly the weapon of choice for international terrorists." (Don Van Natta, "Big Bang Theory: the Terror Industry Fields its Ultimate Weapon," *New York Times*, August 24, 2003 section 4, 1.

6. Mia M. Bloom, "Rape as a Strategy of War," unpublished manuscript 2004.

7. Yoni Fighel, "Palestinian Islamic Jihad and Female Suicide bombers." October 6, 2003 ICT website. www.ict.org.

8. As stated previously, Scott Atran argues that as a result of Akras' martyrdom, Saudi Arabia sent 100 million dollars to fund the Al 'Aqsa Intifada.

9. Sophie Claudet, "More Palestinian Women Suicide Bombers Could Be On The Way: Analysts." *Middle East Times,* March 1, 2002. . Accessed

10. Graham Usher, "At 18, Bomber Became Martyr and Murderer." *The Guardian*, Saturday March 30, 2002.

11. Yoram Schweitzer, "A Fundamental Change in Tactics." *Washington Post*, October 19, 2003, B03.

12. For a full discussion on this issue see Amrita Basu, "Hindu Women's Activism and

the Questions it Raises," in Amrita Basu and Patricia Jeffrey (eds.), *Appropriating Gender: Women's Activism and Politicized Religion in South Asia* (London: Routledge, 1997.

13. Dimitri Sudakov, "Shamil Besayev Trains Female Suicide Bombers" *Pravda*, May 15, 2003.

14. Libby Copeland, "Female Suicide Bombers: The New Factor in Mideast's Deadly Equation" *Washington Post* April 27, 2002, C01.

15. Anatoly Medetsky, "Court Tries Alleged Tverskaya Bomber" *St. Petersburg Times*, March 30, 2004.

16. Steven Lee Meyers, "From Dismal Chechnya, Women Turn to Bombs," *New York Times*, September 10, 2004.

17. Clara Beyer, "Messengers of Death: Female Suicide Bombers."

18. After the Iranian revolution, the clerical regime created informal cadres of women to fight the war, though the Islamic republic could not bring itself to employ women martyrs. Reuel Marc Gerecht, "They live to die," *Wall Street Journal* April 8, 2002, http://www.aei.org/news/filter.,newsID.13787/news_detail.asp.

19. Leila Khaled, *My People Shall Live: The Autobiography of a Revolutionary.* (Edited by George Hajjar. Foreword by Glubb Pasha) (London: Hodder and Stoughton, 1973).

20. Philip Baum, "Leila Khaled, Una Combattente por la Liberta" http://www.arcipel-ago.org/palestina/leila_khaled.htm. Accessed November 16, 2003

21. Julie M. Peteet, *Gender In Crisis* (New York: Columbia University Press, 1991), 152.

22. Simona Sharoni and others have alleged that Palestinian women were sexually humiliated in order to force them to inform or collaborate with the occupation authorities. See Simona Sharoni, *Gender and the Israeli Palestinian Conflict* (Syracuse University Press, 1995). Sharoni discusses how the Palestinian honor code is used against them to extract concessions or force collaboration. Allegations also exist concerning women raped in Israeli jails (anonymous Palestinian source, name withheld).

23. Gregg Zoroya, "Woman Describes the Mentality of a Suicide Bomber." *USA Today*, March 22, 2002

24. Reuven Paz, "Suicide Terrorist Operations in Chechnya: An Escalation of the Islamist Struggle," ICT- International Policy Institute for Counterterrorism, http://www.ict.org.il. Accessed July 10, 2003; and Nabi Abdullaev, "Suicide Attacks Take Rebel Fight to a New Level," *The Moscow Times*, May 16, 2003, 3.

25. Frazier, "Abandon Weeping for Weapons."

26. According to Dr. Samiya Sa'ad Al-Din, *Al-Akhbar* (Egypt), February 1, 2002.

27. Agence France Presse April 12, 2002.

28. Giles Foden, "Death and the Maidens" *The Guardian*, July 18, 2003.

29. *Kul Al-Arab* (Israel), February 1, 2002

30. *Al-Sha'ab* (Egypt), February 1, 2002

31. Sophie Claudet, "More Palestinian Women Suicide Bombers Could Be On The Way: Analysts." *Middle East Times,* March 1, 2002. www.metimes.com/2K2/issue2002–9/methaus.htm

32. Graham Usher, "At 18, Bomber Became Martyr and Murderer."

33. Matti Steinberg, Interview with the Author, September 2002.

34. Peter Beaumont, "Woman Suicide Bomber Strikes." *The Guardian* 28 January 2002. www.guardian.co.uk/international/story/0,3604,640597,00.html

35. Middle East News Online, January 28, 2002.

36. *Al-Sha'ab* (Egypt), February 1, 2002.

37. Ibid.

38. *Al-Sharq Al-Awsat* (London), January 31, 2002.

39. Ibid.

40. Nasra Hassan, "An Arsenal of Believers," *The New Yorker*, November 2001.

41. *Al-Sharq Al-Awsat* (London), January 31, 2002; February 2, 2002.

42. Arin Ahmad is another woman who was caught after she changed her mind and refused to detonate her explosive device. Vered Levy-Barzilai, "On Suicide Bombers and Humanity," June 21, 2002.

43. Arnon Regular, "Mother of Two Becomes First Female Suicide Bombers for Hamas." *Ha'aretz*, January 15, 2004.

44. Ibid.

45. *Al-Sharq Al-Awsat* (London), February 2, 2002

46. MENA news agency, Cairo, in English 2111 gmt 2 Nov 03

47. http://www.metimes.com/2K2/issue2002–4/women/fadlallah_condones_female. htm. Accessed November 14, 2003

48. Yassin's comments were reported in *Al-Sharq Al-Awsat* (London), January 31, 2002.

49. John F. Burns and Greg Myre, "Suicide Bomber Kills at Least 19 in North of Israel," *New York Times* October 5, 2003.

50. For a full list of names of women suicide bombers, see Debra Zedalis, "Female Suicide Bombers" Strategic Studies Monograph, Carlyle Barracks, June 2004, 3-6

51. "Bin Laden Has Set Up Female Suicide Squads: Report," *Arab News,* Dubai, March 13, 2003.

52. Cited by Roman Kupchinsky, in "Smart Bombs with Souls," in *Organized Crime and Terrorism Watch* 3, no. 13 (April 17, 2003).

53. Dimitri Sudakov, "Shamil Besayev Trains Female Suicide Bombers" *Pravda,* 5/15/2003

54. Ibid.

55. "Inside a Chechen Bomber's Mind." *BBC News* September 4, 2003.

56. Michael Fredholm, "The New Face of Chechen Terrorism," *Central Asia—Caucasus Analyst*, September 24, 2003

57. Lilya Tsingiyeva, chairwoman of the Chechen Interior Ministry, told Interfax. Sudakov, "Shamil Besayev Trains Female Suicide Bombers".

58. Steven Lee Meyers, "Female Suicide Bombers Unnerve Russians." *New York Times,* August 7, 2003.

59. Medetsky, "Court Tries Alleged Tverskaya Bomber."

60. Interfax, Available at http://edition.cnn.com/2003/WORLD/europe/07/25/russia. belts/index.html. Accessed July 2003.

61. David Holley and Kim Murphy, "Russians Say Terrorists Downed at Least One Jet;

Traces of an explosive are found. Two Chechen women, one on each plane, are suspected." *LA Times*, August 28, 2004, A1.

62. Steven Lee Meyers, "From Dismal Chechnya, Women Turn to Bombs," *New York Times*, September 10, 2004.

63. Owen Matthews, "So Warped by Hate, They Will Kill Anyone to Take Revenge Against Russia," *Daily Mail* (London), September 4, 2004, 8.

64. Meyers, "Female Suicide Bombers Unnerve Russians."

65. Ibid.

66. Interviews with the author, (names withheld) Batticaloa, Sri Lanka November 2002.

67. Neloufer De Mel, *Women and the Nation's Narrative: Gender and Nationalism in 20th Century Sri Lanka*. New Delhi. Kali for Women, 2001, 203–32

68. Frances Harrison, "Up Close with the Tamil Tigers." BBC World.

69. Ann Adele (Balasingham), *Women Fighters of the LTTE*, ii.

70. Tamil sources, Personal correspondence with the author November 26, 2003.

71. Robert I. Rotberg, *Creating Peace in Sri Lanka: Civil War and Reconciliation* (Washington, DC: Brookings Institution Press, 1999), 25. After the assassination of Gandhi, Dhanu's father, A. Rajarattinam, was posthumously honored by Prabhakaran as having contributed to Tamil culture and public service (M.R. Narayan Swami, *Inside an Elusive Mind* [Colombo: Vijitha Yapa 2003], 232; Ana Cutter, "Tamil Tigresses: Hindu Martyrs." http://www.columbia.edu/cu/sipa/PUBS/SLANT/SPRING98/article5.html. Accessed October 6, 2003

72. Ibid.

73. Neloufer De Mel, "The Body Politics, (Re)presenting the Female Suicide Bomber in Sri Lanka." http://www.aucegypt.edu/igws/deMel.pdf, 12. Accessed November 20, 2003.

74. In July 1997 three national human rights commissions established in 1994 found that there had been 16,742 disappearances since July 1988.

75. Interview with the author, Colombo, Sri Lanka October 25, 2002.

76. Rajasingham-Senanyake in Rotberg, *Creating Peace in Sri Lanka*, 62.

77. Tamil sources, Personal correspondence with the author November 26, 2003.

78. Rotberg, *Creating Peace in Sri Lanka*, 9.

79. According to Sherine Xavier, director of the Home for Human Rights in Colombo, cited by Ana Cutter, "Tamil Tigresses: Hindu Martyrs." http://www.columbia.edu/cu/sipa/PUBS/SLANT/SPRING98/article5.html. Accessed October 6, 2003.

80. Bernard-Henri Levy, *Reflections on War, Evil, and the End of History* (France: Grasset and Fasquelle, 2001).

81. Swarna Jayaweera, "Monitoring and Evaluation of the Implementation of the Beijing Platform for Action and the Outcome of the 23rd Special Sessions of the General Assembly—Sri Lanka." http://www.unescap.org/wid/Proceedings/Country%20paper-Sri%20Lanka-Swarna%20Jayaweera.pdf. Accessed November 20, 2003.

82. Boaz Ganor, Discussions with the author, November 2003.

83. Fighel "Palestinian Islamic Jihad and Female Suicide bombers." http://www.ict.org.il/articles/articledet.cfm?articleid = 499. Accessed November 15, 2003.

84. Israel's security forces are aware of more than 20 cases in which women were in-
    volved in sabotage activity against Israeli targets. "The Role of Palestinian Women in
    Suicide Terrorism," January 2003 http://www.mfa.gov.il/mfa/go.asp?MFAH0n21o.
    Accessed March 2003; Libby Copeland, "Female Suicide Bombers: The New Factor
    in Mideast's Deadly Equation" *Washington Post*, April 27, 2002.
85. Israeli Security Sources, "Blackmailing Young Women into Suicide Terrorism," Feb-
    ruary 12, 2002, http://www.mfa.gov.il/mfa/go.asp?MFAH0n2ao. Accessed July 2003.
86. Barbara Victor, *Army of Roses: Inside the World of Palestinian Suicide Bombers* (New
    York: Rodale Press, 2003). However, family shame can be misconstrued based on a
    variety of factors. If this was a key explanatory variable, then we should expect to
    see more suicide bombing among females which we don't (yet) observe.
87. Interview with the author, April 12, 2004.
88. Schweitzer, "A Fundamental Change in Tactics." The financial incentives are real
    and amount to between $10,000 to $25,000 to compensate the martyrs' families.
89. Two of the three women were killed by the LTTE en route to meeting the author
    for an interview in November 2002. The third woman understandably went into
    hiding and so I was unable to conduct the interviews personally. The information
    was derived from the reports given to the international aid organization.
90. Sandro Contenta, "Student 'Had Wish to Become a Martyr.'" *Toronto Star*, March 1,
    2002.
91. Giles Foden, "Death and the Maidens," *The Guardian*, July 18, 2003.
92. Ibid.

8. CONCLUSIONS AND PROSPECTS FOR THE FUTURE: IS SUICIDE
   BOMBING INEVITABLE IN THE UNITED STATES?

1. Ivo Daalder and James M. Lindsay, "Trust Clarke: He's Right About Bush." Op-ed,
   The Globe and Mail, March 26, 2004.
2. Daniel Pipes, "America's Muslims Against America's Jews" *Commentary* May 1, 1999
   and *Militant Islam Reaches America* (New York: Norton, 2002), 201–202.
3. Matt Levitt, *Targeting Terror: U.S. Policy Toward Middle Eastern State Sponsors and
   Terrorist Organizations, Post-September 11* (Washington: Institute for Near East
   Policy, 2002).
4. Porter Goss Interview with George Stephanopoulos, May 18, 2003 and Bruce Hoffman, "The Logic of Suicide Terror," *Atlantic Monthly*, June 2003, 40–46.
5. January 10, 2003 according to Muzi.com-News "Hamas Urges Iraq to use Suicide
   Bombers." Accessed February 13, 2003.
6. John F. Burns, "Iraqi General Says 4,000 Volunteered for Suicide Attacks" New York
   Times, March 31, 2003.
7. Neil MacFarquar, "An Arab Martyr Thwarted," *New York Times*, November 2, 2004.
8. Intelligence Sources, Interview with the author, November 2003.
9. Interview with the NYPD Counter Terrorism Unit, November 11, 2004.
10. Christine Spolar, "Terrorist Memo Raises Questions on War's Impact, Vacuum
    May Have Invited al Qaeda," *Chicago Tribune*, February 16, 2004.
11. Text of Zarqawi letter was translated by the Coalition Provisional Authority in Iraq

and published in Dexter Filkins, "Could the Job in Iraq be Working?" *New York Times* February 9, 2004. The full text of the letter is available at www.globalsecurity. org/wmd/library/news/ iraq/2004/02/040212-al-zarqawi.htm.

12. Ibid.
13. Spolar, "Terrorist Memo Raises Questions on War's Impact."
14. Richard A. Clarke Interview with Leslie Stahl on *60 Minutes*, "Clarke's Take on Terror" March 21, 2004.
15. Michael Scheuer, interview with Steve Kroft, *60 Minutes*, November 14, 2004.
16. Ibid.
17. Ned Parker, US adopts Israeli model of collective punishment for Iraq" http://www. dawn.com/2004/01/17/int5.htm.
18. Dexter Filkins, "Tough New tactics Tighten U.S. Grip on Iraq." *New York Times*, December 7, 2003.
19. Ibid.
20. Ned Parker, "US adopts Israeli model of collective punishment for Iraq."
21. Filkins, "Tough New tactics Tighten U.S. Grip on Iraq."
22. Ibid.
23. Ibid.
24. Interview with the author, New York, October 14, 2004.
25. Jeffrey Gettleman, quoting Moqtada Al Sadr in "Violent Disturbances Rack Iraq from Baghdad to Southern Cities." *New York Times*, April 4, 2004.
26. Reuters, "Shiite Militia Marches in Iraq To Back Cleric Critical of U.S." *New York Times*, April 4, 2004.
27. Reuters, "Iraqis Condemn Falluja Attacks, Warn of Bloodshed." *New York Times*, April 2, 2004.
28. Bruce Hoffman, "The Leadership Secrets of Osama Bin Laden: The Terrorist as CEO" *The Atlantic Monthly*, April 2003.
29. Hoffman, "The Logic of Suicide Terror," 40–46.
30. The Israeli Defense Force (IDF) sources place the number of suicide attacks in excess of 500.
31. Bruce Hoffman, "Atlantic Unbound: The Calculus of Terror." *The Atlantic Monthly* May 15, 2003.
32. Maurice R. Greenberg, William F. Wechsler, and Lee S. Wolosky, *Terrorist Financing*, Report of a Special Task Force Sponsored by the Council on Foreign Relations, November 14, 2002, at
http://www.cfr.org/pdf/Terrorist_Financing_TF.pdf. The current 2004 version reasserts the original findings and expands upon them. Mallory Factor, Lee S. Wolosky, William F. Wechsler, Council on Foreign Relations Update on the Global Campaign Against Terrorist Financing
http://www.cfr.org/pub7111/william_f_wechsler_lee_s_wolosky_mallory_factor/update_on_the_global_campaign_against_terrorist_financing.php.
33. Seymour Hersh, "King's Ransom. How Vulnerable are the Saudi Royals?" *The New Yorker*, October 22, 2001.
34. Chair of the 9/11 Commission Governor Thomas Kean Interview with Tim Russert, *Meet the Press*, April 4, 2004.

35. Seymour Hersh, "King's Ransom."
36. Statements made by Mohammed Karzai and President Musharraf to the author, September 22 and 25, 2003.
37. Sydney Jones, "Jemaah Islamiyah in South East Asia: Damaged but Still Dangerous," *Asia Report* no. 63, August 26, 2003.
38. AH Nayyar and Ahmed Selim, et al. "The Subtle Subversion: the State of Curricula and Textbooks in Pakistan: Urdu, English, Social Studies, and Civics" (Islamabad: Sustainable Development Policy Institute, 2002).
39. Richard A. Clarke, "Testimony before the National Commission on Terrorist Attacks Against the United States" (9/11 Commission), March 24, 2004, http://news.findlaw.com/hdocs/docs/911rpt/clarke32404.pdf.
40. Bruce Hoffman, "The Leadership Secrets of Osama Bin Laden: The Terrorist as CEO" *The Atlantic Monthly*, April 2003.
41. Clarke Interview with Stahl.
42. I am grateful to Gideon Rose for this suggestion.
43. Al Jazeera website, www.aljazeera.com.
44. http://www.whitehouse.gov/news/relases/2004/09/20040907-8.html. Town hall meeting and Q&A session in Des Moines, Iowa.
45. https://www.qal3ati.com/vb/showthread.php?t=115812 cited by Yigal Karmon, http://www.memri.org/bin/opener_latest.cgi?ID=SA1404
46. Al Jazeera, "Bin Laden Warns of Retaliation for Iraqis Killing," November 3, 2004: aljazeera.com.
47. Mike Scheuer Interview, *60 Minutes.*
48. Hoffman, "The Leadership Secrets of Osama Bin Laden."
49. Ibid.
50. Excerpted from Hoffman, "The Leadership Secrets of Osama Bin Laden."
51. According to Richard A. Clarke, "In the ensuing 30 months [since 9/11], al Qaeda has morphed into a decentralized network, with its national and regional affiliates operating effectively and independently."
52. The Bali Bombings are one such example of this, they were perpetrated by the JI (Jamiyat al Islamiyya) but not ordered by al Qaeda.
53. Hoffman, "The Logic of Suicide Terror."
54. Nichole Argo, Interview with the author, August 25, 2004.
55. Kavkaz-Tsentr news agency web site (in Russian), 8 Feb 2004.
56. Osama Bin Laden's videotape, transcript available on www.aljazeera.com or http://memritv.org/Search.asp?ACT=S9&P1+312.

INDEX

War/U.S. occupation; September 11,
2001 terrorist attacks
UNP. *See* United National Party (Sri
Lanka)
Uribe, Alvaro, 133
USS Cole attack (2000), 166
Uzbekistan conflict, 131–132

value rationality, 85, 222*n*27
Van Bruinessen, Martin, 105
Varshney, Ashutosh, 77–78, 84
Velioglu, Sheikh Huseyin, 92, 100, 114
Victor, Barbara, 98, 163

Waldman, Amy, 213*n*5
Walter, Barbara F., 21, 22, 45
Weathermen (United States), 146
Weinstein, Ira, 228*n*12
Wines, Michael, 128
women. *See* female roles
World Trade Center: bombing (1993), 166,
182, 183. *See also* September 11, 2001 at-
tacks

World War II, 4, 13–16, 205*n*41, 206*nn*46, 51
Wye Accord, 25

Yassin, Sheikh Ahmed: assassination of, 31,
93; and female roles, 98, 149–151, 152; and
public opinion, 24, 25, 28; on terrorism
as weapon of the weak, 3–4
Yastrzhembsky, Sergei, 129, 158
al-Yazuri, Ibrahim, 28
Yeltsin, Boris, 126, 229*n*29
Yezhiyev, Imran, 157
Yezhkov, Sergei, 132
Yilmaz, Halil, 117–118
Youssef, Ramzi, 183
Yussef, Sheikh Hassan, 149

al-Zahar, Mahmoud, 211–212*n*84
Zakaria, Fareer, 221*n*17
Zarqawi, Abu Musab al, 170–171, 172
al-Zawahiri, Ayman, 187
Zawilski, Valerie, 163
Zealots, 4–5, 8–11, 204*n*22
Ze'evi, Rechavam, 33